JAPAN: An Anthropological Introduction

JAPAN:
AN ANTHROPOLOGICAL INTRODUCTION

HARUMI BEFU
Stanford University

Japan

An Anthropological Introduction

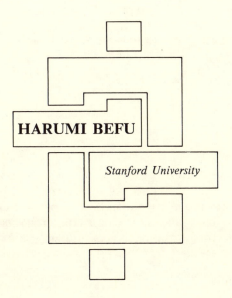

HARUMI BEFU

Stanford University

CHANDLER PUBLISHING COMPANY
An Intext Publisher
SAN FRANCISCO • SCRANTON • LONDON • TORONTO

ILLUSTRATION CREDITS

The photographs in Chapter One are reproduced by courtesy of the Archeological Museum, Meiji University, Tokyo, Japan.

The photographs that appear on the following pages are reproduced by courtesy of Frank J. Shulman, Center for Japanese Studies, University of Michigan, Ann Arbor, Michigan: 40, 68, 72, 110, 115, 133, 147

The remaining photographs are from the personal collection of the author.

The maps are the work of Joseph M. Roter.

Book Designed by Joseph M. Roter

To my parents

Contents

Illustrations

Photographs

Maps

Tables and Diagrams

Preface

Like most other scholarly works, this book is a product of the efforts of many people, even though it may bear a single name as its author. It is literally impossible to acknowledge all the numerous persons who provided scholarly criticism, material assistance, and moral support in bringing this book to its conclusion. To the following individuals, however, I must express my special gratitude.

To Professor Keith Brown, for his critical comments, particularly on Japanese kinship, which were valuable in crystallizing my thinking on the subject. To Professor Chester S. Chard, who with his vast and at the same time detailed knowledge of the culture history of the Pacific area, provided me with constructive criticism on the chapter on the cultural background of Japan. To Professor Robert Cole, who made extremely helpful comments on the basis of his special knowledge in the area of industrial relations. To Dr. John B. Cornell, for devoting many of his precious hours making painstakingly detailed and extensive comments on all parts of the book. To Professors George DeVos and Takao Sofue, for examining my analysis of Japanese personality and providing useful comments to update my observations. To Professor Edward Norbeck, for making available a manuscript of his book on Japanese religion and society, which was particularly useful in preparing the chapter on religion. To Professor David W. Plath, for making an astute overall evaluation of the book as well as specific comments on various sections. To Professor Kurt Steiner, political scientist, for suggesting revisions on matters dealing with government. To Professor Mitsuo Suzuki, whose generous evaluation of the manuscript gave me confidence that the book will be of some contribution to Japanese Studies. To Professors Ezra P. Vogel and H. Howard Wimberly, for their suggestions for change, both general and specific, which enormously improved the book. To Professor David E. Young, who through our close association over the past years helped me see Japanese esthetic styles in a perspective which is consistent with my general view of Japanese culture and personality.

In addition to these individuals who supplied me with intellectual stimulation, I must also acknowledge my sincere thanks to the following persons who provided more technical, but none the less substantial assistance. They are Miss Carolyn Nomura, for helping prepare bibliographic entries with painstaking accuracy and for reading the manuscript for stylistic corrections; Mr. Frank J. Shulman, for making available his personal collection of photographs for many of the illustrations in this book; and Mrs. Anne Gamble, Mrs. Solveig Stone, Miss Kathryn Case, and Mrs. Nuri Wyeth, for the accurate typing of the manuscript at various stages of completion.

A great deal of work on the manuscript for this book was carried out in Japan in 1969–70 while I was on a grant from the National Science Foundation (GS 2370). The field data I was then collecting on institutional and motivational factors in interpersonal relations in Japan were in many ways directly useful in revising and updating various parts of the manuscript. I greatly appreciate the generous support of the National Science Foundation and would like to express special thanks to Dr. Richard W. Lieban, the then Program Director for Anthropology, who administered my grant with much patience, understanding, and effectiveness. Many of the ideas and materials in this book, especially those in the chapters on rural life and kinship, are based on research which was made possible through grants-in-aid from the Wenner-Gren Foundation for Anthropological Research (#1425 and #1657) and a grant from the National Science Foundation (GS 985). Their financial support is gratefully acknowledged. Thanks are also due the Committee for East Asian Studies of Stanford University and its parent body, the Center for Research in International Studies for providing generous financial support which greatly facilitated completion of the book.

Lastly, let it be noted that the book reached its final completion only with the patient and warm understanding of my wife Kei and the joy and pleasure in life continually and abundantly supplied by my two adopted children, Marina and Justin.

H. B.

JAPAN: An Anthropological Introduction

Japan in Asia

Introduction

On the small islands of Japan, lying off the Asiatic continent across the Pacific Ocean from the United States, over a hundred million people make their living in an area roughly comparable in size to the state of California. This book is about these people—how they came to be what they are, how they live, and how they feel.

There are several reasons why the study of Japan is worth our while. For one thing, coming out of a feudal era only a hundred years ago, Japan has become a world economic power easily rivaling most Western nations. In most indices of economic development Japan ranks among the top three or four nations of the world, along with the United States, the Soviet Union, the Federal Republic of Germany, and Great Britain. Outside Europe and besides the United States, Japan is in fact the leading economic power, so much so that in recent years Japan has been investing billions of dollars all over the world. There are Japanese electronic, textile, and other industrial plants in Southeast Asia, Latin America, and Africa. Japan has provided millions of dollars in direct economic assistance to the underdeveloped nations of the world, and the amount continues to increase.

For the United States, moreover, Japan occupies a special place in the world. Economically, Japan and the United States form important trade partners, the United States selling raw materials to Japan and Japan selling processed goods to the United States. Militarily, the United States has maintained a large number of strategic defence bases and other installations and training grounds throughout Japan under the security pact signed between the two nations. Culturally, much Japanese influence has been felt in the United States in art and architecture, and in general has permeated the daily life of Americans in more ways than most of us realize. In addition, thousands upon thousands of military personnel, their dependents, tourists, and others from the United States have visited Japan since the close of the Second World War. They have formed a broad basis at the grass roots level of a lasting popular interest in things Japanese.

1

Visitors to Japan will be impressed by the massive concrete buildings, smart shops, modern highways, and fast trains. They will see congestion at stations, smog-infested cities, bumper-to-bumper traffic, rivers and coastal waters polluted by industrial wastes.

They will see men working for wages, shop owners looking after their customers, university students demonstrating for this or that cause, mothers caring for their children, young people talking about the latest fashion, and they may get the impression that Japan is not much different from the West. Beyond these and other similarities with the West, however, lie differences —from the use of chopsticks to the use of the Japanese language, from enjoyment of the tea ceremony and flower arrangement to modes of thinking and of relating to one another. Both similarities and differences demand explanation. Rather than simply caricature Japan as a mixture of the old and the new, it is important to understand why Japan is like the West in many respects and yet remains distinct from it in many others.

To help do this, we shall distinguish throughout the book between *traditional* Japan and *modern* Japan. By traditional Japan is meant the Japan of the feudal period, particularly the late feudal period known as Tokugawa or Edo (1603–1868). The cultural developments leading to this period certainly played a crucial role in shaping Japanese culture as we know it now. For this reason, most of the first chapter is devoted to outlining such developments. But Japan began a new era in the Tokugawa period, with its centralized political structure, Confucian-based political and moral ideology, the rise of a mercantile economy, and a rigidly stratified social system. In this period of two and a half centuries, Japan prepared itself for entering the subsequent era of rapid modernization, a process which was in part forced upon Japan by the arrival of black ships from the West, threatening Japan's security. Modern Japan, then, began with Japan's attempt to rid itself of the threat from the West and become an equal with the world's military, political, and economic powers. This process of modernization obviously must be seen against the background of traditional Japan—how on the one hand traditional cultural patterns and institutions have aided or hindered the modernization process; and on the other, how these patterns and institutions have been transformed by the forces of modernization. These are some of the central questions to be considered throughout the book.

To answer these questions from the anthropological standpoint would mean several things: to clarify the origins of Japanese culture and people, to interpret its cultural history from the earliest times to the present, and to account for the relationship among the components of the culture, such as ideology, social structure, personality formation, and economic development. In order to carry out these tasks, we must use many different approaches.

Archaeology forms the backbone of the deciphering of cultural origins. Accordingly, we shall devote a good portion of the first chapter to summarizing and interpreting archaeological findings as related to prehistoric Japan. At the same time, we shall consider the biological origins of the Japanese and the linguistic affinities of their language. When we combine archaeological, physical anthropological, and linguistic data, there emerges a picture of Japanese prehistory more complete and clearer than if one relied singly on any one of these methods. Although in Japan as in the West, the interpretation of the period of documented history is generally left to professional historians, we shall take a brief look at Japanese history insofar as it is necessary background for an anthropological understanding of modern Japan.

The study of kinship systems and rural communities have been two of the principle concerns of anthropologists, and we shall look into changes in the form and function of kinship, marriage, and family institutions in Chapter Two and the organization and development of village Japan in Chapter Three. We would first like to know what is unique and different about the kinship system of traditional Japan. Once the basic patterns are understood, we can examine the interplay between the kinship system and political and economic development in modern times. A crucial question here is whether and how kinship aids or hinders these processes. Rural Japanese communities even in traditional days were never completely isolated, closed, and autonomous. Such an image of traditional communities is erroneous. Only in comparison with subsequent times can we say that they were smaller, more isolated, closed, and autonomous. How did village Japan become more open, and what were some of the consequences? These are some of the central topics of Chapter Three.

In the next chapter we shall consider religious beliefs and systems in both rural and urban Japan. We are not here concerned so much with the theological bases and distinctions of Shintoism and Buddhism and of various sects, old and new, which are subjects for philosophers of religion, as with the actual beliefs and practices of the common folk, which may indeed be at great variance with theologians' lofty views of what religions are supposed to be. In examining the so-called new religions, we shall see how religion is responding to the changing situations of large cities.

This discussion provides us with a transition to an analysis of Japan as an urban, industrial society. We shall consider in Chapter Five how the system of social stratification changed during the transition from the traditional agrarian-period to modern industrial times. Since the class system is closely related to the economic structure, it is appropriate to treat here the changing human relations in work and industrial organization. Lastly, as education is an important component in determining one's social class and ability to move up the social ladder in an industrial society, we shall take a brief look at the role of education in Japan. The purpose of this chapter is to draw anthropology out of its traditional concerns with cultural history, kinship, the rural community, religion, and the like, and bring it face to face with issues relevant to modern urban, industrial society.

The personality make-up of the Japanese has been one of the long-standing interests of anthropological students of Japan. Starting with the wartime interest which Americans had in their enemy, the field has continued to attract attention, and by now we have a considerable amount of information on the subject. We shall explore in Chapter Six certain selected aspects of the Japanese personality, particularly the nature of emotional interdependence that Japanese feel, their attitude toward time, nature, and human nature, and their ethical and esthetic values.

I have said earlier that a central theme of this book is the changing and developing processes of Japan. It is fitting, therefore, to conclude the book, after treating several substantive topics, with a discussion in Chapter Seven theorizing on processes of modernization. The significance of this discussion lies in the spectacular speed with which Japan became a modern nation. This chapter, therefore, will try to provide some answers to the question of how Japan succeeded in modernizing itself at a miraculous rate.

This book is meant to be an anthropological introduction to Japan for those who have only a modest amount of background either in anthropology or Japanese culture. It is not, in short, intended as a work for specialists on Japan. The content of this book consists largely of digests and summaries of the findings of a large number of scholars, although the writer's own views cannot help being expressed in the selection of topics and the organization of materials. In addition, I have tried in places to present my own interpretations of Japanese culture, which are different from those previously expressed by others. I hope they will be an aid in a better understanding of Japan.

Sources cited in the text are listed alphabetically at the end of this book. In addition, at the end of each chapter I have provided a reading list of from seven to ten titles relevant to the chapter. In preparing these lists I selected as much as possible titles from among sources which are relatively easily available in most college libraries. Also, I tried not to duplicate the titles in the list at the end of this volume in the chapter-end bibliographies, so that the two lists, one at the end of the chapter and the other at the end of the book, would complement each other.

A number of Japanese terms, in roman transliteration, are used in this book. In many books of this nature a glossary of these terms is provided, in which translations of the terms are expected to serve as handy, synoptic definitions. In this book, I have avoided providing a glossary of this type because they too often give the misconception and erroneous impression that there is nothing more to the Japanese terms than their English counter-parts. The truth is that many of the Japanese terms require an extended discussion for their accurate understanding. I have tried to provide such discussion in the text. The Japanese terms are indexed at the end of the book, and readers are encouraged to find the meaning of the terms in the text.

1 Cultural Origins and Historical Background

The Preceramic Age

How long man has lived on the islands now known as the Japanese archipelago has been a subject of considerable discussion among archaeologists in recent years. Until 1949, it was the commonly accepted notion that man's presence in Japan went no further back than the first appearance of pottery there, then assumed to be no more than four or five thousand years before Christ. This view is now completely controverted, although there are a few who refuse to accept the new view. As older and older prehistoric sites are uncovered, the origins of human occupation in Japan are pushed back further and further. It is now certain that Japanese prehistory goes back at least to the Late Pleistocene, and possibly still further back, although for the most remote period we have little more than stone implements and a few fragments of human bone as evidence of man's existence (Serizawa, 1965, p. 113).

The long stretch of time from the beginning of culture to the appearance of pottery in Japan is commonly called the preceramic or non-pottery age. One should not assume, however, that this age is represented by one homogeneous culture. On the contrary, it is a period in which many heterogeneous cultures existed, some side by side and some following others. The over 350 preceramic sites uncovered since 1949—the date of the first major excavation of a preceramic site at Iwajuku in Gumma Prefecture—have yielded enough material to work out a tentative classification and chronological ordering of various cultures, or "industries," as Paleolithic cultures are often called.

An industry consists of a number of types of stone tools used for different purposes by a people possessing a common culture, but it is often identified by one principal tool type. The identifying tool types of the oldest industries of Japan are the so-called hand-axe and the chopper-chopping tool, of which there are many subtypes. Those found at Sōzudai, Ōita Prefecture,

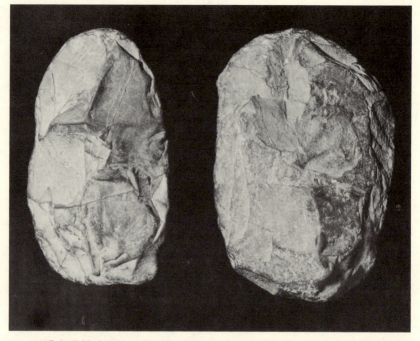

A Paleolithic hand-axe from Iwajuku, Gumma Prefecture, about 10 cm. long.
As older and older prehistoric artifacts are discovered, the origins of human
occupation in Japan are pushed back further and further.

are some of the oldest tools yet discovered in Japan (Serizawa, 1965). The
Sōzudai assemblage is tentatively given a date corresponding with the Riss-
Würm Interglacial of Europe. Other identifying tool types include pear-
shaped hand-axes from Gongen'yama, Gumma Prefecture, and oblong
specimens from Iwajuku.

Some of these early implements are claimed to have close resemblance
in form and technique of manufacture to those found in surrounding areas
of East Asia; for example, tools of the Gongen'yama I and II assemblages
with those of the Patjitanian industry of Java, the Gongen'yama III with
the Hoabinhian culture of Indonesia (Maringer, 1957a and b), and the
Sōzudai with the Choukoutien (Loc. 1) in northern China where the famous
Peking Man was discovered. When the similarities are pointed out in these
cases, there is at least an implicit suggestion of historical relation, that is,
the derivation of these Japanese industries from elsewhere. Evidence is far
from clear-cut, however, and it is entirely possible that some of the latter
industries of Japan evolved independently out of earlier ones, rather than
having diffused from outside.

The next stage in the development of the preceramic culture of Japan is
characterized by blade and knife-blade industries of several varieties. Typo-

logically, a "blade" is a more or less elongated stone implement struck from a core, with or without further trimming applied to it. The blades of Tarukishi in Hokkaido are fairly large, about fifteen centimeters long, with parallel sides. Their cross-section is either triangular or trapezoidal. The knife-blades of Moro, Tokyo, on the other hand, are much smaller, being about five centimeters long, and have a pointed tip and fairly extensive retouch, especially at the base. The Sugikubo type is similar to the Moro type, but is about three centimeters longer. Another type of knife-blade, known as the Kō type, is made by a very specialized, "Setouchi technique" (cf. Kamaki, 1965, for details of this technique) in which the bulb of the percussion—the portion which is struck in flaking the piece off from the core—is located, not at an end of the length of a piece as is usually the case, but at the middle of the length of the blade. This technique may have originated in response to the rock material—a type of andesite—principally used for this type of tool. Some of the techniques of manufacturing blades may have been derived from the "Aurignacoid" hunting tradition of northern Eurasia (Chard, in press).

Next in the tentative chronological order we are following are industries whose dominant features are the various types of pointed tools. It is entirely possible that these point industries evolved out of the previous knife-blade industries, since typologically speaking the latter are often cruder versions of the former. In a rough fashion, we may distinguish two groups of point industries, one with and the other without a "tang," or stem. The point industry at Etchūyama in Yamagata Prefecture, for example, contains tang-less points. These points are almond-shaped and semi-bifacial, i.e., one side is extensively retouched but the other side is only moderately retouched. The length varies from about five to fifteen centimeters.

Tanged points are mostly completely bifacial. Some, such as those found at Nakabayashi, Niigata Prefecture, have serrated edges. Others, like those of Tachikawa, Hokkaido, are characterized by grinding at the base of the stem. Some of these industries appear close to the end of the preceramic sequence in Japan; they are found either immediately underlying a level containing Jōmon pottery, as at Nakabayashi, or found in actual association with it, as at Kamikuroiwa, Ehime Prefecture and Yanagimata, Nagano Prefecture. A pottery-containing level (Level 9) at Kamikuroiwa has been dated to be over 10,000 years old.

Along with pointed-blade industries, we must also consider microlithic industries of various types as marking the terminal stage of the preceramic sequence of Japan. The striking feature of the microlithic industries of Japan is the small blades of about four centimeters long; hence the designation "microblade industries." These blades are struck either from all around a conical core, as are those of Yadegawa, Nagano Prefecture, or from one end of an elongated core. The elongated core is prepared in at least two distinct fashions, one more characteristic of northern Japan, as exemplified by those from Shirataki (Loc. H), Hokkaido, and the other of southern Japan, as seen in those from the Fufui cave site (Levels 2 and 3), Nagasaki Prefecture. At Fukui (Level 3), microblades were uncovered with pottery. This level has been given a radiocarbon date of 12,700 years.

Gravers and other tools from Araya, Niigata Prefecture. These tools link Japan with the wider cultural tradition of the Northern Hemisphere. (The right top piece is about 5.3 cm. long.)

A significant point about Japanese microblade industries is that they are by and large part of the wider cultural tradition of the northern North Hemisphere stretching from Lake Baikal in Siberia to Alaska. This is not to say that the method of manufacture is uniform throughout this wide stretch of land, or that the dates of microblade industries in different parts of this area are known to correlate with one another. Still, these microblade industries of the North form a unit when contrasted with the geometric microliths which characterized the mesolithic stage of the tropical and subtropical Old World. It should be mentioned for the sake of accuracy, however, that some of the microliths unearthed in southern Japan do show characteristics of geometric microliths, although they constitute only a small minority in the microlithic industries of Japan.

Before concluding this section on preceramic industries, it is worth reminding ourselves that though we have discussed merely the criterial tool types of various industries, each industry consists of many tool types, so that the identifying tool type of one industry may be a minor type in another and the two industries may in fact be historically related. For example, crude forms of pointed tools are sometimes found in knife-blade industries, suggesting a possible, though not an inevitable evolution of the former out of the latter. Also to be remembered is the fact that although our discussion was in terms of four groups of industries, there are in fact dozens of distinct industries or cultural traditions, many of which existed contemporaneously.

One may wonder what kind of social organization might have been observed during the preceramic age. Preceramic peoples of Japan must have hunted wild animals and gathered wild plants for subsistence. This much is easy to guess. To carry out such an economy, they probably lived in small bands whose members were related to one another by blood, marriage, or perhaps even both. Service (1962) has speculated, without specific reference to Japan, that at the earliest stages of human society man lived in what he called "patrilocal bands," whose core members were consanguineally related males and which required the male members to obtain their wives from outside their own band. Fried (1967) has also suggested a similar stage of "simple egalitarian society" at the beginning of human history. While there is nothing in the Japanese preceramic data to deny the existence of such social organization as Service and Fried postulate, at the same time there is nothing to support it. Verification of these writers' contentions will require closer analysis of archaeological data in the framework of their ethnological theories.

Who, biologically speaking, were the peoples who possessed these preceramic cultures of Japan? The only basis for inferring the physical type of man is skeletal remains, and there is very little evidence of this sort so far excavated. The so-called "Ushikawa man" consists of fragments of the femur and the humerus. The "Mikkabi man" is represented by fragments of the skull, pelvis, and femur, and the "Hamakita man" by a molar and fragments of the skull, clavicle, molar bone, ulna, and humerus, all found in one level, and also a fragment of tibia from a lower level. The investigator, Suzuki, (1965, 1966) concludes that the Ushikawa man, of the Upper Middle Pleistocene, while clearly Hominid, is not Homo sapiens. The Mikkabi man and the Hamakita man, on the other hand, are regarded as Homo sapiens and probably ancestral to the later Jōmon man. (Incidentally, both the Ushikawa Man and the Hamakita man are supposed to be females.) In spite of the investigator's detailed analyses, the meagerness of the evidence cannot help but render his suggestions highly tentative.

The Jōmon Period

As we saw, some of the microblade and tanged point industries contain pottery, and thus mark the end of the preceramic sequence and the beginning of the earliest ceramic culture. The earliest pottery of Japan, such as that found at Fukui III, Nagasaki Prefecture, goes back approximately 12,000 years, according to the radiocarbon analysis (Morlan, 1967; Serizawa, 1967). Whether such early pottery should be called Jōmon has been a point of much debate. Also, some prominent Japanese archaeologists like Sugao Yamanouchi have staunchly refused to recognize the phenomenally old radiocrabon dates of Japanese pottery.

These dates make Japanese pottery easily the oldest known in the world, robbing the Near East of the claim, and inevitably raise the question of the origin of pottery. Several alternative hypotheses can be entertained. One might claim that in the Old World pottery was invented only once—in Japan—and diffused to other parts of the world. One may even be bold enough to suggest the diffusion of the Jōmon pottery to the New World (Meggers, Evans and Estrada, 1965). Alternatively, one might assume that pottery diffused to Japan from elsewhere, perhaps continental Asia, where pottery had been invented at some as yet unknown locality—a view favored by some scholars because the earliest Japanese pottery is not "crude" enough to be man's first attempt at pottery making. Or one may suggest a multiple origin hypothesis, namely that pottery was invented more than once in the world and that Japanese pottery is merely one of several such cases.

Pottery is the best indicator of regional variations and chronological changes in the Jōmon culture. The analysis of Jōmon pottery design and style is bewilderingly complex for beginners and would simply confuse the reader. Suffice it to say that local variations persisted throughout the Jōmon period, while at the same time there were certain Japan-wide trends in the transformation of Jōmon pottery, e.g., in the shift from a pointed bottom to a rounded bottom and then to a flat bottom in the course of the development of Jōmon culture. On the basis of ceramic analysis, the Jōmon period is divided into the five phases of Initial, Early, Middle, Late, and Final, to which some add an Incipient phase preceding the Initial. Thus the pottery found with microliths and tanged points would belong to the Incipient phase. In this survey, we are not concerned with the details of pottery style but wish to use the chronology based on pottery analysis as a device for discussing other cultural developments.

Broadly speaking, the Jōmon people were hunters and gatherers, as both the floral and faunal remains and the stone and bone-antler tools used in the collecting economy clearly indicate. More than 300 species of edible plants and animals have been identified from Jōmon sites, including

Middle Jōmon period pottery
figurine from Kaido, Nagano
Prefecture. (About 40 cm. high)

shellfish, fish, land and sea mammals, birds, reptiles, nuts, and fruits. Stone arrowheads, wooden bows, stone spearheads, fish hooks, harpoon heads, dugout canoes, and other cultural remains provide abundant testimony of the kind of economic life the Jōmon people led. There were important regional as well as chronological variations in the economy. Coastal sites, for instance, show a heavy dependence on sea life for subsistence, which naturally was not the case in the interior. Dependence on sea mammals, as evidenced by harpoon heads, etc., came into existence only in the late Jōmon period and was limited to the northeast coast of Honshū.

There have been some recent suggestions that Jōmon people cultivated plants, an idea supported by the presence in large quantities in the Final period of stone adzes, which could have been used for cultivation, and serrated stone tools, which could have been used as sickles (Esaka, 1967; Ishida and Izumi eds., 1968, pp. 15–73; Kimura 1963). Cultivation may have been based on the swidden technique, where a plot of land is cleared by burning trees and shrubs, the resulting ashes being the sole fertilizer. As the soil depletes nutrients in subsequent years, new plots are cleared. This type of cultivation, with millet, soy beans, etc., as main crops, was in fact practiced in Japan until only a few decades ago. Another mode of agriculture, suggested by Kokubu (1966), is the cultivation of tuber crops, along with raising domestic pigs.

Mori (Mori, 1966, pp. 38–39) has suggested the possibility of rice cultivation, at least on a small scale, toward the end of the Jōmon period, an idea supported by the discovery of Jōmon pottery with impressions of rice grains. Since rice had long been cultivated on the continent by this time, it is entirely possible that rice cultivation diffused to Japan before the following Yayoi period. This possibility, however, leaves open the question as to why rice growing did not spread widely and rapidly then as it did in the early Yayoi. The answer may be that success in rice cultivation involved the wholesale adoption of a variety of technological and economic activities. Diffusion of rice cultivation at the end of the Jōmon probably was not alone sufficient to offer an alternative economy to the successful hunter-gatherer of the Jōmon, whereas the wholesale adoption of a whole new way of life centered around rice growing at the beginning of the Yayoi enabled the new economy to challenge the old one successfully.

Shelters of the Jōmon period, said to resemble those of Siberian aborigines, are about twenty square meters in floor space. They have a subterranean floor and are either circular in outline or rectangular with rounded corners. Post holes are located along and just inside the outline of the floor plan. The hearth, marked with stones, is situated near the center of the house. Shelters are often found in clusters, suggesting definite settlement patterns. Watanabe (1966) has suggested relatively lengthy occupation of settlements, rather than a nomadic life in which seasonal movement is involved, on the basis of such features as the fairly large and deep post holes (commonly 30 to 50 centimeters in diameter and 25 to 90 centimeters deep for the main pillar), the evidence of repeated use or expansion of a shelter, and the presence of stone structures too large and heavy for ready and frequent transportation, such as stone circles, stone pillars (presumably of symbolic nature), etc. Such a settled way of life is in agreement with the incipient agriculture suggested above for the terminal Jōmon period, and as Watanabe argues, is "pre-adapted" to accepting the intensive wet rice cultivation of the following Yayoi period, which required permanent settlement.

The Jōmon social organization might have remained at the "band" level of Service's scheme or have achieved the "tribal" level. In Service's definition, the tribe consists of a number of segmentary groups which can coalesce for political or military purposes and disband when the task is over. The Tribal level is achieved when there is ecological pressure for survival exerted by surrounding groups. For this reason, it was probably achieved, if at all, toward the end of the Jōmon and in the areas of exceptional economic success where increasing population put demographic pressures on the area.

In contrast to the preceramic age, skeletal remains of the Jōmon people are quite abundant. A recent study by K. Kobayashi (1964) of a small sample of thirty-eight pubic bones of both sexes of individuals above the estimated age of eighteen shows that the greatest majority died before reaching forty-five, the greatest number of deaths occurring from thirty to thirty-four years of age. If younger age groups are also considered, one can see how short the life expectancy of the Jōmon people was. The burial custom practiced toward the end of the Jōmon period—that of placing the dead inside a jar, with or without another jar as a cover—is a feature that indicates some amount of cultural continuity with the following Yayoi period. Another custom revealed by Jōmon skeletons, namely teeth-filing and teeth extraction, shows a possible cultural affinity to southeast Asia, where such practices have been seen among aborigines until recent years.

The several sites where dozens of skeletons—up to 300—have been found together can serve as a basis for an analysis of population genetics. This relative abundance of skeletal remains, at least from the Middle Jōmon period on, enables us to make considerably more precise inferences about the physical character of the inhabitants than we could for the preceramic age. The basic issues related to the biological characteristics of the Jōmon people may be phrased as follows: What is the relationship of the Jōmon population to the subsequent prehistoric, historic, and modern populations of Japan and the surrounding areas? Comparisons of Jōmon skeletons have been made with those of the following Yayoi period, of the Tomb period, of the later, feudal periods, and of contemporary Japanese. Jōmon remains have been also compared with the Ainu of Hokkaido and Sakhalin, with Koreans, Chinese, Micronesians, and other groups in the areas surrounding Japan. A few of these comparisons will be discussed here.

A word should be said about the Ainu, since they have an important place in the question of the origin of the Japanese. Now living mostly in Hokkaido, the Ainu are a population whose physical features are markedly different from the Mongoloid Japanese. Some authorities like Howells (Howells 1959, pp. 286–287) and Montagu (Montagu 1960, pp. 447–448) claim resemblances and even genetic affinity of the Ainu to the Caucasoid stock of Europe in such features as the heavy distribution of hair throughout the body, protruding supraorbital ridges, thin lips, and well-developed jaws and chin. Howells (Howells, 1959 p. 284) has even referred to the Ainu as being "incontestably White."

Several alternative historical relationships may be conceived among the Ainu, the Jōmon, and the modern Japanese. Ignoring a certain amount of genetic exchange among them from time to time, the following three alternative hypotheses may be considered (Diagram 1.1). The first hypothesis is that the modern Ainu and the modern Japanese originated from the same stock, from which one group branched off and formed the Jōmon population, who later became the modern Japanese. The second hypothesis is that

	1	2	3
Modern Period	Ainu Japanese	Ainu Japanese	Ainu Japanese
	Jōmon		
Historic Origins	Ainu	Jōmon	Ainu Jōmon

Diagram 1:1. Three Alternative Hypotheses on the Relationship among the Ainu, Jōmon, and Modern Japanese.

the Jōmon population split into two groups, one of which became the modern Ainu and the other the modern Japanese. The third hypothesis considers the Ainu and the Jōmon as separate genetic populations from the early Jōmon or even from the preceramic age and the Japanese as being derived from the Jōmon stock. In this last hypothesis, whether the Ainu are the older group than the Jōmon in Japan or vice versa remains moot.

Attempts to test these hypotheses have been made principally by three-way comparisons of characteristics of the Jōmon skeletons, the modern Japanese, and the modern Ainu. In these comparisons, the Jōmon group is more like the Ainu than the Japanese in certain respects but more like the Japanese in certain others. One is thus forced to make a composite picture of all measurements and observations to assess which group the Jōmon people resemble more. The results of such composite comparisons are inevitably inconclusive and difficult to interpret.

As has been mentioned, many Westerners have favored the third hypothesis, linking the Ainu with other "proto-Caucasoids," such as the Australian aborigines and some American Indians. Howells (1966), apparently reversing the earlier view, has recently favored the second hypothesis on the basis of a complex set of statistical analyses. Japanese specialists, such as Hasebe (1956) and Suzuki (1956), are inclined to believe that the Jōmon people more closely resemble modern Japanese than the Ainu, the implication being that the Jōmon people were the principal genetic contributors to the present day Japanese, and that there has been an overall genetic continuity from the Jōmon period to the modern day, with only minor amounts of later admixtures.

What language was spoken during the Jōmon period? This may sound like an absurd question since archaeological evidence speaks no language. But we may be able to pose the question in the following manner: Was Japanese possibly spoken then? What about Ainu? Although Hattori and Chiri (Hattori and Chiri 1960, p. 307) have revived the suggestion earlier made by various scholars that Ainu and Japanese are possibly historically related, the dominant view is that the two languages are probably unrelated. If the Jōmon people were biologically ancestral to the Japanese, and if the two languages are unrelated, the chances that Ainu was spoken by the Jōmon people, though not completely absent, seem slim.

As for the Japanese language, its probable genetic relationship to Korean has been argued on the basis of cognates which are not loan words, grammatical similarities, and phonological comparisons far more convincingly than on its possible relationship to other languages such as Ainu or Austronesian. It should be evident that in this historical analysis, we must reconstruct and compare proto-Japanese and proto-Korean, artificial constructs which characterize ancestral languages. A comparison of the modern languages themselves, which have gone through centuries of change, would yield erroneous results. For example, Japanese and Ainu have been alleged to be related because both have five similar vowels; but ancient Japanese had eight instead of five vowels, making this point of similarity irrelevant to a possible historical relationship.

Grammatical similarities between Japanese and Korean include (1) word order, (2) absence of noun inflection, and (3) lack of comparatives in adjectives. Phonologically, both languages have what is called vowel harmony. That is, only vowels of a given group can occur together in a given word, and vowels of different groups cannot so occur. This vowel harmony is a characteristic feature of languages of the Altaic linguistic stock. On this and other bases, Japanese and Korean have been tentatively assigned to this linguistic stock. An interesting sidelight on the question of the genetic affinity of Japanese is Murayama's claim (1962) that Japanese is more closely related to Tungus than to Korean among Altaic languages. If this is true, the interpretation of Japanese cultural history would have to undergo a major revision.

It is worth noting that Japanese and Chinese are totally unrelated languages, genetically speaking. To be sure, the Chinese language has had enormous influence in terms of loan words and phonology in historic times. Genetically, however, Japanese is not derived from Chinese, which is a member of the Sinitic stock, entirely apart from the Altaic stock.

Assuming that Japanese and Korean are genetically related, we can apply the lexicostatistical technique to estimate how far back the two languages diverged from one another and became separate languages. This technique assumes that there is a uniform rate of change in a set of certain carefully chosen words—most of them related to the human body and common natural phenomena. A comparison of these words in two related languages will reveal the proportion of historically related words. When a special formula developed by Morris Swadesh is applied, this proportion provides the probable date at which the two languages became separated.

According to Hattori's application of this technique to Korean and Japanese (Hattori, 1956, p. 128), their separation came about 6700 years ago. This length of time suggests that proto-Japanese language speakers probably came from Korea to Japan during the Early Jōmon period, some four or five thousand years after pottery appeared in Japan. It is interesting in this connection that the pottery of one of the Early Jōmon styles (from Nishikaratsu) of northern Kyūshū shows a close resemblance to the "comb-designed" pottery of Korea (Otomasu, 1965, p. 253). Characterized by thin parallel incisions, made, as it were, by scratching with the teeth of a comb. But before any inference can be drawn regarding possible migration or diffusion from Korea during this period, this Korean pottery must be demonstrated to be of the same age as the northern Kyūshū pottery in question.

The question still remains as to what language was spoken in Japan before the proto-Japanese of Altaic derivation. Although many candidates may be proposed, the strongest contender among them is Austronesian, a linguistic group spoken throughout the Pacific and Southeast Asia. Japanese may be basically Altaic, but in terms of vocabulary and sound patterns there are many points of similarity between Japanese and various Austronesian languages. It is possible, then, that an Austronesian language was spoken in Japan early in the Jōmon period, and was then to a large extent obliterated by the intrusive Altaic language. (Ōno, 1957, pp. 186–200; and Ōno, 1962). This view, however, is at variance with the oft-voiced notion that proto-Japanese was brought over by bearers of Yayoi culture in about 300 B.C., an Austronesian language having been spoken throughout the duration of the Jōmon Period. (Ōno, 1957, pp. 198–199).

Where did Jōmon culture come from? The hypothesis that the early Jōmon language is Austronesian points to a southern origin. Indeed, Oka (1965) has suggested similarities, though superficial, between Jōmon pottery designs and designs on New Guinea specimens. The custom of teeth extraction and teeth filing, too, reminds us of similar customs in Southeast Asian tribes. These data would support the view that Austronesian cultural elements contributed to the formation of the Jōmon culture. Although an Austronesian contribution to the Jōmon culture cannot be denied it is likely that during the eight or nine thousand years of the Jōmon period, cultural influences reached Japan from all surrounding areas.

The Yayoi Period

The Yayoi culture marks a definite and radical departure from the preceding Jōmon. This is not to deny any cultural continuity from the preceding period. Indeed, cultural continuity is evident in ceramic tradition, burial customs, shelter forms, etc.; the use of stone tools and also some amount of hunting and gathering continued throughout the Yayoi. But changes in cultural contents from the beginning of the Yayoi are drastic as well as dramatic, and there is no question that a whole new way of life was ushered in at the beginning of the Yayoi, about 300 B.C., plus or minus fifty years.

The most important innovation of this period was unquestionably the introduction of the cultivation of wet rice, which ultimately came from Southeast Asia—the heartland of the domestication of wet rice. The analysis of remains of rice grains and artifacts of the Yayoi period points to central China as the closest provenience of Japanese wet rice cultivation. Apparently elements of rice cultivation diffused from central China across the China Sea to southern Korea and Japan, rather than taking the land route up through north China, down the Korean Peninsula and then reaching Japan. That north Kyūshū, the gateway to Korea, was the earliest place to adopt the Yayoi way of life is abundantly attested to archaeologically. Yayoi culture quickly diffused eastward to roughly what is now the border between the Kinki and Chubu regions. Beyond this point, to the east and north, diffusion was somewhat delayed. Moreover, rather than a relatively clean replacement of the preceding Jōmon culture with the new one as in western Japan, there is a considerable amount of blending between the persisting Jōmon culture and the invading Yayoi culture, probably reflecting the difficulty of adaptation of the tropical plant to the colder climate of the northeastern half of Japan. It is also possible that toward the end of its period, the foraging economy of the Jōmon culture was declining in southwestern Japan and was ready for new cultural stimulation, whereas in the northeast it was still vigorously thriving and resisted the encroachment of a faltering economy based on a tropical plant. One might remember in this connection that Yayoi culture never diffused to Hokkaido.

Cultivation of rice, even at the primitive level of the early Yayoi, is a complex affair requiring knowledge of soil conditions, irrigation and drainage, the technique of harvesting husking, and storing rice, methods of cooking, etc. Merely the number of kinds of tools used, as evidenced in the excavation of early Yayoi sites such as those at Karako, Nara Prefecture, reveals that rice cultivation came to Japan fully developed. This implies that at least initially, when rice growing was first introduced to north Kyūshū, there was a migration of people equipped with knowledge of rice cultivation, perhaps from southern Korea. Possibly because of this, the Yayoi sketetal remains of north Kyūshū show resemblances to those of neolithic south Koreans. (Kanaseki, 1966). After this initial introduction, however, this migration need not have continued, since the natives who learned the method could then transmit the knowledge to their neighbors, or the natives of north Kyūshū could then migrate and spread rice cultivation to other parts of Japan.

Excavated and reconstructed Toro site (Yayoi Period), Shizuoka Prefecture.

Rice paddies and irrigation ditches of this period suggest that rice cultivation assumed a fairly complex form from the beginning of the Yayoi. Some archaeologists have hypothesized the presence of political leadership to coordinate and execute irrigation projects. In the Philippines, however, the extensive and intricate paddy system of the Ifugao or Kalinga of Luzon is associated with a political structure of the most modest sort. It is thus unnecessary to assume that any extensive political coordination or control of labor was needed to build the irrigation systems of Yayoi Japan.

Although Yayoi culture began in north Kyūshū, it quickly diffused to the Kinki area of central Japan. Kinki immediately established itself as a rival cultural center throughout this period, and from the subsequent Tomb period on it successfully replaced north Kyūshū as the cultural center of Japan.

The success of Yayoi technology is in part attributable to the use of iron tools. Because iron corrodes in the moist atmosphere of Japan, iron artifacts of the Yayoi period are unearthed only rarely; but there are iron finds such as the sickle, knife, arrowhead, and fishhook. While iron was used for the manufacture of utilitarian implements for daily living and subsistence, bronze was used primarily for non-utilitarian or ceremonial objects.

There are two major categories of bronze objects of Yayoi culture: "swords" and "bells." Both come in several definable types. Some of the chronologically earlier swords were made in China, but other swords and all bells were presumably made in Japan. Chinese swords have a shape and metallic consistency which indicate that they can be used for fighting. The bells are from about four to forty inches in height. Although some of them were used to produce sound, most of them show no indication that they were so used. The distribution of bells is by and large restricted to Kinki, Shikoku, and Chūgoku regions. Swords have a much wider distribution, including Kyūshū and Chūbu as well as the aforementioned three regions.

Some of the swords of earlier periods are found in burial sites in association with individual burials. Since only some of the burials are associated with swords and these burials tend to have other ornamental goods like necklaces, bracelets, and mirrors, the common interpretation is that these individuals had a special political and/or religious status in the community. Swords, however, later became dissociated from burials and tend to be found by themselves, often in groups, as bells commonly are. These swords, and also bells in general, are thought to have religious significance for the corporate community, rather than any symbolic meaning for certain individuals.

These considerations suggest that at least toward the end of the period, Yayoi social organizations recognized certain individuals as occupying a status superior to the rest of the community and as having some, though not much, political authority. The social organization may very well correspond with what Service (1962) has called "chiefdom" or Fried (1967) has designated as "rank society."

The Tomb Period

There is no question that rice cultivation, introduced on a major scale at the beginning of the Yayoi period, brought about fundamental changes in the culture. However, the phenomenal effects of this new economy were not seen until the following Tomb period, when from about A.D. 250 one begins to find burial mounds of influential men being built throughout western Japan. So far 2160 tomb mounds, large and small, have been identified. Whether mound building was initiated by diffusion from Korea and also whether it first began in Kinki or in north Kyūshū are points of heated debate. Mound building had modest beginnings in the late Yayoi, mostly in north Kyūshū, only a short distance from Korea, and thus one cannot ignore the burial mounds of Korea as a possible stimulus to its beginnings in Japan, or if not its beginnings, at least to further elaboration in size and structure.

At any rate, tombs of the Tomb period are markedly different from the modest burial mounds of the Yayoi period. They are much larger in scale, and often shaped like an old-fashioned keyhole or a rectangle. From the Early Tomb period, one finds mounds up to 200 meters long. The size gradually increased until about the early fifth century; thereafter the size on the whole decreased, although the number of tombs explosively increased in the sixth and seventh centuries. The largest tomb, belonging to Emperor Nintoku is 475 meters long and has three moats surrounding it. It is estimated that about 20,000 terra cotta figures known as *haniwa* were placed around the mound and that 26,000 cubic meters of stones were used as part of the inner structure.

Earlier tombs utilized natural hills and knolls, on which dirt was piled to make them into a standard form. Inside, early tombs had a small chamber containing a coffin; later ones had a passageway and a larger chamber and in general manifested technical improvement in construction over the earlier tombs. Inside, there were a large number of burial goods, such as mirrors (Chinese and Japanese imitations), beads, bracelets, necklaces, agricultural implements, and swords, From the latter half of the fifth century, the inclusion of continental type equestrian equipment becomes noticeable. It is about this time also that large quantities of weaponry are added to burials. This fact has given rise to the theory of the conquest of Japan by nomadic horseback riders from the Asiatic continent, most vociferously expounded by Egami (1962, 1968). Whereas, the theory goes, rulers of the Early Period were by and large civil-religious leaders oriented toward

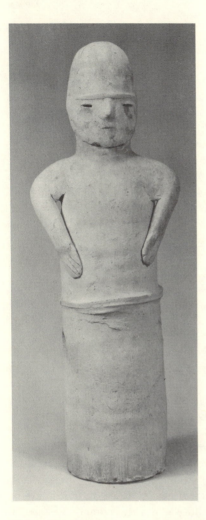

A terra cotta figure known as *haniwa*.
It has been estimated that as many
as 20,000 of these were placed around
Emperor Nintoku's tomb. (59 cm. high.)

the welfare of the community and agricultural success, later rulers were military-religious leaders oriented toward political control and expansion through military conquest.

An interesting sidelight on Egami's theory is Hattori's lexicostatistical data which place the split between the Japanese language (using the Kyōta dialect for this purpose) and the Ryūkyūan language (Shuri dialect) at about A.D. 500 (Hattori, 1955). It is plausible to imagine that some of the inhabitants of Kyūshū fled to the Ryūkyū islands to the south to escape the domination of the new military power from the continent and that the speech of these refugees became the Ryūkyūan language, while the speech of the remaining people later became present-day Japanese. The nomadic conquerors presumably adopted the native speech. Attractive though this theory is, we have no clear evidence from continental Asia of migration of a military group in the third to fourth century through Korea to Japan. (Ishida ed., 1966, p. 74). At any rate, it is not necessary to invoke foreign invasion in order to explain the sudden increase in military equipment in the late fifth century. Weaponry could have been imported without the invasion of foreigners and used by native Japanese rulers in response to, for example, a population explosion resulting from success in rice cultivation and the consequent need for more territory.

The political significance of tomb builders, cannot be ignored entirely, however one might interpret the data. Large tombs of over 200 meters in length with thousands of *haniwa* placed around them cannot be built overnight by a small group of families; nor would such a group have any need for gigantic mounds to bury one or two individuals. Assuming these tombs were built for political leaders, how powerful might such rulers have been? Japanese archaeologists tend to exaggerate the extent of the political power of these rulers, calling them "dictators" or "despots" and suggesting their exploitation of the peasants. On the basis of the sheer amount of labor involved in the construction of these tombs, however, there is no need to assume political control of a large mass of people. It is sometimes suggested that it took twenty years to build the tomb for Emperor Nintoku. This would mean that on the average less than four cubic square meters of stones had to be transported per day in order to pile up the 26,000 cubic meters of stones and that only about three *haniwa* had to be made per day to make the necessary 20,000 *haniwa*. Thus in terms of the amount of daily labor, construction of even the largest tombs need not imply coordination and exploitation of a large labor force. Moreover, to claim that people were exploited or enslaved in building the tombs assumes that they totally lacked the willingness to participate. It is entirely possible that participation in the construction of religious centers was an honor or at least an unquestioned duty. It is also possible that the occasional labor service did not interfere very much with subsistence activities and was not exceedingly onerous or unpleasant. More careful analysis of labor requirements for tomb construction—of the sort which Erasmus (1966) and Kaplan (1963) have done with Meso-American monument building—is urgently needed in order to have interpretations which are more closely related to factual information.

The reason for the gigantic size of the tombs, therefore, seems to lie elsewhere than in the despotism of rulers desiring self-aggrandizement and exploitation of the people. The reason might have been found in some symbolic function the tombs served. For example, it might have been necessary to impress peasants with the authority of the ruler, since peasants in the early Tomb period, coming out of the Yayoi communal stage, were not accustomed to the kind of status disparity observed in the later Tomb periods. Also, under the ever increasing political expansion and military

The tomb of Emperor Sujin, Nara Prefecture. So far, 2160 tomb mounds, large and small, have been identified. (330 m. in length, including the moat.)

conquest of neighboring territories, integration of a number of hitherto independent political units was problematic, and the construction of tombs of rulers, perhaps with the aid of people of all territories, served to help unite the expanding state.

Y. Kobayashi (1959,) has suggested, in interpreting the relationship among various tombs, that a ruler in the Nara basin held paramountcy not only in Kinki but as far as north Kyūshū and Kantō. The major evidence for this argument is the Chinese mirrors, made from the same molds, which are found in tombs throughout western Japan but in the greatest number in the Kinki region. Kobayashi interprets this distribution to signify the political superiority of a Kinki ruler, who gave these mirrors which he obtained from China to rulers of neighboring petty states as a symbol of their subordination. Since the mirror has had a magico-religious significance in Shinto throughout Japanese history, it would not be farfetched to assume that political leaders, who were most likely also religious leaders, used mirrors as symbols of their power. The tomb of Ōtsukayama, near Kyōto, which holds the key position in Kobayashi's theory, is dated to be around A.D. 300. Thus this theory holds that a considerable amount of political unification was effected very early in the Tomb period.

Intriguing though this theory is, there are difficulties. For one thing, while there are tombs as far as Kyūshū which contain mirrors presumably given by the Nara ruler, there are many tombs in intervening areas which do not contain such mirrors. These areas presumably were not subordinate to Nara. How did the Nara ruler maintain control over distant nations if there were enemies in between? Second, establishment of such large-scale political unification so soon after the Yayoi is problematic, especially since evidence of military power is only modest about that time. Third, the nature and extent of the political domination which Nara enjoyed are ill-specified. Political domination suggests complete control of subordinate powers, but it may be more realistic to envision political alliances that Nara maintained with whichever petty state it could persuade, partly through shows of force but also through other means such as economic sanction and magical power.

We have reviewed two opposing interpretations of evidence from the Tomb period. Egami, in his nomadic equestrian military conquest theory, favors the view that large scale political power first arose in north Kyūshū, Japan's gateway to the continent, and then moved to the Kinki region. Kobayashi's theory, on the other hand, supports the view that political domination began in Kinki and that the power which arose there extended to surrounding regions, including north Kyūshū. In making inferences about political organization on the basis of archeological evidence, there is the constant danger of assuming that cultural diffusion—of mirrors and equestrian gear, for example—must imply political control. There is no necessary relationship between the two, and such inferences are not warranted without other kinds of supportive evidence.

At any rate, some time during the Tomb period, one ruler did emerge victorious among the various contending powers. He and his descendants came to be known as the emperors of Japan. By the end of this period, Japan clearly achieved a level at which rulers had organized power behind their authority, thus deserving the designation "state" either in Service's or Fried's terminology.

The Historic Period

The Emergence of Civilization: Great and Little Traditions

The end of the Tomb period gradually merges into the documented period of Japanese history. The oldest documents in Japan, *Kojiki* and *Nihon Shoki,* presumably written in the early eighth century, contain accounts of earlier times which are only in part factual, the remainder being mythological and legendary in varying degrees. These myths and legends, however, enable us to engage in indirect reconstruction by correlating them where possible with archaeological data and ethnographic and historical information from areas surrounding Japan. Comparison of the myths in these documents with those of continental Asia and the Pacific has indicated historical connection with and cultural diffusion from those parts of the world. Also, archaeologists and historians have attempted with partial success to correlate legendary tales and personalities in these documents with archaeological findings. Not to be forgotten in this connection are Chinese documents describing the customs and manners of Japanese people. Interpretation of these data is extremely difficult, and there is as much controversy as agreement.

With these written documents, Japan entered the fully historic period, a period which is traditionally the concern of the historical discipline rather than anthropology. What follows is a synoptic treatment within the anthropological framework of a few historical factors that are relevant to the understanding of modern Japan.

Politically, the Tomb period may be characterized as a primitive state, and the earliest historic period marks the beginning of "classical civilization" in Japan, a civilization that came into being as a result of the fusion of the indigenous Japanese tradition and the Chinese civilization of the T'ang Dynasty, which was massively and actively imported from the seventh century on. It is important to observe that without the fairly elaborate political structure already developed in the Tomb period, a civilization could not have been built in Japan. Japan had been in contact with the continent from time immemorial, and items of Chinese civilization had been diffusing to Japan for hundreds of years without having substantial influence on Japanese culture. By the seventh century Japan was "ready" to start a civilization, albeit in a small way compared with China.

It was at this time that the Chinese writing system was imported, and that Chinese became the official language in which to preserve records, much as Latin was the official language of the Church in the Middle Ages, regardless of the local vernacular language. Chinese governmental organization, complete with all the ministerial and lesser offices, was imported *in toto* whether or not such offices had any use in the context of the Japanese government. (Crump, 1952.) The capital of Heijō (the present Nara) was planned and laid out after the model of the seventh century Chinese capital of Ch'an-an. Buddhism, then the officially approved religion of China, was imported and espoused by court aristocrats. Confuscianism, the official doctrine of the Chinese state, was also introduced in Japan, although it did not have much influence in Japan until the Tokugawa period.

I have said that Japan became a civilization with the wholesale introduction of Chinese culture. One important mark of civilization, as distinct from the primitive state, is the difference between the style of life of the ruling elite and that of the ordinary people. (Befu, 1967). As the ruling aristocracy learned to read and write Chinese, the people were left behind as illiterate peasants. As the rulers espoused the high religion of foreign origin, and engaged in esoteric discourse on Buddhist sutras, the peasants were content with the practical efficacy of their folk Shinto beliefs handed down from former times. Buddhist temples of massive size were constructed one after another, and the splendor of Buddhist art—in architecture and iconography —symbolized the power and prestige of the rulers. Meanwhile, peasants worshipped their primitive deities in their humble makeshift shrines. As court nobles busied themselves with organizing and reorganizing the government (with little effect on the people) and vied for power and favor from the Emperor, the masses continued tilling the soil and minding their business in their village communities.

Thus the beginning of civilization meant that the gap between the rulers and the ruled widened, and two distinct cultural traditions came into being: the "great tradition" of the rulers on the one hand and the "little tradition" of the masses, or rather a series of "little traditions" as followed in different regions of Japan, on the other. But there were important countering processes which operated to relate the rulers to the ruled, so as to effect and maintain a unified political structure and an integrated culture. For example, the administrative system of the government reached down to the peasant communities through a variety of means, e.g., the proclamation of state ownership of all land and initiation of a taxation system imported from China. Another way that the great tradition was related to little traditions was dissemination of the teachings of Buddha by missionary Buddhist priests who traveled throughout the countryside. Obviously, priests had to interpret the esoteric philosophy of Buddhism and make it understandable to illiterate peasants; and the latter further interpreted the preaching in the light of their own experience and knowledge about the workings of the supernatural world. Herein lies one reason why ordinary Japanese Shintoism and Buddhism never constituted completely distinct religions. At any rate, elements of the great tradition began to permeate down to the village level, but always with modification and adaptation before being incorporated into the little tradition.

Cultural Crystallization

From about the ninth century on, after the initial period of almost indiscriminate importation of Chinese culture, Japan almost completely ceased contact with China and began a period of integrating the borrowed elements with the native tradition, eliminating some and modifying others. A large number of offices in the original bureaucratic structure transplanted from T'ang China were found to be useless and dropped. The examination system, which was open to all men in China, was highly modified to fit the traditional Japanese system of recruiting court officials from among court nobles. Japanese esthetic style began to reassert itself in various forms of art, architecture, and literature in combination with Chinese elements. For example, Buddhist sculpture and architecture began to reflect a distinctly Japanese style. The Chinese writing system became modified to allow the Japanese language to be recorded in the *kana* syllabary. This new writing system was used most effectively by court women during this period, who produced literary pieces of high quality, such as the *Tale of Genji*, while their brothers were still discoursing in Chinese and considered writing in Japanese below their dignity.

All in all this was a period spent assimilating the superior culture imported from the continent. Foster (Foster, 1960, pp. 227–234) has introduced the concept of cultural crystallization in his attempt to show how the total potential impact of the Hispanic culture on Spanish America "is channeled and limited by the successful efforts of new hybrid cultures to achieve reintegration and stability." Although there is a major difference in the process of acculturative influence between Spanish America and Japan, one involving conquest and the other not, Foster's concept of cultural crystallization seems to apply to Japan after the ninth century. In Japan, too, there was cultural selectivity, adaptation, and fusion until a new, stabilized synthesis developed which combined both the indigenous Japanese culture and imported Chinese elements.

The Imperial Institution

From the beginning of the historic period, if not before, the emperor was an indispensable political institution in Japan. An important characteristic of the Japanese emperor is his semidivine quality. Governance has been regarded in Japan as an activity inseparable from religious affairs: the emperor ruled in accordance with the will of his ancestors and other deities. His semidivine quality was derived from the presumption that he alone was the lineal descendant of the Sun Goddess, the mythological founder of Japan. This genealogical relationship conferred upon the emperor divine legitimacy to rule. The emperor alone among mortals was given the power of legitimating any government of Japan.

In the early days, the emperor was both the official high priest and the political ruler of the nation. As time went on, particularly since the ascendancy of the Fujiwara family in the ninth century, the emperor's power to rule was taken over by the Fujiwara and various other families which came and went in rather rapid succession until modern times. But no matter who came into power and controlled the nation, his power remained brute force until and unless it was legitimated by the emperor. It is this indispensable role which in an important way perpetuated the emperor as a political institution for over a thousand years and kept his office from being annihilated on many occasions in Japanese history when it came precariously close to destruction. At the same time, efforts to win the emperor's official backing have been the source of a good deal of political struggle in Japan, for the adversaries of the man who won it automatically became imperial enemies and illegitimate seekers of power.

This traditional Japanese concept of political legitimacy, in which sovereignty resides in one person, sharply contrasts with the modern Western counterpart, in which sovereignty resides in the people and is delegated to elected representatives. After World War II, with the adoption of a new constitution in Japan, sovereignty was transferred to the people, and the emperor lost his indispensable political function. A momentous implication of this fact is that the imperial institution can now be destroyed without causing a fundamental crisis in the political structure.

Feudalism

Another important development in Japanese history is the emergence of a feudal political order. With the decline in the power of the emperor from the beginning of the ninth century, local powers, monastic institutions, and court aristocrats gained tax exemptions for their estates. As they acquired more and more land, they effectively subverted the imperial taxation system by reducing the amount of taxable land to a small fraction of the total. The emperor in effect became merely one of the many landholders. Worse yet, with the rise in power of the Fujiwara family, the emperor lost control of his own court.

This decline in the central power reached another ebb when the *samurai* (warrior) deputies of title holders to estates began exercising independent power, thus becoming *de facto* rulers of provincial territories while title-holding court aristocrats stayed in the capital, busied themselves in poetry contests and other polite games of the court, and competed for high-ranking titles which in fact carried no power. At first the power of provincial warriors was not legitimate because it was obtained through usurpation without imperial sanction. However, when the Minamoto family, one of the most successful warrior groups, took virtual control of the whole nation in the twelfth century, the emperor conferred on them the title of *shōgun,* thus legitimizing the power of the Minamoto. Minamoto distributed provinces to his followers according to their merit and favor. Thus he began a period of feudalism which, while going through a number of transformations in its structure and changes in the ruling families, was to last until the middle of the nineteenth century.

Perhaps the most important division in the long feudal period is that between the decentralized form, in which subordinates of the *shōgun* retained a considerable amount of power and control over their respective provinces, and the centralized form, in which the *shōgun* managed to exercize a great deal of control over his subordinates called *daimyō.* Centralized feudalism began with the brief rule of Toyotomi Hideyoshi at the end of the sixteenth century and culminated during the 250 year hegemony of his successor, the Tokugawa family.

Several significant points should be made about Japan's feudalism. First, it resulted in the establishment of a military government and raised the status of warriors from mere executors and administrators of court orders to powerful rulers, of whom even the court aristocracy had to take heed. Second, military rule meant that the society sanctioned male dominance. The former high status of court noblewomen, who made themselves well known for their literary talent and romantic affairs, was now gone. Arranged marriage and even political marriage, in which women were simply pawns in the political chess game, became a common practice among warriors. To be sure, peasants were not on the whole affected by the institution of feudal male dominance.

Third, a political system based on personal loyalty became entrenched in feudalism. It is important that kinship as such was not a crucial consideration in the feudal system, as can be seen from a number of occasions during the feudal period when kinsmen as close as brother and brother or father and son fought against each other for power. Fourth, this personal relationship between the leader and the follower was rationalized into the normative concept of *on. On* is personal indebtedness which binds subordinates to their leader. It is a debt which the subordinate accrues as his master or lord grants a favor, a benefice like land, which the subordinate desires but cannot obtain in any other way because he does not control the resource. This favor, or debt, is to be repaid by the subordinate in the form of personal loyalty and service. As we shall see in subsequent chapters, the political value of *on* has played an enormously important role in Japan's modernization.

Fifth, the feudal military regime emphasized extreme asceticism, perfection of behavior, industry, austerity, and lack of concern for worldly things. Zen Buddhism, whose philosophy was in harmony with these warrior values, naturally appealed to warriors and was widely accepted by them. It helped to elaborate, perfect, and systematize the warrior's way of life, which now became the dominant part of the great tradition.

In addition, centralized feudalism, perfected in the early Tokugawa period, has special significance for modern Japan if only because this period immediately preceded the modern period and thus provided the "base line" for Japan's modern transformation. We shall use the term "traditional" with respect to Japan's past to refer to the culture of the Tokugawa period.

The political, social, and economic institutions of the nation were carefully and rigidly laid down in the early Tokugawa period. Warriors, peasants, artisans, and merchants were frozen into their respective castes, in that order of hierarchy; mobility and marriage between caste lines was strictly forbidden. When in the modern period, the former warriors and their descendants took control of the Meiji government and removed the caste barrier, the values and the style of life of the warrior caste began permeating down to the common people, in part through incorporation of these values in the new legal codes, such as the family law, and in part through formal and informal media of instruction and mass communications. This process, here called "samuraization," is analogous to the process whereby, in the beginnings of Japanese civilization, the great tradition was disseminated to the masses. In samuraization, the process was more effective and rapid. At the same time, the spread of warrior values was challenged by the influence of the West, which began coming into Japan at a rate similar to the importation of the T'ang civilization earlier in Japanese history. As we shall see, the resultant process of the modernization of Japan was a complex interplay between traditional warrior values and the foreign values coming from the West, as well as the more indirect social and political effects of imported industrial capitalism.

Japan as a Borrower

From prehistoric times Japan has experienced cultural diffusion from surrounding areas. We cannot be sure of the nature of diffusion in the early prehistoric times. But we know that at least since the beginning of the Yayoi period, the direction of diffusion has been overwhelmingly inward—into Japan from neighboring areas rather than the other way around. This pattern of cultural borrowing reached a new peak at the beginning of the historic period when a massive importation of Chinese culture took place, followed by another peak which began with the end of feudalism and the beginning of the modern period.

It is well to remember that Japan has always been at a periphery of major cultural centers, or what Kroeber has called "cultural climaxes," where most of cultural innovations occur and from which these innovations diffuse. Historical and geographical circumstances have made Japan principally a borrower or receiver of cultural innovations. As Kroeber has remarked, there are very few basic inventions which can be attributed to the Japanese. (Kroeber, 1948, p. 745). Rather, Japan has expended its energy in integrating what it borrows with the indigenous culture. Japan's uniqueness, according to Kroeber, lies in its ability to work out "stylistic" refinements of borrowed elements.

We noted earlier that after a period of major Chinese influence, Japan went through the process of synthesizing and crystallizing a new culture. At present Japan has not ended its period of massive Western influence. Given the present trend of worldwide technological development, moreover, it is not likely that Japan will be able to afford a period of seclusion and indulge in reconstituting its culture. Rather, bombardment by foreign influences on the one hand and the selection, adaptation, and synthesis of foreign elements on the other will have to continue side by side.

This intensive cultural borrowing has gone hand in hand with a feeling of inferiority which Japanese have toward donor cultures. In the language of social psychology, the reference group of the Japanese has always been a culturally or technologically superior nation. We do not know how this feeling of inferiority came about, although ultimately it probably has to be analyzed in relation to the desire of the Japanese to improve their cultural status relative to superior cultures.

The Peasant Community

The Peasant community is an enduring Japanese institution that cannot go unmentioned. Peasantry as a status contrasts with the ruling elite and the city dwellers. Peasants are politically subordinate to the former, as is evident in the requirement that they pay taxes and accept laws created by the rulers largely for their own benefit. They maintain an economic symbiosis with the latter but are socially distrustful of them. Peasants remained the major economic contributor to the state until well into the modern period.

In the decentralized period of feudalism, lower echelon foot soldiers and peasants were indistinguishable. The same individuals took up arms in time of war and tilled the soil between battles. In centralized feudalism a sharp line was drawn between peasants and warriors, and a distinct peasant way of life began to develop, although emulation of the warrior way of life—

within the limits set by sumptuary regulations—continued, especially among wealthier peasants. It is important to keep in mind this sharp difference in the style of life and in social institutions between peasants and warriors in the Tokugawa period. There was no one, homogeneous traditional Japanese culture: there were the peasants and the warriors, and also the court aristocracy and the city folk, each leading its own way of life (R.J. Smith, 1960).

Peasant communities of the Tokugawa period tended to be more politically autonomous, economically self-sufficient and socially self-contained than their later counterparts. But even in the Tokugawa period, political relations obviously tied villages to the state (Befu, 1965). Peasants, especially those near cities, sold crops to city people and bought merchandise from the city. Social contacts with neighboring communities and important regional religious centers kept peasants aware of the world outside them.

The modern period in Japan was inaugurated by the abolition of the feudal regime and the establishment of the Meiji government, which was intent on modernizing Japan as quickly as possible and thereby ridding Japan of Western military and economic threats. This story of Japan's modern transformation will be the central concern of the remainder of this book; but it must be seen against the backdrop of Japan's historical past and tradition.

SUGGESTED READINGS

Beardsley, Richard K.
1955   "Japan before history: a survey of the archaeological record." *Far Eastern Quarterly* 14: 317–346.

Befu, Harumi and Chester S. Chard
1960   "Preceramic cultures in Japan." *American Anthropologist* 62: 815–849.

Egami, Namio
1962   "Light on Japanese cultural origins from historical archeology and legend," in Robert J. Smith and Richard K. Beardsley, eds., *Japanese Culture, Its Development and Characteristics.* Viking Fund Publications in Anthropology No. 34, pp. 11–16.

Ishida, Eiichiro
1962   "Nature of the problem of Japanese cultural origins," in Robert J. Smith and Richard K. Beardsley, eds., *Japanese Culture, Its Development and Characteristics.* Viking Fund Publications in Anthropology No. 34, pp. 3–6.

Kindaichi, Kyosuke
1949   "The concepts behind the Ainu bear festival *(kumamatsuri),*" *Southwestern Journal of Anthropology* 5: 345–350.

Ōno, Susumu

1962   "The Japanese language: its origin and its sources," in Robert J. Smith and Richard K. Beardsley, eds., *Japanese Culture, Its Development and Characteristics.* Viking Fund Publications in Anthropology No. 34, pp. 17–21.

Reischauer, Edwin O.

1964   *Japan Past and Present.* New York: Alfred A. Knopf. (A brief overview.)

Takakura, Shin'ichiro

1960   "The Ainu of northern Japan: a study in conquest and acculturation," trans. and annot. by John A. Harrison. *Transactions of the American Philosophical Society,* n.s., vol. 50, part 4.

Watanabe, Hitoshi

1964   "The Ainu: a study of ecology and the system of social solidarity between man and nature in relation to group structure." Tokyo University: *Journal of the Faculty of Science.* Sect. V. 2: part 7, pp. 1–164.

Yawata, Ichiro

1962   "Prehistoric evidence for Japanese cultural origins," in Robert J. Smith and Richard K. Beardsley, eds., *Japanese Culture, Its Development and Characteristics.* Viking Fund Publications in Anthropology No. 34, pp. 7–10.

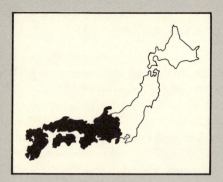

KEY

1. Kagoshima	17. Hyōgo	33. Yamanashi
2. Miyazaki	18. Kyoto	34. Kanagawa
3. Kumamoto	19. Wakayama	35. Tokyo
4. Ōita	20. Osaka	36. Chiba
5. Fukuoka	21. Mie	37. Saitama
6. Saga	22. Nara	38. Ibaraki
7. Nagasaki	23. Shiga	39. Tochigi
8. Kōchi	24. Fukui	40. Fukushima
9. Tokushima	25. Ishikawa	41. Yamagata
10. Kagawa	26. Gifu	42. Miyagi
11. Ehime	27. Aichi	43. Akita
12. Yamaguchi	28. Shizuoka	44. Iwate
13. Hiroshima	29. Nagano	45. Aomori
14. Shimane	30. Toyama	46. Hokkaidō
15. Okayama	31. Niigata	
16. Tottori	32. Gumma	

SEA OF

HONSHU I.

Chūgoku

14
16
12 13 15 17
18
25 30
24
26 29
33
6 5
11 10 23
27 28
4 8 9 20
7 3 19 22 21
2
1

Kyūshū

KYŪSHŪ I.

Shikoku

SHIKOKU I.

Kinki

Chūbu

HOKKAIDŌ I.

46

Hokkaidō

JAPAN

N

HONSHU I.

Chūbu

45

43

44

41   42

Tōhoku

31

40

PACIFIC OCEAN

32   39

37   38

35   36

34

Kantō

– – – Regions
——— Prefectures

JAPAN:
Regions and Prefectures

2 Kinship, Ritual Kinship, and Paternalism

The Concept of the Stem Family

The most important kinship unit in traditional Japan—recall that we are referring to the pre-modern, feudal period—was the group called *ie,* or the stem family. The structure and function of the *ie* began to modify themselves from the early modern period, and its characteristic features are rapidly disappearing. Yet the development of modern Japan cannot be understood without regard to this group.

The stem family consists of all those who commonly reside together and share social and economic life. It is primarily composed of close kin as its core, but may include distant kin and non-kin, e.g., employees, insofar as they reside with the core kinship group and participate in its social and economic life. It is, in addition, a corporate group, that is to say, it perpetuates itself from generation to generation beyond the life span of any single member of the group. After the retirement or death of its head, the stem family is continued through succession and inheritance, usually by one of the offspring, who stays with the parents after marriage and maintains the family line. This contrasts with the nuclear family of the United States, which starts when a couple sets up coresidence and, after the birth, maturation, and departure of the children, dissolves when one or both of the couple dies.

Although the term "household" is often used as an alternative translation to "stem family" for *ie,* this usage will be avoided here since there is a separate Japanese term *setai* which closely corresponds to the English term "household," meaning a residential, domestic unit, irrespective of the genealogical or kinship composition of the group. The national census of Japan commonly reports household composition, and sociological use of census reports must therefore be made with caution. There is another Japanese term *kazoku,* meaning a domestic unit composed of individuals related by blood or marriage, which is safely translated as "family." In actual usage, both scholarly and everyday, the terms *ie, setai,* and *kazoku* are often confused.

One important way in which the stem family of Japan differs from the Western family is in the treatment of non-kin. In the West, a non-kin or a distant kin residing with a family is not, strictly speaking, a member of the family, and a sharp distinction is made between members and non-members, kin and non-kin. In the Japanese stem family there is no such sharp distinction. This is not to say that there is no distinction whatever, or that Japanese can not tell the difference between them, but that in actual treatment of members a non-kin may be assigned a role similar to a kinsman's role. It should be admitted, however, that there was a tendency for non-kin to have an inferior status in the structure of the stem family. Numerically, non-kin constituted a fair percentage of members of stem families in the late Tokugawa Japan. In some areas upwards of 30% of stem family members have been reported to belong to the category of non-kin or distant kin (Nakano, 1964, pp. 194–276).

The importance of non-kin in the stem family is not simply numerical. This blurring of the demarcation line between kin and non-kin, i.e., not regarding kinship as an absolute criterion for recruitment into the stem family, has functional significance in numerous ways. For example, this feature has enabled Japanese to move out of the kinship context and adapt relatively readily to a non-kinship situation. It also explains why Japanese readily adopt non-kin when a family lacks a child to take over the family line and are not concerned if there is no actual continuity of blood. Too, this feature laid the basis for the efflorescence of ritual kinship and other family-like institutions in the early modern period.

What is of primary importance in the conception of the stem family is the economic pursuit of the group, and how each member contributes toward it, rather than how he is related through kinship to other members. The stem family is not realistically conceivable when the economic activities of the group are left out of consideration. To the extent that non-kin contribute toward this end, they are vital members. Thus the stem family is not, strictly speaking, a kinship unit, but an economic organization. It is illuminating to note in this connection that according to Japanese folklorists the Japanese terms *oya* and *ko,* which mean in modern Japanese "parent" and "child" respectively, originally referred to a leader of a work group and its members (Yanagita, 1937). Kinship considerations in such a group were of minor importance, granting at the same time that in most cases such work groups in traditional Japan involved kinsmen as the core. As work and home began to separate during the inception of the modern period of Japan, *oya* and *ko* began to have a strictly kinship meaning devoid of economic considerations. We shall see that the Japanese term *kazoku* (family) denoting a kinship-based domestic group as a separate concept from *ie,* is also of modern origin.

A fisherman couple waiting in their boat. The economic activity of
the family is an essential part of its definition.

Although the stem family was basically defined by coresidence, as stated
above, one proviso is necessary. Close kin living away from home for any
duration remained members of the stem family, and were subject to the
control of the family head. This situation continued until they returned
home or became fully absorbed into another stem family, e.g., through
marriage or adoption. In the modern period, too, until the adoption of the
new constitution after World War II, the stem family was legally responsible for and held control over its members even though they might move
away, e.g., to go to school away from home. Although the legal status of
the family head was changed after the war, his moral responsibility as head
of a family still remains.

As suggested above, the headship of a stem family was an extremely
important position. For the head was vested with the authority to control
its members and the responsibility to provide them not only with material
sustenance but moral guidance as well. He was responsible for managing
the family property, carrying on the family occupation, and caring for
deceased ancestors by, for example, officiating at their memorial services.
The headship was important, and its relinquishment either through death
or retirement and the succession of an heir were crucial events. Retirement
marked an end to the exercise of authority, after which the retired head

retained much respect but little formal power. Paralleling the retirement of the head was his wife's relinquishment of authority over cooking and other domestic matters to the heir's wife.

The importance of this headship is reflected in the convention of Japanese family sociologists of indicating family composition in relation to the family head: the head, his father, his mother, his wife, his oldest son, etc. It is also reflected in the special position of the heir. Because the head alone exercised authority in the stem family and controlled even his brothers and sisters, the heir, who was destined to assume this position, was socialized early into his special role. A differential and favored treatment of the heir and inculcation of his special responsibilities characterized his socialization. His siblings were in turn taught to show respect and deference to the potential head of the family.

Although succession by the oldest son was the dominant pattern, there were variant forms which should be mentioned. In some areas of northern Honshū, the oldest child, regardless of the sex, was expected to remain with the parents. If the oldest child was a girl, a man was brought into her home as her groom, and he assumed the actual headship. Thus the headship was always carried on by a male, although the line of genetic continuity shifted between sexes depending on the sex of the oldest child. In another variation, distributed mainly on the southern coast of Japan, the youngest child— usually the youngest son—succeeded, while older children moved out.

Whatever the pattern of succession, the stem family could not operate without a clearly defined headship. This meant that when the family lacked an appropriate person to be recruited into the headship, e.g., no son in the region where the oldest son was to take over the headship, some alternative method had to be resorted to. Many such alternatives were available. (Befu, 1962). The most common method was to "adopt" a man to marry one of the daughters, in case there is no son. Adoption was executed simultaneously with his uxorilocal marriage. In the absence of any child, a child of either sex might be adopted; if a boy, he would later take over the headship, .or if a girl, she would marry uxorilocally a man who would become the head. One notes in these patterns of succession, a relative absence of concern for unilineal descent, patrilineal or matrilineal, although in practice a son takes over the headship more often than an in-marrying male.

The concept of *kazoku* (family) as exclusively a kinship unit was first introduced from the West. When the civil code was promulgated under the Meiji Constitution, it incorporated the Western concept of the family, combining it with Confucian ideals, in both of which non-kin had no legitimate place. In practice, of course, the traditional stem family was not immediately replaced by the legal conception of family, and has persisted, though in decreasing degree, until the present time. The gradual decrease in the proportion of non-kin and an increasingly sharp separation between

A mother and her son. Succession by the oldest son is
the dominant pattern in Japan.

kin and non-kin in the stem family has not been so much due to the legal change mentioned above as to economic and social changes brought about as a result of modernization. Because of the modern emphasis on efficiency and industrial technology and the attendant labor shortage and wage increase, small traditional occupations found it difficult to compete with the new sources of employment in recruiting labor forces. As this happened, the hitherto vague distinction between kin and non-kin became sharpened, *bona fide* wages had to be paid to non-kin rather than just spending money, and also non-kin felt relatively freer than kinsmen to leave the business. At the same time, the stem family as a social group and its business as an economic enterprise, which were once undifferentiated, began to constitute separate spheres of life. The family head and his son participated in both spheres as before, but the head's wife now spent most of her time with the family, whereas non-kin employees restricted their activities by and large to the business sphere. Thus the stem family gradually began to assume the character of the legal family as defined in the civil code.

Structure and Size of the Family

Family Structure

To obtain some notion of the structural variation of the stem family in traditional Japan, let us review Koyama's studies (1959, 1962) of the census records of a village for a sixty-year period from 1802 to 1861. His analysis reveals that families went though a variety of structural stages (Diagram 2:1). For example, a married couple (type 1) has children and becomes a nuclear family (type 2; 66.7% of type 1 shifted to type 2). The children mature and the son marries, bringing in his wife and thus creating a lineally extended family (type 3; 26.1% of type 2 shifted to type 3). The former head grows old and retires and the married son becomes the head of the family; the family is now a collateral extended type (type 4; 50% of type 3 shifted to type 4). The siblings of the new head of the family move away; by this time the head had his own children, creating a three-generational lineal family (type 5; 44.8% of type 4 shifted to type 5). With the death of the senior couple, the family reverts to type 2 (61.3% made this shift).

A little calculation would show that only a small percentage of the families in this community followed the entire sequence from type 1 to type 5. That is, this sequence shows only a tendency, with a large number of cases deviating from it. For example, if a family of type 3 had one son, the son might marry and become the family head, thus creating a family with a head, his wife and his retired parents (type 6; 21.7% of type 3 shifted to type 6). Then this family type would most naturally expand into type 5 (54.5% made this shift), or if the retired parents died before procreation, it will revert back to type 1, a couple without children (6.1% made this shift).

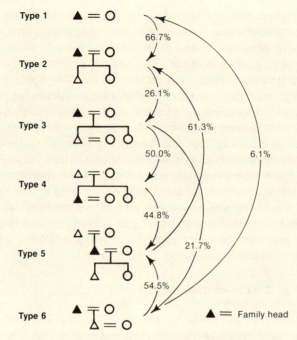

Diagram 2:1.   Domestic Cycle in a Tokugawa Village
(Adapted from Koyama, 1959).

Three important conclusions may be drawn from this analysis. First, to speak of *the* family type of traditional Japan, as if there was only one principal type, is a gross distortion of fact. Such a view is predicated on the assumption that a traditional society is simple in structure, that the reality comes close to whatever is the stated ideal of the society, and that with modern changes it becomes more and more complex. Such an assumption is usually an expression of our lack of detailed empirical knowledge about the past, coupled with a functional bias inherent in social sciences, which regard past, traditional societies as homogeneous and static. What is revealed in Koyama's analysis is that even in traditional Japan it is difficult to speak of any central tendency or a major structural type of family and that a great deal of variability obtained in the family structure.

Second, although we often speak of *the* domestic or family cycle of a given community, there are in fact many sequential patterns which a family of a given structural type can follow. In fact, the sequence followed by a given family is seldom a closed cycle, in which all the families go through all the stages in a given sequence and return to the first stage, to repeat the whole sequence again. Rather, the sequence of stages which a given family follows in the sixty-year period is almost unique, seldom repeated by any other family of the community.

Third, the nuclear family in a structural sense, corresponding to types 1 and 2 here, does not dissolve with the marriage of children and the parents' death as it does in the West, but instead shifts and expands into other structural forms. This is precisely because the family in traditional Japan was a stem family, a corporate unit which perpetuated itself regardless of the structure it might assume at any one moment. Since the traditional family system required junior sons to move out of the family of orientation and set up their own stem families, it was inevitable for these newly established stem families to be nuclear in form. This observation necessitates a distinction between the structurally nuclear family of the West and that of traditional Japan. I shall use the terms "conjugal (nuclear) family" for the former and "stem (nuclear) family" for the latter.

A grandfather and his grandchildren.

This distinction is crucial in understanding the development of the modern Japanese family system. It is often said in family sociology that industrialization has the effect of creating nuclear families at the expense of various traditional forms of the extended family. Koyama's data show that in his sample 28.9% of all families were nuclear in an agrarian community of traditional Japan. But as we have seen, these nuclear families do not dissolve in one generation but transform themselves into various other types because they were stem nuclear rather than conjugal. What industrialization does is to create the conjugal type of nuclear family. Therefore, with the inception of the industrialization of Japan, conjugal families began existing side by side with the traditional stem families of various forms and increasing in proportion at the expense of the latter.

An analysis of the 1920 census shows that in that year about 60% of all Japanese families were nuclear (irrespective of whether stem nuclear or conjugal) and about 40% extended. Koyama's limited sample surveyed in 1956–57 (Koyama, 1960) shows that the proportion of nuclear families further increased to about 80%, reducing extended families to a small minority. This increase in the nuclear family, compared with Koyama's figure for the Tokugawa period, has been in part due to a demographic factor. The population of Japan at the beginning of the Meiji period was less than 35,000,000, but it doubled by 1940 and is now in excess of 100,000,000. This rapid increase meant that increasing numbers of junior sons had to move out and set up nuclear families. Thus even without the effects of industrialization, the sheer effect of demographic increase is capable of increasing the proportion of nuclear families. We have no way of knowing how many or what proportion of the nuclear families of 1920, or of the present for that matter, are stem nuclear and how many are conjugal. We can only conjecture that because of Japan's rapid industrialization, an increasing proportion of nuclear families is now conjugal rather than stem nuclear.

Demographic Trends

A word may be said about the overall demographic trends in Japan. Traditional Japan, like practically all other agrarian traditional societies, was characterized by a relatively static population, in which a high birth rate was roughly matched by an equally high death rate, with particularly high infant mortality. With the advent of the modern age, the death rate, especially of the new born and infants, rapidly decreased, while at the same time life expectancy began to lengthen. These factors caused the population to increase rapidly, at the rate of around five per thousand in the early Meiji, around fifteen per thousand from 1920 to 1955, ignoring some fluctuations. Since 1955 the rate of increase has dropped to about ten per thousand, due in large measure to the decreasing birth rate. Table 2:1 shows these trends.

These demographic transitions from high birth and death rates through high birth rate and low death rate to low birth and death rates follow the pattern observed by Western nations (Davis, 1963). As a background to the decrease in birth rate, one must understand that the success of industrialization made attainment of a high living standard possible. From the point of view of individual Japanese, attainment of a high standard of living involved delaying marriage and keeping the family size down. A number of methods of population control were known and used in the Tokugawa period. Infanticide and abortion were widely practiced by poor peasants who could not afford to feed an additional mouth. In modern times, infanticide is practically never resorted to. Use of contraceptive devices, on the other hand, has

TABLE 2:1.

RATES OF POPULATION INCREASE, 1872–1965

Year	Rate of Increase (per 1,000)
1872	5.1
1880	8.6
1890	8.7
1900	11.7
1910	13.6
1920	14.7
1930	14.2
1940	13.0
1950	16.1
1960	9.3
1965	8.0

spread widely. Also, abortion has been legalized in postwar years and is resorted to by millions of women every year, the estimated number of abortions exceeding the number of live births. However, the ratio of abortions to live births has been steadily declining since 1959. This relative decrease in abortion has been accompanied by an increasing use of contraceptive devices. In 1967, 53% of surveyed couples were currently using one device or another (Anon., 1968).

Family Size

Turning now to the size of the family, we compare data for 1920, the earliest date for which we have reliable data, with those for 1960. Census reports show *household* size, not family size. Although the difference between them is negligible for our purposes, it is important to keep in mind that we are using one as an approximation of the other. As Table 2:2 shows,

TABLE 2:2.

COMPARISON OF HOUSEHOLD SIZE, 1920 AND 1960

Household Size	1920	1960
1	5.7%	4.7%
2	12.5	12.7
3	15.2	16.0
4	15.3	18.9
5	14.5	17.2
6	12.6	13.2
7	9.5	8.4
8	6.3	4.7
9	3.8	2.3
10	2.2	1.1
11 and over	2.3	0.8
	100.0%	100.0%

the household size has shrunk in the forty-year span. Percentages of households with four through six members have increased at the expense of larger households—those with seven or more members. Percentages of smaller households of one to three members, on the other hand, have remained fairly constant. Table 2:3 directly shows the trend in the average household size from 1920 to 1965.

TABLE 2:3.
AVERAGE HOUSEHOLD SIZE, 1920–1965

Year	Nationwide	Urban	Rural
1920	4.89	4.47	4.99
1925	4.88	4.43	5.01
1930	4.98	4.61	5.11
1935	5.03	4.74	5.18
1940	5.00	4.62	5.25
1945	4.85	4.25	5.20
1950	4.97	4.45	5.34
1955	4.97	4.73	5.32
1960	4.56	4.36	4.95
1965	4.08	3.90	4.51

Marriage, Residence, and Divorce

Marriage and Residence

Marriage in Japan has always been monogamous, although concubinage was practiced to some extent—mostly in cities by wealthy individuals and some *samurai*. Although the concubine and her children occupied a legally recognized status in the society, their status was inferior to that of the legitimate wife and her children in terms both of general regard by the people and of inheritance and succession. Although concubinage has been practiced, the great majority of Japanese men have had no concubine, and the source of sexual gratification outside the home was by and large limited to the entertainment they sought in gay quarters. The entertainment world of *geisha* girls emphasized and symbolized the traditional segregation of sexual gratification from marriage, which was considered primarily a means for perpetuating the stem family.

In traditional Japan, the marriage practices of the peasants differed radically from those of the warriors. The peasant practices are important for us because of the sheer number of people involved, the warrior practices because of their implications for the modern period. Let us therefore briefly review both.

In traditional Japanese peasant society marriage was contracted between members of hamlet community; it was based on romantic love and was established through one's own choice. Premarital sexual relations were approved between such partners. However, any attempt on the part of a girl to attract men of other communities or on the part of a boy to flirt with girls of neighboring hamlets was strongly disapproved. Such attempts were met with definite sanction, including physical punishment, meted out by the youth group of the village.

When the relationship became securely established between a man and a woman, a member of the youth group went to the parents of the prospective bride and groom to ask for permission for marriage. Since permission was almost always granted, this amounted not so much to asking for their permission as to reporting of the forthcoming marriage. The go-between's role in this situation was a perfunctory one—what Gamō has called "pro forma go-between" (1967)—compared with his role in a truly arranged marriage where neither partner has any prior knowledge of the other— Gamō's "substantive go-between." Most commonly, a relatively simple ceremony was performed to legitimate the relationship between the partners as marriage; but the partners did not change their residence immediately. They continued to sleep where they had been sleeping, usually either their respective natal homes or their youth lodges, whichever was the practice in the region. After this ceremony, however, there usually was a shift in the work arrangement. In general, either the bride or the groom, again depending on the local practice, spent a certain portion of time working for the partner's parents. The groom would do farm work and the bride farm work and domestic chores. This residential work pattern lasted until the previous, co-residential couple in the groom's home, such as his parents or his older brother and his wife, moved out or retired from active life. This post-marital residential arrangement may be called "duo-patrilocal" (Gōda, 1958). Even after the permanent move, the bride visited her parents frequently; and for the delivery of the first one or two babies, she commonly returned home, as a bride still often does in present-day Japan. This close and continued relationship was possible because of the proximity of the spouse's natal home (Ōmachi, 1963).

Some variant forms of marriage and residence among peasants of traditional Japan may be briefly mentioned here. One variant is matri-patrilocal residence, in which the groom first moved over to his bride's natal home and lived there for a certain duration, providing labor services to his in-laws, and then brought his wife back to his natal home, a practice in limited areas of northern Honshū. A variant form still more limited in distribution was permanent duolocal residence, which was probably practiced only in one small area in the mountainous central Japan. In this form, man and wife never lived together, but stayed for life with their respective blood relatives. When children were born, they stayed with their mothers (Befu, 1968). A third variant is uxorilocal residence, where a man goes to his wife's home to live permanently. We have encountered this form of residence above in discussing adoption practices. As noted, it occurs in northern Japan where by custom the oldest child regardless of sex stays home and marries an incoming spouse. Uxorilocal residence results when the oldest child happens to be a girl. in this case, on the average only 50% of marriages would be uxorilocal. Full 100% uxorilocal residence, together with matrilineal descent, has been claimed to be the rule in the late prehistoric and early historic Japan. But the evidence is contradictory and does not warrant ready acceptance of the claim.

Marriage among the ruling warrior caste was of another world entirely. The fact that the two families generally lived in widely separated areas and had no knowledge of each other prompted the use of a go-between in initiating the marriage. Needless to say, the partners to marriage themselves had little or no previous acquaintance with one another until the day of the wedding. Marriage abruptly brought the bride over from her home to the groom's on the day of the wedding, at which time marriage was consumated. This type of marriage among warriors was a contract between families and a means of perpetuating the family. Suppression of individual desires in the choice of mates and after marriage in one's general conduct for the sake of the well-being of the corporate family was demanded of both husband and wife. In this context, any mutual affective gratification, including sexual satisfaction, which tended to undermine the corporate interest of the family, was understandably suppressed. The male dominance of the society, however, enabled men to find sexual satisfaction in the entertainment world, whereas women were not allowed to seek such gratification outside the marriage.

Japan's modernization coincided with the samuraization process—the spread of the ideology of the ruling warrior class. Through introduction of the warrior ideology in a modified form in the Civil Code and through incorporation of this ideology in the school curricula, the prestigeful warrior marriage and family customs began to supplant the local peasant forms. Although even now there are isolated pockets, especially on small offshore islands, where traditional peasant forms still remain, by the end of World War II marriage and the family in the countryside were almost completely transformed. It is in a way curious that as industrialization proceeded in Japan, the marriage practice shifted, at least in numerical dominance (no less that 70% of the population was rural at the close of the Tokugawa period) from romantic marriage to arranged marriage. This does not mean that industrialization and the consequent social mobility, the rise in women's status, etc., did not promote romantic marriage, but that the forces favoring romantic marriage were countered by a strong ideological factor favoring arranged marriage. The net effect was that as arranged marriage began to be the rule, the traditional romantic marriage of rural Japan disappeared; at the same time, in cities, romantic marriage, fostered by a wholly different set of factors, began to rise slowly, at a speed checked by the countering samuraization process.

It is only in the postwar years, partly through the 1948 Civil Code, that romantic marriage has been given a stamp of legal as well as popular approval. In face of these radical legal and attitudinal changes, one now finds the actual practices lagging behind. Romantic marriage is not universally practiced and people do not find the social environment conducive to carrying it out (Blood, 1967). For one thing, Japanese find it difficult to meet potential partners for a romantic relationship. Most college students, for example, do not have the financial resources to be married. Moreover, there is a general disapproval of student marriages on the assumption that serious study does not or should not allow time for married life. Also, girls and their parents alike consider college students a risk since they have no permanent employment, and their future is very uncertain. Once a man starts working, his social life is much limited to the work situation. Yet if a student does not happen to meet a suitable girl in college, he is not likely to meet another.

Young people who do not go to college are no better off in this regard. High school graduates, whether they commute to work from home or move to a place near their employment, generally do not find appropriate social settings to meet people of the opposite sex for serious romantic purposes except at the place of employment. The casual meeting of such a person, without a proper introduction, at parties, for example, or coffee shops, or recreational facilities, is not approved of in Japan as a way of finding a marital partner. Some are fortunate enough to find a mate at the place of work, but these are numerically insignificant.

There is in addition a psychological problem. As we shall see in the section on the Japanese personality, there is a tendency for Japanese to feel particularly comfortable in a situation in which they are interacting with people with whom they have a relatively deep emotional commitment. The other side of this coin is that they feel inhibited from approaching a stranger or casual acquaintance of the opposite sex with a potentially serious intent such as marriage. Moreover, a more or less serious, "steady" relationship between an unmarried man and woman with no definite intention of marriage is still frowned upon as improper. Yet, having dates with several persons one after another is considered "loose." For these reasons, young people tend to rely on parents, friends, and other intermediaries, at least for the initial introduction. Even in the urban middle class, which is more "emancipated" than any other group, only about one-half of Blood's sample couples met each other without any intermediary (Blood, 1967, p. 36). It may be noted here that these intermediaries screen and select out for introduction those whom they judge to be potentially appropriate partners.

While the new romantic ideology began spreading in cities, where it finds social and economic factors supporting it, its diffusion into rural areas has lagged behind. For example, in Koyama's rural-urban comparison of the family system, it was found that 59.6% of the rural sample proposed marriage through a go-between, as against 31.9% of the city sample (Koyama ed., 1960). Also, a larger percentage (49.4%) of the city sample than the rural sample (31.9%) responded that the partners to the marriage themselves were more interested in contracting their marriage than their parents, who more or less went along with the children's desire, whereas a larger proportion (23.3%) of the rural sample than the urban (8.7%) responded that their parents took the initiative in their marriage and that the partners were satisfied with the outcome.

Divorce

A similar complex interplay of traditional ideology and modern social and economic forces is seen operating on the divorce rate in Japan. Family sociologists have generally blamed increasing technological development as being at the root of increasing divorce rates in the United States. Curiously, the divorce rate in Japan has on the whole steadily declined since the start of the modern period, except for the relatively sharp rise during and immediately after World War II (Kawashima and Steiner, 1960). The following table (Table 2:4) comparing the divorce trends in Japan and the United States, calculated on a per 1000 population basis, shows the opposite trends in the two countries.

How are we to comprehend these contradictory trends? Kawashima and Steiner's analysis (1960) is instructive here. We have seen that through the process of samuraization, the values and institutions of the warrior caste permeated the common people. Part and parcel of this process was the spread of the ideology of the warrior family system which emphasized male dominance, combined it with patrilocal residence and fused it with the concept of the corporate family. As a consequence, a bride moving into her husband's father's home found herself on trial, to be sent back home if found incapable of adapting to the "tradition" of her husband's family, or unable to produce a child. Since her husband's parents were the guardians and upholders of the family tradition, a good deal of "fitting into the family tradition" meant for the bride to get along well with her in-laws and receive their approval through demonstrations of submission and service to them. In fact, the marriage was often not registered with the government for more than a year after the wedding, for fear that she might have to be sent back home. Should this occur before registration, and it would normally occur early in marriage, at least the bride's legal record would not show divorce but remain unblemished. Thus if these cases of extralegal divorces are included in the statistics, divorce rates in early modern Japan would be even higher than shown in Table 2:4.

TABLE 2:4. COMPARISON OF DIVORCE RATES IN JAPAN AND
THE UNITED STATES (RATE/ 1000)

Year	Japan	United States
1890	2.69	0.5
1895	2.62	0.6
1900	1.43	0.7
1905	1.26	0.8
1910	1.17	0.9
1915	1.10	1.0
1920	0.99	1.6
1925	0.86	1.5
1930	0.79	1.6
1935	0.70	1.7
1940	0.66	2.0
1945	—	3.5
1950	1.01	2.6
1955	0.84	2.3
1960	0.74	2.2
1965	0.78	2.5

Sources:
Japan:1890–1935, Kawashima and Steiner, 1960; 1960 and 1965, based on *Asahi Nenkan,* 1967.
United States: 1890–1935, U.S. Bureau of the Census, *Statistical Abstract of the United States: 1940;* 1940–1960, U.S. Department of Health, Education, and Welfare, Public Health Service. National Center for Health Statistics, 1967; 1965, U.S. Bureau of the Census, *Statistical Abstract of the United States:1968.*

The high divorce rate in early modern Japan can be attributed to the spread of this legally supported samurai family ideology, and its steady decrease to the slowly but surely increasing effects of industrialization, which began to undermine the traditional warrior ideology, with the result that parents-in-law were divorcing the bride less and less. But this effect was not strong enough to make itself felt on the increase in conjugal marital problems. This hypothesis is supported by the fact that divorce rates have been higher in rural than urban areas of Japan. In postwar years, the legal support of the traditional family system has disappeared because of the revised constitution and phenomenal industrial development. It appears that while the traditional family ideology is becoming less important as a cause of divorce, industrialization is becoming more so. For example, the postwar rise in the status of women, brought about by industrialization, has affected divorce. Also affecting divorce patterns are the changes in divorce law, which have now equalized the right to initiate divorce between the sexes. In recent years, by far the great majority of divorce cases are brought to court through the complaints of wives rather than husbands (Shikata, 1966, p. 259). When one realizes that in traditional Japan and before World War II it was extremely difficult, even when it was at all possible, for a wife to sue her husband for divorce, while for the husband it was a fairly simple matter, the reversal of the situation is dramatic and indicative of the changing role relationship between man and wife.

Role Relations in the Family

As the family and marriage have gone through structural changes in the modern period, attitudes toward values related to interpersonal roles within the family have also changed. In analyzing the changes, however, one suffers from a lack of detailed empirical studies from before the war, let alone from traditional days, making it difficult to assess the extent of change with any degree of accuracy.

We do know the ideology of the traditional family system—how it should have operated, how one should have behaved toward others in the family context, etc. What we do not know is to what extent people then adhered to such ideals. Ideally, age, generation, sex, and the manner of recruitment (i.e., whether one was born into the family or moved in through marriage or adoption) were the four major determinants of relative rank in the family. That is, generally speaking, those older in age commanded respect and authority from those younger, and those in an older generation from those in a younger generation, and men from women. Problems arose, of course, when there was conflict among these criteria, e.g., when an older person happened to be of a younger generation, as might happen between an uncle and his nephew. Complex patterns of resolution of such conflicts had been worked out, which we cannot go into here. An example will suffice. A mother would have authority over her infant son, but she must gradually relinquish it as he grew older, especially if he was the oldest son, who would take over the family. But as we shall see in the chapter dealing with personality, this mother's relinquishment of authority in the sociological sense did not necessarily mean loss of psychological control over her son.

According to these four criteria, the husband-father had authority over his wife and children. His position was further given legal sanction if he were the head of the family. It goes without saying that authority went hand in hand with responsibility. The husband-father had the responsibility of looking after those who lived in his family. But the primary emphasis was on the authority of those in the superior status. Children were taught respect and obedience to parents and older siblings from infancy. Obedience and respect were instilled through various institutionalized means, among which inculcation of the value of *on* played a major role.

The concept of *on* implies indebtedness in a social sense and also a hierarchical relationship between the *on*-giver and the receiver. It is this concept which justifies the hierarchical relationship not only between parents and children, but between emperor and subject, teacher and pupil, employer and employee, and any other pair which stood in vertical relationship to one another. The superior in this vertical dyad has access to resources which the subordinate wants but lacks—be they nurture, political protection, skill, knowledge, or employment. Though this concept of *on* first becomes inculcated into an individual through socialization in the context of the parent-child relationship, the concept itself is not bound to the kinship context, as is the concept of filial piety. It is instead capable of being generalized into semi- and non-kinship contexts.

Like monetary debt, social indebtedness to one's parents must be repaid. Repayment takes various forms. In the parent-child relation, the repayment is rationalized by the Confucian concept of filial piety. Filial piety in the broadest sense means everything from paying verbal respect to parents and pleasing their whims to supporting them in their old age.

These values were particularly strongly adhered to by the warrior caste in feudal times, but spread rapidly among common people through the samuraization process in the early modern period. They were incorporated in the school curricula in various forms, but particularly strongly expressed in the so-called moral lessons (*shūshin*) which were required of pupils of all school grades.

Signs of postwar changes in the roles and values defining relationships among family members are observable everywhere. There is presently a strong tendency toward egalitarianism. Criteria of differential status, such as age, generation, and sex, though by no means completely gone, are nonetheless far less important than before. As an expression of this, in many urban middle class families, the traditional kinship terms for father and mother, which connote respect and deference, are now replaced by the English loan words "papa" and "mama."

In Koyama's previously mentioned survey, only a small percentage of the urban sample favored living with their parents or support of parents by their children. An equally small proportion of the respondents preferred the oldest son to have special privileges in succession and inheritance. Adoption of a child for the purpose of continuing the family line was also favored by a minority of urban respondents. A majority, though by no means all, of the rural sample, on the other hand, still adhere to values supporting the traditional family system. These changes have not proceeded without a price. For example, the plight of old people who cannot find sons or daughters to support them has become a public concern of late. For most old people, the retirement allowance paid by the employer and the public assistance provided by the government are scarcely enough to support them. Surveys show that a great majority of Japanese nearing retiring age are quite worried about the financial prospect of their life after retirement. The real problem, however, is not simply financial, but social; these aged people must now learn to live by and large by themselves, separated and

Old men gathered in a shrine rest area. The plight of old people who cannot find sons or daughters to support them has become a public concern of late.

away from their children, playing a role quite unfamiliar to the society and to themselves. Even when they live with their children, they do not always enjoy the respected position that their parents formerly did and whatever task they perform around the house is usually menial and non-essential, like running errands, sweeping, etc., which only helps to lower their status in the family (Morioka, 1967). It is a comment on the time that a recent best-selling novel, *The Hateful Age* by F. Niwa, depicted a crabby old woman who moved from the home of one grandchild to another because she was not wanted by any of them or their spouses.

Another major change is that the husband has become less capable of making demands on his wife. At the base of this change is the increasing number of women bringing income home, estimated to be as high as 60% for working wives, including those who have temporary, part-time work at home (Fuse, 1967, p. 47). When the wife is working, she tends to have more say about household finances, especially regarding major purchases. At the same time, a mother working away from home tends to depend on her mother, mother-in-law, sister, or others for taking care of the children while she is working, and these caretakers assume an important role not only in caring for children but in making or helping make decisions affecting children.

In the countryside also, the status of women has risen, but in part for an additional reason. As we shall see, the number of farm families has been fairly constant until recently. This means, for one thing, that the same families have been continuing without new ones being established. Consequently, a farm bride would move into a long continuing family, most likely where parents-in-law are still living, rather than establish a nuclear family. This undesirable feature is coupled with the attraction which the city offers young people. Young people in rural areas, including girls, would prefer to go to the city for jobs and marriage, where they are not likely to live with their in-laws. These factors have caused a dire scarcity of women willing to marry into a farm family. To secure a bride, therefore, farm families have been forced to upgrade their treatment of the daughter-in-law, giving her more free time, for example, to attend meetings and participate in club activities and allowing her to make decisions in more areas of life than before.

Extended Kinship Relations

Dōzoku

In any type of extrafamily kinship relations in Japan, there are two separate aspects or levels, one interfamily and the other interindividual (Matsushima and Nakano, 1962, pp. 56–62). Conventionally, the *dōzoku*, the kindred, and other extended kin relations we shall discuss are regarded as social systems whose constituent units are families, that is, their structures are defined in terms of the relationship among families. But, while this is the proper perspective, it does not mean that individual members of these constituent families act simply as agents of the family-based systems. The aspect of interpersonal relations in these kinship systems constitutes a separate, but nonetheless legitimate dimension, which is often forgotten in the institutional treatment of Japanese kinship. Our primary emphasis will be on interfamily relationships, but it is well to remember that there is the interpersonal aspect of kinship.

The most important extended kinship structure in traditional Japan is the so-called *dōzoku*, for the elucidation of which we owe Ariga more than anyone else (Ariga, 1939, 1943, for example). Structurally, the *dōzoku* is composed of several stem families organized into a hierarchical group, with one family at the top, known as the main family (*honke*), and the others called branches (*bunke, bekke,* etc.), occupying subordinate positions in the system. The hierarchy, which implies political, economic, and ritual disparity among families, may involve more than two levels, some families being branches of branches.

There are numerous ways in which a branch may be established, only some of which will be listed here as illustrations. (1) Because of the primogenitural rule, the oldest son would normally take over the headship of a farm family, and the junior son would leave. If the family has enough resources, it will set up some of the junior sons as branches. The main family would build a house for a junior son, provide it with furnishings, food, farm implements, and give him a piece of land. The land in all probability would not be sufficient for subsistence, and would be supplemented by a rental of additional land from the main family. (2) Alternatively, a branch may be set up, with the same economic arrangements as above, for a daughter who would marry uxorilocally a man adopted into the group. In this case, adoption, marriage, and branching might take place simultaneously. (3) A junior son of a branch might come to the main family to live in and work as a handy-man or farm hand, and after fifteen or twenty years of service, be set up as a branch. In such a case, the newly established branch would be a branch of the main family and not a branch of his natal family. It is important to keep in mind this disregard of genealogical relationships, and the emphasis on economic considerations in the organization of the *dōzoku*. (4) Non-kin may be set up as branches also. A non-kin working as a servant or handy-man might be set up as a branch like a kin after so many years of service. (5) Or, a non-kin who migrates into the community may be allowed to establish a household as a branch of the main family of the local *dōzoku* group without a period of live-in service.

Thus while the core of the *dōzoku* remains a kinship group, it readily incorporates non-kin as legitimate members. In this sense, the *dōzoku* is a stem family writ large, if one recalls our discussion of the nature of the stem family. Like non-kin in the stem family, branches set up by distant kin and non-kin tend to have inferior status in the *dōzoku*, compared with those established by immediate kin, and the economic resources allotted to them by the main family at branching tend to be correspondingly more meager. The genealogical relation of the main family branches in a hypothetical *dōzoku* are represented in Diagram 2:2. This diagram shows interpersonal relationship, as distinct from inter-family relationship. The latter are diagrammed in Diagram 2:3.

It is important to note the dominant position which the main family commands vis-a-vis its branches and branches of branches. Economic supremacy of the main family is basic to the working of the *dōzoku* as a corporate group, and it was the basis of its social and political superiority. The main family owned the largest amount of land among all members of the group. Since it rented out land to branches, the latter were forever dependent on the main family for subsistence. The branches, in short, owed their very existence to the main family. And this debt was *on,* and had to be repaid in various institutionalized forms, among which payment of the rent on the rented land constituted only a small segment. Branches were expected to help out the main family in various agricultural, ceremonial, and other events in which extra labor was required by the main family. In

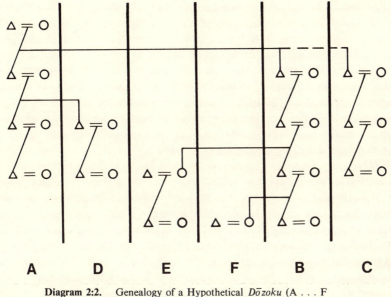

Diagram 2:2. Genealogy of a Hypothetical *Dōzoku* (A . . . F represent family lines).

turn, the main family was morally obligated to "look after" the branches in the broadest sense of the term. This obligation included providing cash or subsistence whenever a branch was in need and lending material assistance, guidance, and leadership in the execution of funerals, weddings, and other ceremonial events. Branches were expected to seek counsel from the main family regarding disposition of their members and property, and the main family had the responsibility (which may also be interpreted as a right)

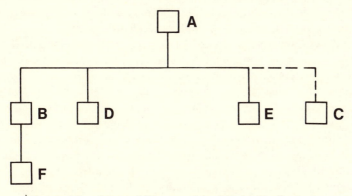

Diagram 2:3. Structural Diagram of the *Dōzoku*. Family C was established by a non-kin; family E was established as a branch of A by a man from family B (see Diagram 2:2) who worked in family A.

to advise the branches. The main family also provided the ritual leadership of the *dōzoku* in that the whole group venerated its guardian deity (who may or may not be its founder), and the main family was in charge of officiating at ceremonies for ancestor worship.

It is not difficult to see that the *dōzoku* as a corporate group functions best when the group is localized. If a member of the group left the area, he could no longer fully participate in the social and economic activities of the group. Such a member, however, retained inactive membership which he could activate upon returning, and whereby he could claim the rights and privileges of a full-fledged member.

While the discussion above of the *dōzoku* describes the system as it operated in farming areas of some parts of northern Honshū, it also existed in essentially the same form in premodern and early modern urban Japan, in Osaka (Ariga, 1959), Kyoto (Adachi, 1959; Nakano, 1964), Nara, and Sakai (Nagashima, 1959). The best described urban *dōzoku* are the pharmaceutical groups in Kyoto (Nakano, 1964). Among them one sees the same structural arrangement as in their rural counterpart. There was the main family, which controlled the greatest amount of capital resources among all members. The main family included, besides the head and his immediate kin, distant kin and non-kin who worked in the store or helped with household chores. Branches were established roughly in the same manner as those in the rural *dōzoku*—by junior sons, daughters' in-marrying husbands, distant kin, and non-kin workers. They were either given a certain amount of resources to open stores as branches of the main family store, or established as "commuter" branches, whose heads commuted to the main store and continued to work there. The political, economic, and ritual relationships which tied the main family with its branches were the same as in the rural *dōzoku*.

The economic, political, and ritual dependence of the branches on the main family in a *dōzoku* meant that the group could not exist as a corporation if the branches became completely independent of the main family. Dependence, however, is a matter of degree. In the modern period, as the branches became less and less dependent on the main family, especially in economic matters, and as some branches began to move away without any prospect of returning, the *dōzoku* became less and less corporate. Although this process began before World War II, the major blow to the rural *dōzoku* came with postwar land reform, which took tenanted land away from the main family and distributed it among the tenant branches. The urban *dōzoku* disintegration began much earlier because the inroads of modernization were felt first in cities. Increased wages, the introduction of Western employment practices, the availability of formal technical training in school, etc., dealt heavy blows to the urban *dōzoku* system. By the early part of this century, it was well on its way toward disintegration.

At present there is no longer any corporate *dōzoku* with the original economic base. Yet many Japanese, especially in rural areas, think of themselves as belonging to a *dōzoku* group, using one or another of several variant terms, such as *ikke, jirui, kabu,* or *maki.* They have in mind primarily the structural relationships in the *dōzoku* between the main family and its branches and not the functional aspects. This relationship is validated, if at all, only by the annual participation in the memorial ceremony for the founding ancestor or the guardian deity of the group and other deceased members of the group. Many Japanese social scientists do not consider this type of group a *dōzoku,* using the term only when the group is strongly corporate.

Social scientists theorizing about the *dōzoku* have asked whether or not the *dōzoku* is a descent group, and if so, what rule of descent it observes. Most social scientists who have analyzed the *dōzoku* system have regarded it as a descent group (Befu, 1963; Brown, 1966; Gamo, 1962; Kitano, 1951; Oikawa, 1939). Others (Ariga, 1947; Nakane, 1967; Nakano, 1957) have regarded the *dōzoku* as a localized group consisting of families sharing economic activities, in which the internal kinship structure is not of primary importance. Reflected in this debate appears to be a confusion between the interfamily and interpersonal levels of analysis discussed above, both of which are of course observable in a *dōzoku* group. Those who argue that the *dōzoku* is a group composed of families is analyzing its interfamily aspect, whereas those who insist it is a descent group are focusing their attention on the interpersonal aspect, as they must since descent is defined in terms of a specific kind of relationship between individuals rather than between families.

When we examine closely the interpersonal aspect, however, we see that it is not quite accurate to regard the *dōzoku* strictly as a patrilineal group, since in practice it does rather freely allow in-marrying men and non-kin to become members of the group. To be sure, the core of the group does tend to be composed of patrilineally related kin. Practice aside, in ideology, Brown (1966) has maintained, it is a cognatic group, allowing as a rule either a male or female link as the basis of membership. I tend to believe that ideally a *dōzoku* is a patrilineal group in that the first choice for extablishing branches is given to a male descendant; but if there is none alternative courses of action are taken. That such alternative actions are resorted to quite often is simply a reflection of the adaptability of the kinship system to the local situation. Such a reflection does alter the picture of the *dōzoku* as practiced, but it does not alter its ideology.

Other Descent Systems

In addition to the *dōzoku* there are other principles of organizing kinsmen in rural regions of Japan which should be at least briefly mentioned.

On the Amami Islands just south of Kyūshū there is a kinship system in which a kin group consists of the following kinsmen and their paternal and maternal ancestors: (1) ego's parents, (2) ego's paternal or maternal aunt's husband, (3) ego's wife, (4) ego's daughter's husband, and (5) ego's son's wife. In this system, ego has the obligation to attend funeral and memorial services of any kinsmen listed here (Ōyama, 1960). A similar but somewhat different system is reported from northern Honshū (Ueno, 1967). Ueno reports that ego's affiliation to a kin group in a coastal village in Iwate Prefecture is based on a patrilineal link to some ancestor and on his mother's patrilineal link to some ancestor. These examples further illustrate the complexity of regional variations in cultural practices which we already saw in relation to marriage and residence.

Kindred

All the groups discussed above are ancestor-oriented descent groups of one sort or another. In addition, we should mention the bilateral kindred —a circle of kinsmen to whom ego is related through paternal, maternal, affinal, and filial links without the consideration of linkage with specific ancestors. In one of the best documented analyses of such kindred, Yonemura (1966) reports of a kindred organization in Okayama Prefecture, where members assist each other in such diverse activities as financial support, agricultural activities, house repair and roof-rethatching, and mutual visiting at ritual occasions such as the New Year, fall festival, mid-year memorial services (o-Bon), and weddings, childbirths, and funerals. Yonemura points out that in these activities of the kindred it is the interpersonal rather than interfamilial relationship which is emphasized. It is important to note that the disintegration of the dōzoku has gone hand in hand with the relative weakening of the corporate structure of the stem family; and correspondingly the individually-based kindred has become relatively important (Befu, 1963). This is not to imply that the dōzoku and the kindred do not coexist in the same social setting. They often do; Yonemura's work, for example, shows that the kindred and the dōzoku organizations are superimposed in the village he studied.

Familism, Ritual Kinship, and Paternalism

In concluding this chapter, a word should be said about the relevance of kinship and family to the society as a whole. It is well to recall at the onest the absence of a clear-cut distinction between kin and non-kin in traditional Japanese society, which is evidenced in a variety of ways. We recall that the stem family consisted of both kin and non-kin, without a sharp line of demarcation between them, and that the legal separation between them came about with the promulgation of the Civil Code in the late nineteenth century. In adoption, too, we saw that there is no strong feeling that the adopted person must be related by blood. Here again, one sees the Japanese attitude that kinsmen were not a special category of people, but relatively freely interchangeable with non-kin. Another example is the relatively loose use of kinship terms in addressing non-kin. Terms such as *ojisan* ("uncle"), *obasan* ("aunt"), *niisan* ("older brother"), and *neesan* ("older sister") are freely used in addressing non-kin in situations calling for light-hearted, somewhat joking, but intimate relations (Norbeck and Befu, 1958). One may recall in this connection that the terms *oya* and *ko* have in the past meant leader and follower, regardless of the kinship relation.

Given such cultural background, it is not surprising that the Japanese would institutionalize the extension of kinship attitudes toward non-kin through formal organization of ritual or fictive kinship relations and groups, and that they would extend the kinship ideology to non-kinship contexts and use it as a "charter" for the justification of other social units, including the whole nation (Befu, 1964; Bennett and Ishino, 1963). Let us examine these two kinds of extension—institutional and ideological—more closely.

The institutionalized extension is the so-called ritual or fictive kinship and is based on several components of the kinship system seen especially strongly in the *dōzoku* system. They are: a hierarchical organization under a single leadership, a functionally diffuse and particularistic relationship between the leader and the followers, protection and assistance of the followers by the leader in return for their loyalty and service, and the norm of *on* (indebtedness) and the obligation to return the debt (*on*) as the ideological basis of the system. Such ritual kinship groups utilized terms clearly implying semikinship statuses, such as *oya-kata* (or "parent status") and *ko-kata* (or "child status"). Such a group may be composed of one leader and one follower, as sometimes happened when the relationship was contracted at life crises such as birth, maturation, and marriage; or it may involve a dozen or more families or individuals. When a number of families are organized into a ritual kinship group, as in rural Yamanashi (Hattori, 1955), the group differs from the *dōzoku* very little in structure, function, and ideological basis. It is noteworthy that in the *dōzoku* the main family is often called *oyakata* and branches *kokata*, further blurring the line between kinship and non-kinship. Ritual kinship groups organized on an individual rather than a family basis were seen in cities among stevedores, labor gangs and street-stall merchants, and mine workers.

One should not idealize the ritual kinship institution as a wonderful adaptive measure the society had worked out. Ideally, it works to the advantage of both the *oyakata* (patron-leader) and the followers, just like a true kinship group, but exploitation often occurs. If we define "exploitation" as the uncontrolled and arbitrary use of power for the benefit of the leader at the expense of the followers, such exploitation has been seen in ritual kinship groups. It occurs to the degree to which (1) the leader lacks affective consideration for his followers, which may happen because the leader and the follower often have limited contacts which do not allow emotional bonds to develop between them; (2) the leader fails to internalize the moral obligation, or the norm associated with his obligation to "look after" his followers; and (3) the follower cannot find alternative courses of action, as when jobs are scarce and cannot be secured easily if he leaves his leader. For example, in some occupations, such as mining or in the underworld, ritual kinship groups have monopolized the trade. If one left his group without a reason satisfactory to his leader, or if he were ostracized by his group, the news was transmitted to all other groups of the trade, which maintained a gentlemen's agreement not to accept such an individual. This enables an *oyakata* who is so inclined to exploit his followers.

Systems resembling the true ritual kinship system in varying degrees operate in many groups and situations where there is no explicit declaration of ritual kinship relations. The same features of the ritual kinship institution discussed above are observable among most schools of traditional Japanese arts and crafts, such as flower arrangement, the tea ceremony, dancing, pottery, etc. (Nishiyama, 1959). Here again, the system is vulnerable to exploitation by the master. The resources monopolized by the master are the skills essential for the art or craft and the power to grant a license to teach. "Exploitation" enters in the form of the expensive fees required by the masters and the rebates which a school's headquarters, known as *iemoto,* collects at the time of licensing and on other occasions.

Another area in which a similar, ritual kinship-like institution is observable is in small businesses with only a few employees. The employer and employees are in a particularistic relationship where the legalistic, contractual conception of the relationship between labor and management loses significance. This work organization, to be elaborated on in Chapter Five, is remniscent of the traditional situation where the family and work were inseperable and is in fact a historical outgrowth of this situation.

In large modern business firms, the sheer size of the organization, involving thousands of workers, precludes any possiblity that the institution of ritual kinship will develop. Also, for various reasons, universalistic legal regulations governing labor-management relations tend to operate more strictly in large companies. In addition, the large size of such organizations and the huge volume of work, together with a complex internal specialization requiring the coordination of many segments, demand a relatively rational organization. All these factors militate against formation of kinshiplike or ritual kinshiplike organization. What developed, nonetheless, in the early modern period and continued until World War II was the *ideology* of paternalism, according to which the whole company was regarded as one big family and the mangement was to be considerate to the workers as parents would be to children. We shall examine the details of this "managerial paternalism" more closely later.

Lastly, until the end of World War II, the government propagandized the ideology that the whole nation was at least figuratively one family, with the Emperor as the parental figure, symbol of nurturance and authority, much as the real father or ritual father, but with an aura of sanctity added. This ideology was buttressed by the value of *on,* indebtedness emanating from the person of the Emperor which all subjects were required to repay, if necessary with their lives.

Thus one sees that the institutional and ideological components of the Japanese kinship and family systems have widely ramifying implications for the whole society. This mode of analysis gives causal and logical priority to the family system, out of which other systems have developed. There seems to be psychological justification for this mode of analysis as well: the individual in the family setting learns through socialization certain psychological processes which are useful later in life in non-familial contexts. In a purely structural analysis, however, it is probably more prudent to say that a paternalistic structure and ideology have characterized Japanese society as a whole, and that one expression was seen in the family structure and other expressions in ritual kinship, in industry, and in other areas of social life. Although paternalism is seldom seen in a pristine form in contemporary Japan, elements and aspects of it are still seen everywhere in varying degrees.

SUGGESTED READINGS

Befu, H. and Edward Norbeck
1958   "Japanese usages of terms of relationship." *Southwestern Journal of Anthropology* 14: 66–86.

Bennett, John W. and Leo A. Despres
1960   "Kinship and instrumental activities: a theoretical inquiry." *American Anthropologist* 62: 254–267.

Blood, Robert O.
1967   *Love Match and Arranged Marriage, A Tokyo-Detroit Comparison.* New York: The Free Press.

Cornell, John B.
1964   "Dōzoku: an example of evolution and transition in Japanese village society." *Comparative Studies in Society and History* 6: 449–480.

Koyama, Takashi
1961   *The Changing Social Position of Women in Japan.* Paris: UNESCO.
1964   "Changing family composition and the position of the aged in the Japanese family." *International Journal of Comparative Sociology* 5: 155–161.

Morioka, Kiyomi

1967   "Life cycle patterns in Japan, China and the United States." *Journal of Marriage and the Family* 29: 595–606.

Plath, David W.

1969   "Japan: the after years," in *Aging Around the World,* eds. Donald O. Cowgill and Lowell D. Holmes. New York: Appleton-Century-Crofts.

Sano, Chiye

1958   *Changing Values of the Japanese Family.* Washington, D. C.: Catholic University of America Press.

Vogel, Ezra F.

1961   "The go-between in a developing society: The case of the Japanese marriage arranger." *Human Organization* 20: 112–120.

3 Rural Life

The Japanese Peasant Community

Social life in rural Japan was traditionally carried out by and large in the context of the rural community called *mura*. Generally during the Tokugawa period, peasants lived in village communities which to a large extent constituted their social world. These communities were by and large self-sufficient economically and suffered little political interference—aside from tax matters—as far as internal operations were concerned.

A great majority of contemporary rural communities in Japan are direct descendants of the Tokugawa *mura* in the sense that there is historical continuity in the community's existence back to the traditional period and that most families can trace their histories within the community back to the same period. The term *buraku* is generally used in the social sciences to describe the modern descendants of the mura. The English term "hamlet" has been used as a translation of *buraku* and will be used in this book.

We have little reliable information as to how large these rural communities were in the traditional period. But there is no reason to believe that the size of rural communities has drastically changed until now. According to the 1960 World Agricultural Census, the average rural settlement size in Japan was sixty-four households, which for our purposes can be taken to mean that the average *buraku,* or hamlet, had sixty-four families (Fukutake, 1967, p. 82). We may assume that an average rural community of the Tokugawa period contained about fifty or sixty families.

As the modernization of Japan proceeded on all fronts from the early Meiji, rural districts underwent administrative reorganization from time to time in order to adjust to the nation's changing political and economic situation. One aspect of this reorganization was the amalgamation of administrative units into larger and larger groups. An increasing number of hamlets became subsumed under one administrative village, or sometimes

A rural community in Nara Prefecture. During the Tokugawa period
these communities were by and large economically self-sufficient.

an administrative township. Through this and many other processes of
modernization during the last hundred years, the *mura* of the Tokugawa
period have evolved and transformed and today there are probably more
new features than ones remaining from the past. Indeed, peasant life in
Japan has gone through such drastic changes that one may even doubt the
wisdom of the use of the term "peasant" in reference to most contemporary
rural Japanese, if we understand by the term a fatalistic attitude, a distrust
of outsiders, the lack of capital for reinvestment, the absence of risk-taking,
and the like. Nevertheless, community life is still the basic social world
beyond the family in rural Japan.

The Economic Base

Rice Growing as a Way of Life

As we saw in the chapter on the cultural origins of Japan, agriculture as
the dominant form of subsistence—with rice as the staple crop—was ushered in from the continent in the early Yayoi period in the third century
B.C. In the following two millenia, rice growing became deeply entrenched
in the rural life of the majority of Japanese peasants, to the extent that rice
is not simply a source of subsistence but is a cherished as well as relished
food. That rice has been the staple crop does not necessarily imply that

peasants subsisted principally on rice. On the contrary, in the feudal past most of the harvested rice had to be given up in the form of tax, rent, or economic exchange, and peasants subsisted by and large on less valued cereals such as wheat, barley, and millet of several varieties, which they grew "on the side" on less fertile land or as winter crops. Nonetheless, rice growing was *a way of life,* deeply affecting the individual, the family, and the community. We can begin to appreciate the pervasive significance of rice in traditional Japan by noting that rice was the basic unit of economic exchange, measure of wealth, and symbol of political power.

A labor exchange group pulling rice seedlings. Rice growing was a way of life in traditional Japan, deeply affecting the individual, the family, and the community.

Given the economic and cultural significance of rice, it is not surprising that there are innumerable varieties of rice, each one adapted to a special need, such as taste, shortness of growing period, early ripening, resistance to cold, drought, or disease, etc. While some of these have been developed by inventive individual farmers, most of them in modern times have been developed through government-sponsored research, notably at agricultural experiment stations throughout the country. These varieties vary as to yield per unit area, taste, and profit per unit volume. Any farmer must therefore choose among several varieties locally available in order to maximize profit.

Ecological Factors

A crucial consideration for the analysis of rural life in Japan is the fact that rice-growing depends on irrigation rather than natural precipitation. Water is generally drawn from a nearby river or lake through a complicated set of dams, gates, and canals which lead water into individual rice fields, and the water source must be shared by a large number of farmers. A water shortage necessitates arrangements for equitable distribution of the water; and excess water, e.g., due to over-precipitation, must be eliminated. In traditional Japan, the size of each basic irrigation system was rather small, and it was more or less coterminous with the extent of the farm land owned by members of a given hamlet community. To the extent that the sharing of water calls for cooperation, this irrigation system helps produce community solidarity, and conversely, creates friction between neighboring communities which derive water from the same ultimate source.

Transplanting rice seedlings. The sharing of water calls for
cooperation and helps to promote community solidarity.

In the past one hundred years, irrigation networks have been organized into larger and larger systems, in order to make more rational use of water. Bringing into one large system several irrigation systems which previously competed for water enlarges the social sphere of cooperation, as those sharing the same water source are organized into an irrigation cooperative. This cooperative collects a small amount of dues and in turn manages the irrigation system under its jurisdiction, doing such work as installation and repair of gates, pumps, and bridges and cleaning of ditches. It should not be thought that the communities under the newly created, larger irrigation system form a unit as cohesive as each individual community once did. Because of the sheer increase in the number of people involved, all cannot have intimate, face-to-face relations as they did before. Other forces of modernization to be discussed below have necessarily loosened community solidarity, too.

Factors of Productivity

Productivity of land is basically a function of three major factors: land, labor, and technology. Where land and technology are limited, as they were in traditional Japan, a large amount of labor must be expended per unit area to increase productivity. With increasing application of technological knowhow in the form of machinery, chemical fertilizer, insecticides, weed killers, weed retardants, etc., Japanese farmers have been able to increase productivity by a large percentage since the beginning of the modern era. This is evident from the drastic decrease in the proportion of farm households from 44.2% in 1930 to 29.6% in 1960. In 1967 the agricultural work force was down to 19.3% of the total work force of the nation. Roughly, this means that while in 1930 it took about 44% of all households to feed the nation, in less than forty years not even 20% of the total work force was needed to feed the nation. Even then the nation has so much surplus rice that the government has begun subsidizing farmers for curtailing their rice production and is experimenting in feeding it to livestock. As mentioned earlier, the number of farm households remained about the same until recently. For although junior sons generally went to the city to find employment and daughters, except for the case of the uxorilocal, *mukōyoshi* marriage, left home to marry, an heir always remained behind to carry on the family line. However, since the mid-1960s whole families have begun to migrate to cities, selling or leaving behind their entire property. One reason for this migration is that in these days of rapid economic development and high standards of living, farmers are unable to make ends meet unless their land is highly productive. This fact has forced poor farmers to give up their ancestral occupation and leave for the city. At present, depopulation of remote, rural areas of low productivity has brought about serious consequences to rural communities, for without sufficient personnel the community cannot be organized as it used to be. Lack of sufficient labor force, for example, has forced either curtailment or abandonment of many activities. Those farmers living close to urban centers, on the other hand, have found it lucrative to sell their land for industrial, commercial, and residential purposes. Many in fact are making a killing doing this.

The application of technology in Japan is directed primarily toward maximizing productivity per unit area of severely limited land, whereas in the United States agricultural technology is applied basically to maximize productivity per unit labor, which is highly expensive. It would be a careless generalization, therefore, to say that Japanese agricultural economy is becoming like the American counterpart only because both utilize mechanized, "labor-saving" equipment and other technological aids.

Cultivating the fields. The application of technology in Japan is directed primarily toward maximizing productivity per unit area of severely limited land.

In terms of acreage, about one-half of Japan's agricultural land is given over to growing rice. Non-rice crops are grown not only in the remaining half of the land but also, in winter, on land where rice is grown in summer. This is another aspect of the intensity of Japanese agriculture: not only is each unit area of farm land intensively cultivated, but a good portion of it is used for growing more than one crop a year. Non-rice crops include cereals, such as wheat, barley, millet, etc., and fruits, vegetables, and root crops. These are grown in part for home consumption and also in part for obtaining cash. The dairy industry, though growing, is still a minor one in Japan.

Forestry

Japan is a mountainous country, and only approximately 16% of the land is cultivable. Although the great majority of people, both rural and urban, live on the plains, there are a substantial number of rural people living in the mountains and engaged in lumbering or charcoal making, either exclusively or in conjunction with farming. Though the percentage of people involved is relatively small, lumbering and charcoal making have been important elements of rural economy.

Fishery

A third type of rural economy, in addition to farming and forestry, is fishing. As in forestry, the total number engaged in fishing is relatively small, about 144,000 in 1961. The sheer length of the coast line of this island nation, the presence of numerous natural harbors, and the relative abundance of sea products have provided a rare opportunity for the Japanese to exploit the marine environment. Consequently, the Japanese have added to their diet a large variety of sea products, from seaweeds and shellfish to deep sea fish like bonito and tuna. These sea products provided the only major source of protein, in addition to soy beans, in traditional Japan since the Buddhist injunction against meat eating centuries ago. In modern times, with the relaxation of the taboo, meat eating has become quite common. Even now however, Japanese obtain more protein from the sea than from the pasture.

Sea products are caught by many different techniques, which vary depending on the specific product involved, and one may also distinguish between traditional techniques and modern ones. The introduction of Western-derived, technologically advanced means of catching certain types of sea products has vastly improved the efficiency of fishing. It made some traditional methods obsolete and catching certain species whose methods cannot be modernized (like the sea urchin and sea slug) uneconomical. These changes have had social consequences for fishing villages. Those which could not adapt to the modern changes have been left behind and become poor, while those which have managed to make the changes have been relatively prosperous. Also, with the introduction of modern methods, e.g., with the use of large ocean-going deep-sea fishing boats, the scale of fishing has greatly increased, with the consequence that the capital outlay has become so large that large fishing operations have been taken out of the hands of ordinary fishermen and become dependent on capital sources available in cities, or more recently, in fishing cooperatives.

Just as there are ecological bases to unite farmers, there are ecological reasons for fishermen to cooperate. Commonly, the offshore sea of a hamlet is communal property and strict regulations govern how and who may operate fishing boats in the area. Also, many types of fishing require the cooperation of families, e.g., large deep-sea fishing boats require a crew of many men, who generally come from a given hamlet. Often one of the wealthier families owns the boat, which is captained by a man of another influential family of the community and manned by men of the same community. Such a fishing boat has manifested a ritual kinship organization in the structure of the crew, with the skipper as *oyakata*. Certain types of large nets must be pulled in from the shore by a large number of people. Factors such as these have served to maintain a corporate structure in fishing communities.

Non-agricultural Occupations

People living in rural Japan are not all engaged in farming, forestry, or fishing. A growing number make their living by other means. There are small retailers who operate stores in the front part of their house and sell dry goods, hardware, clothing, etc. to meet the daily needs of farmers. There may be a barbershop, a drugstore, or a tobacco shop in the hamlet. Then there are wage earners who commute to a nearby city, the village office, or the local agricultural and irrigation cooperative. As the nation's economy has grown, secondary and tertiary industries, like manufacturing, retailing, and service, have increased and moved more and more into rural areas—in the form of small shops at first, but in postwar years in the form of large factories, as well. Consequently the proportion of the non-agricultural population in rural Japan has grown enormously. At first, nonagricultural workers were few and many wage earners were unmarried junior sons or daughters who made modest contributions to the family budget. But of late, an increasing number of them are either the major contributor to the family budget, farming being reduced to secondary importance, or the sole breadwinners.

In 1935 75% of the farmers were pure farmers, the remainder holding some non-farming occupation as well; in 1955 only 35% were pure farmers. The trend of augmenting income with non-rural occupations has resulted from two factors which are both causes and effects. On the one hand, modern science and technology have enabled farmers to spend less and less time on the farm without decreasing the yield. The resulting free time could be, and is, spent in nonfarming occupations. On the other hand, farming has become an occupation requiring heavy capital outlay—in equipment, commercial fertilizer, various chemicals, etc.—so that in order to pay for the expenses of modern farming and also to keep up with the rising standard of living, the farmer is compelled to hold an additional job which will bring in the needed additional income. This change in the economic picture has drastically reduced the solidarity of the rural community insofar as this solidarity has been based on the presence of common and shared interests as well as the relative absence of individuated interests directed outside the community.

Landholding

One important economic basis of social life in rural Japan in the past was the structure of landholding. Although there has been a great deal of fluctuation in the specific patterns of landholding in Japan in the last hundred years, there has always been a disparity among families in landholding, from large landlords owning hundreds of acres to tenants and farm laborers who owned none. Four basic categories may be distinguished in relation to landholding: the landlord, who rents land to tenants and collects rent; the independent cultivator, who cultivates the land he owns; the tenant who rents land from landlords and pays rent; and the farm laborer, who has no title to land but works for wages. A given farmer often combines two of these categories. Thus a man may be an independent cultivator, but at the same time may rent out a portion of his own land. Or an independent cultivator may not have enough land and rent additional land from a landlord. Japanese social scientists use the following classification, which incidentally serves as a rough social stratification scheme for rural Japan:

landlord
landlord-independent cultivator
independent cultivator-landlord
independent cultivator
independent cultivator-tenant
tenant-independent cultivator
tenant
tenant-laborer
laborer-tenant
laborer

When two categories are combined, the one which is more important economically for a given individual is listed first. Thus if a man is primarily a landlord, but cultivates a little on his own, he is a landlord-independent cultivator, whereas if he makes his livelihood principally as an independent cultivator but rents out a small amount of land, he is an independent cultivator-landlord.

In traditional days, this system of land tenure was by and large confined within a given hamlet, no landlord renting land to outsiders and no tenant renting land from outsiders. This arrangement supported community cohesion to the extent that the economic interests of the community as related to landholding never went beyond hamlet boundaries, although this is not to deny that conflicts of interest between landlords and tenants often became a serious problem.

After the Tokugawa period, concentration of land in the hands of fewer landlords proceeded, partly aided by the abolition of the feudal prohibition of land sale. Landlords bought land not only from within their hamlets, but also from neighboring hamlets; and peasants often rented land from landlords living in other hamlets or even in cities as absentee landlords. Independents, too, began more and more to own pieces of land scattered throughout many neighboring communities. This new pattern of landholding began to change the peasants' social life. Their social horizon began to enlarge: in an important economic sense, they were now tied to neighboring hamlets, and the traditional hamlet became less of a closed corporate entity. Also, when a landlord, an independent cultivator, or a tenant began to have land interests outside his community, he inevitably became concerned with the irrigation system and other ecological and economic factors affecting the whole neighboring area. This interest in extrahamlet affairs also contributed toward breaking down hamlet parochialism and uniting members of several neighboring hamlets.

The post-war land reform initiated by the Occupation and administered by the Japanese government did away with absentee landlordism, reduced resident landlordism and tenancy to an insignificant proportion, and created farmers who are by and large independent cultivators. But the land reform did not intend to distribute the land equally, among all the farmers; there still are families which own many times the land owned by others.

Landlord-tenant Relationship

The landlord-tenant relationship was much more than just a contractual economic arrangement. Ideally, the landlord-tenant relation was characterized by an explicit or implicit ritual kinship relationship, in which the economic arrangement of land rent constituted only a small segment of the total social relations and it is probable that a majority of peasants adhered to this conception. As was discussed in the previous chapter, this relation implied an act of benevolence by the landlord and an act of personal service by the tenant over and beyond whatever the contractual relation legally required. Thus the landlord might agree to reduce the rent in a year of poor harvest, visit or send his wife to his sick tenant, counsel tenants on personal or family matters such as marital problems, advance the tenant cash with low or no interest should he be in dire need, serve as the go-between in arranging marriage of his tenants or their children, or even provide a scholarship for a tenant's promising son. In return, tenants were expected to help the landlord, free of charge, whenever he was in need of extra labor, such as at rice transplantation in spring, weeding in summer, and harvesting in fall. They were expected to help out when the landlord's household had a large gathering, e.g., at wedding, funeral, and memorial services.

In this functionally diffuse and particularistic relationship, when ideally adhered to by both the landlord and tenants, there was no exploitation.

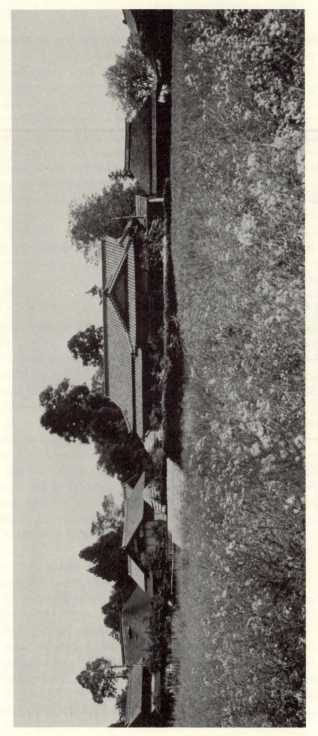

Farm houses for the main family (left) and its branch (right). Ideally, the landlord–tenant relation was characterized by an explicit or implicit ritual kinship relationship, in which the economic arrangement of land rent constituted only a small segment of the total social relation.

77

Both parties were on the whole satisfied with the relationship; neither side felt he "gave" more than was due or received more than he gave. There was a sense of balance in this exchange relationship. This type of relationship existed in many kinds of social contexts in which the landlord-tenant relation was found. It existed in the classic *dōzoku* system of northeastern Japan, in the ritualized kinship *(oyakata-kokata)* relationship of central Japan, and in landlord-tenant relationships which involved no explicit kinship or ritual kinship relation. Generally speaking when found in the *dōzoku* context, the landlord-tenant relation tended to operate ideally, somewhat less so in the ritual kinship context, and even less in the non-ritual kinshhip context. While kinship or ritual kinship obligations served as a conscious reminder to the landlord that exploitation was not appropriate behavior, landlords not encumbered by such a reminder felt freer to promote their desire for personal profit. Their tenants were exploited in the sense that the landlords did not give them the personal considerations which were expected.

Communal Property

Another economic factor with important social implications in rural Japan is communally owned land. Such land was not very large in acreage even in traditional times and generally does not include farmland. It is instead a wooded land—slopes of a mountain, for example—where materials for fuel, fodder, and fertilizer (green manure) could be obtained. In the traditional period, when commercial sources of these materials were nil, the communal land was of crucial importance for everyone. Accordingly, strict regulations governed, and still govern, the duration, extent, and purposes for which the communal land may be used. Access to the communal land is limited to community members and is not automatically granted to outsiders or to newcomers to the community. That access to communal land requires approval by the whole community meant in the past, when there was no other way of obtaining fuel, fodder, and fertilizer, that in effect a new family could not be established, e.g., through immigration or through branching, without community approval.

Control and management of this communal property is naturally of vital interest to the community. These functions are either delegated to the hamlet assembly as a whole, or reserved by the ruling elite of the community, which include officials of the assembly and other old and wealthy families. Even if the whole assembly is formally in charge, often the elite hold the actual control of the communal land. This land is also a focal point for the solidarity of the community in that it is available only to its membership. Trespassing by outsiders causes the community to act together and to punish the transgressor.

Some communities lack such communally held land. Instead certain wealthy families own wooded land which other members of the community are given the privilege of using for specified purposes. In still other communities, such land is owned jointly by a group of wealthy families. In these communities, owners of the wooded land have enormous power. At the time of the land reform after World War II, private ownership of communally used land played an important political role. Although the law specified the limits of landholding allowed to any farmer, there was room for negotiation of details, which was handled through the local land reform committee composed of representatives from landlords, independents, and tenants. While landlords and tenants had diametrically opposite interests—the former wanting to retain as much land as possible and the latter trying to take as much as possible from landlords—tenants were often at a disadvantage in the negotiation. If, for instance, there had been some sort of paternalistic relationship between the landlords and tenants, the tenants felt obligated to make concessions to their former landlords, who were, after all, being forced to give up most of what had rightly belonged to them only because of the intervention of an outside force, over which they had no control. If, on the other hand, the landlord had been an exploitive type, but owned wooded land to which other community members had been granted informal access, he often threatened to deny the villagers future uses of his land in case negotiations did not proceed as he desired. (Only cultivated land, no wooded land, was subjected to redistribution through land reform.) As a result, tenants, who usually made up the majority of the land reform committee, were often intimidated into making more concessions than were legally necessary.

As commercial sources of fuel, fodder, and fertilizer became more and more available, and as peasants began to have access to cash for investment both through increased productivity and through loans from agricultural cooperatives and other sources, peasants began to rely less and less on natural sources available on communal or private wooded land. Wooded land, then, ceased to have the social significance it formerly had in unifying the community, and those who had controlled the land lost the economic basis for their political power in the community.

Kinship and the Family

The Family as the Basic Social Unit

Since kinship and the family have been previously discussed, here we shall refer only to those aspects which are relevant to rural life. The family has always been the basic unit for agricultural production in Japan, there having never been plantations or other large scale systems of production. The cooperation of several families in agriculture is limited to special occasions, such as rice transplantation, irrigation-ditch cleaning, road building, etc. The peasant family has tended to be somewhat larger than its urban counterpart. This large size has manifested itself in two ways: structurally complex families with a large number of members, and structurally simple families with many members. The structurally complex type usually has three generations, with grandparents living with their descendants. It often includes collaterals, such as uncles and aunts. Occasionally, families with large land holdings kept hired laborers who lived with the family as members of the household. Since land is inherited in the family, it is no surprise that the household is the basic managing unit of the land. Since family property is inherited by one child—usually the oldest son—land tends to be kept from fragmenting, as it might under a system in which property is divided equally among all children.

The Family as a Productive Unit

This primogenitural rule has also meant that the successor held authority without sharing it. The family head held a crucial position in the management of the family as a corporation, i.e., in managing productive resources, controlling the members, and taking charge of ancestral rites. All these functions are closely tied in with the economic activities of the family since family members constitute the working force in the field, and decisions as to their disposition, e.g., whether to send them to school, allow them to go to the cities for work, or marry them out, crucially affect productive activities. And ancestors, as we shall see in the next chapter, are guardians of agriculture as much as of the welfare of family members. It is understandable, then, that the family head has held a great deal of authority.

Farm families often retain a productive labor force beyond what is necessary for production. This is particularly true of poorer families with smaller holdings, which use their labor at less than maximum efficiency. Since in farm work, every able-bodied member of a family is working it does not appear that there is a labor surplus, or underemployment, but there is in fact underemployment, or "hidden unemployment," because each one is working at less than full capacity. The fact that peasant families are able to absorb excess population in this form has been important in alleviating unemployment problems. In times of economic recessions in cities, unemployed workers have returned to their native villages and lived with their relatives until the economic situation improved. The rapid industrial development of recent years, on the other hand, has affected farm labor in the opposite direction: the rural population, particularly young people, is leaving the farm in increasing numbers because of the availability of work in urban centers and because of the attractions which the city offers. This exodus has created a drastic labor shortage in the countryside and forced farmers to invest in labor saving devices, with the result that farming has become expensive on the one hand and technically complex on the other.

In the early days of modernization, the peasant family structure was not much affected by industrialization since changes were slow to reach rural areas. Also, problems attendant on population increase—overpopulation and unemployment—were minimized in these early days partly by migration of junior sons and daughters to cities for urban employment in rapidly industrializing areas and partly through the mechanism of "hidden unemployment" discussed above, and to a limited extent through emigration overseas to such places as Korea, Taiwan, Manchuria, and the New World. Since the end of the World War II drastic changes have taken place in the family and kinship structure. With the Occupation-enforced land reform, the main family of a *dōzoku* group was stripped of the economic basis for its authority in the group. Without the superior economic power, the paternalistic relationship which had maintained the corporate structure of the *dōzoku* could not persist any longer. While the main family has retained its prestigeful position in the group and retained relatively more farm land than its branches, the *dōzoku* began to function less as a corporate group and each member family began to act more independently.

Changes in Role Relations

The postwar constitution, which declared the sexes to be equal, and the new civil code based on it, which provided for equal inheritance of property in the absence of a stipulation to the contrary by the property-holder, had a profound influence in boosting the position of junior sons and women. The practice of the family head dominating the family, male dominance in general, and the primogenitural rule no longer received the ideological backing that they did under the older, Meiji constitution. To the extent that there was no apparent danger to the maintenance of one's own family, farmers began to accept the new norms. The family head began to relax his authority and the bride began to receive better treatment from her in-laws. At the same time economic changes began to undermine the traditional family structure. As technological innovations began to flood rural areas, young people were quicker than their parents to learn, understand, and adopt them with success. With rapidly increasing employment opportunities in nonagricultural occupations, junior sons and daughters began to work away from the family farm and live away from the authority of their father. This large scale migration to the cities has been caused by the adoption of labor saving innovations in agricultural practices, and has facilitated such adoption, too.

These developments have weakened the corporate structure of the family as an agriculturally oriented group. Some of the former obligations of the head of the family, such as managing the farm, controlling the other members of the family, and soliciting ancestral aid for the family's occupation, began to lose meaning. The management of the farm increasingly became the responsibility of the younger people, who are more capable of taking advantage of agronomical innovations. Since farming no longer requires the labor of all family members and since junior sons and daughters can and do take on nonagricultural jobs, the head of the family's control of these members also began to loosen. Third, as farm management began to be more and more dependent on scientific and technical know-how, solicitation of ancestral protection and aid in agricultural matters began to lose meaning.

At the same time, peasant families have remained conservative, compared with urban families, because while forces are at work to break down the corporate family structure, there still remain many rural families which are not significantly affected by technological innovations. Also, in spite of technological changes, operating a farm still depends to a considerable extent on traditional features of the family structure. The most important such feature is the inheritance of the property, notably the land, by one child. Since the farm is so small already, any further division would make it impossible for all inheritors to make nearly as comfortable a living as their parents. As a result, the practice of primogeniture continues. Fortunately or unfortunately, the importance of primogeniture and of agriculture as the family occupation is still sufficiently internalized by junior sons and daughters that they do not regard it as an infringement of their rights to have to leave the family without receiving a share equal to the inheritor's. This does not mean that they are completely ignored. The head of the family may feel that they are being short-changed and try to compensate by providing technical or professional training to better prepare them for city occupations. As a result, it is a common phenomenon that junior sons are college educated while the heir, the holder of the family authority, has only a minimum education.

Associations

In the traditional days, there were a number of nonkinship groups in the hamlet community, most of which have persisted into the modern period and are still operating in rural Japan (Norbeck, 1962). The more commonly known groups are: the five-man team (and its descendant, neighborhood associations of various names), age grades, and religious organizations. These groups vary a great deal in their organization, membership composition, and functions. Let us review these associations and consider recent changes in them.

Five-man Team

The five-man team *(goningumi)* was first introduced from China early in Japan's historical period, but soon went into disuse until the Tokugawa period, when it was resuscitated primarily as a policing unit against insurrection, subversion, and other criminal activities. Later in the Tokugawa period, it ceased to have any crucial policing function for various reasons (Befu, 1965). The organization remained, however, throughout the Tokugawa period and persisted into the present day as a subunit of the community, serving as the basic unit of community cooperation and as a relayer of messages to and from the government. Though called "five-man team," actually the group consisted of anywhere from 2 to 10 or more neighboring families; also, various names other than "five-man team" have been used in different localities. The system continues to date, with considerable modification in spite of the temporary post-war injunction by the Occupation against neighborhood associations, including the five-man team, because they assisted in the war effort. This resiliency indicates the importance of this organization in rural Japan. Besides serving as administrative tentacles, in many hamlets they are one of the basic cooperative units for such purposes as road repair, weddings, funerals, roof-rethatching, etc.

An important characteristic of this and many other associations in Japan is its compulsory nature: every family is required to belong to the group. This compulsory membership is one means of eliminating expressions of individual will which may go contrary to the will of the majority, and thus has been an important mechanism of reducing sources disruptive of cohesive group life.

Age Grade System

In contrast to the five-man team, which was originally imposed from above, the age grade system and the Shinto shrine organization are of indigenous origin. Traditionally, age grades were most highly developed in coastal fishing communities and in the southern half of Japan, although they were present in most communities to some extent. Where fully developed, they encompassed practically all age levels from childhood, youth, and adulthood to old age. (Norbeck, 1953). Most of these age grades were divided by sex. Each such group had its internal organization with a hierarchy based on seniority. An initiation ceremony characterized some of them, especially youth groups, where it often involved difficult and painful trials. In central and southern Japan, adult and old age groups, under the name of *miyaza*, often controlled activities related to the Shinto shrine of the community and will be discussed below.

The youth group, organized separately for men and women, was primarily for unmarried people from about ten years of age to thirty. Often, such a group had a special lodge where they congregated at intervals varying from every evening to one or two nights a month. The lodge was usually the house of a prominent family, rather than a special structure of a "community hall" type. The periodic gatherings provided occasions not only for informal entertainment, but for education as well. Younger members learned from older ones, and all members were instructed by the host of the lodge. The host served also as an informal leader and counselor for the group. Youth groups maintained strong internal discipline and provided an important context for socialization. Anyone violating group regulations was punished in varying degrees of severity depending on the specific transgression. In these groups, entertainment and instructions were combined with various services performed for the community, such as cleaning the street, cleaning the Shinto shrine grounds in preparation for a festival, etc. Age groups, too, had compulsory membership: all members of the community of appropriate age and sex category had to join the group. In modern times, when the national government began organizing naton-wide age-graded associations, such as the Greater Japan Youth Association, most of these local age groups became absorbed into the national organization.

Shrine Organization

Among primarily religious associations, the most important for the continuation of the community is the parish organization of the guardian Shinto shrine. Each hamlet community is associated with a shrine, which serves as an abode for a guardian deity *(ujigami).* There are both etymological suggestions (*"ujigami"* roughly meaning "clan god") and historical evidence that such a deity was often originally a guardian god, though not necessarily an ancestral soul, of a kinship group like the *dōzoku.*

Each hamlet thus constitutes a parish of its tutelary shrine, and all members of the community are parishioners; again no one is allowed not to be a member. To validate the status, new born babies are taken to the shrine to report the arrival of a new member. Often the baby is made to cry at the shrine so that the god will know its arrival. This membership was not automatically granted to anyone, however. Immigrants to the community might have to meet a residence requirement of a specified period before being admitted to the parish.

In traditional days, maintenance of the parish organization was often in the hands of the village elite who constituted a *miyaza* (T.C. Smith, 1959, pp. 190–200). At the time of the shrine festival they had a privileged position from which other parishioners were excluded. The priest officiating at annual festivals was generally chosen from among *miyaza* members, who took turns serving as priest. In larger shrines of more than local significance, it is common to have a permanent official priest who is ordained by the national Shinto organization. But at the local level, most shrines are divorced from the national organization, except for a subsidy some of them received before and during the war as a constituent member of the state Shinto organization.

Even in the Tokugawa period, there was a tendency for the *miyaza* membership to enlarge and include those who would not formerly have qualified. This process generally reflected the decline in authority of the village elite in the political life of the community. In more recent years, the practice has been to have at least nominal participation by all members of the community in the shrine festival and on other occasions. But the system of parish representation, whereby the parish is divided into several segments, with a representative from each segment serving on the governing board of the shrine, enables the well-to-do families to become representatives and maintain control of the parish organization, as they formerly did. To be sure, the guardian shrine has much declined in importance in recent years and participation in its organization does not grant much power.

It is important to keep in mind that the function of the village shrine is to protect the community. Peasants relied on the village deity for their general health, the prevention and cure of illnesses, and protection from supernatural forces which cause misfortune in the family. They depended on him for a good harvest, for adequate rain, dispelling of crop diseases, etc.

Three kinds of new forces brought about a weakening of the faith in the guardian god. First, as agronomical and medical sciences began to be applied in the countryside, the need for reliance on magical or supernatural means became less and less meaningful. The village shrine began to occupy a less and less crucial place in the community life, until its function was reduced in certain localities to a purely recreational one at the time of the annual festival. Second, because the village shrine's "sphere of influence" is to a large extent in the area of agriculture, as small shop owners moved into the community, and as commuters began to live in the village in large numbers, the guardian god began to play a less and less important role in the community. This does not mean that shop owners and commuters are completely forgotten or immune from the god's influence; they take appropriate measures to insure that they remain in good terms with him. Third, until the end of the war, Shinto shrines were part of the State Shinto organization, receiving official ranks in the State Shinto hierarchy and entitled to subsidy. After the war, with constitutional separation of religion and the state, village shrines were stripped of ranks and financial support. With this loss of a major financial basis for their operation, many activities, notably the annual festival, had to be substantially curtailed. Although attempts are made to raise funds locally, fund-raising is always difficult because of the general decline in Shinto faith.

Temple Organization

Next to the Shinto shrine organization, the other important religious body in rural Japan is the Buddhist temple. The social significance of

Buddhism has many contrasts with Shintoism in rural Japan. The Shinto shrine's primary concern is here and now—the welfare of an on-going community, its members' physical well-being, and its subsistence economy. Even ancestors and other supernatural beings are conceived of primarily as assisting the living to be able to live as well as possible. In Buddhism, the primary concern is with the other world, with consoling and appeasing the dead and with preparing for departure to the other world.

Secondly, the Shinto shrine looks after the welfare of the community as a corporate group, whereas Buddhism is a religion of and for the family (Embree, 1941). It is for this reason that different families of a given hamlet may be, and are, members of different temples. As a result, in a given area encompassing several hamlets, there are usually a number of temples, one each for a given sect, and each temple draws its membership from throughout the area—very much like the situation in the United States with respect to Protestant churches. Even when a family moves out of the area, it retains membership because its ancestral graves are in the local area, if not on the temple ground, where the temple of that area or parish alone can give necessary memorial services.

A further difference between the village shrine and the Buddhist temple is that no matter what the sect is, a Buddhist temple is always part of the national ecclesiastical organization of the sect, with its headquarters usually in Kyoto. A local Buddhist temple therefore is a branch at the lowest level of a nation-wide hierarchy of temples, which have an organization more or less analogous to the ritual kinship system discussed in a previous chapter (Morioka, 1962). A Buddhist temple, no matter how lowly, almost always has a priest ordained by the national ecclesia. To this extent, compared with village Shinto, village Buddhism is sensitive to the demands of the central authority. A local priest, in short, must receive and execute commands from higher ecclesiastical authorities while at the same time fulfilling the needs of local members, a situation quite foreign to village Shintoism.

As the village shrine organization has an elite group representing parishioners, Buddhist temple organizations, too, select representatives who are commonly well-to-do from each of the nearby hamlets with large memberships. And it is these representatives who constitute the ruling group for the temple organization.

The general decline in religious faith which hit Shintoism has also affected Buddhist temples. Attendance of members at special Buddhist celebrations has declined markedly since World War II. Offerings by members at memorial services of deceased relatives have not kept up with the rising expenses of maintaining the temple. The farm land which many temples owned and depended on as a major source of income was taken away by the postwar land reform, as the law did not recognize corporate ownership of cultivated land. The loss of land has dealt a serious blow to local temples since most of them cannot find an alternative and equally lucrative source of income. Many of them have begun running nurseries and kindergartens for working mothers, not so much out of the realization that for Buddhism to survive it must show concern with this world, as out of the dire necessity of making ends meet.

A roadside monument for the Kōshin-kō,
a community Buddhist association.

In spite of the general decline in the religious faith of the temple members, it is interesting that in rural areas membership itself has not seen a corresponding decline. Even today no family is willing to neglect its ancestors entirely. Since Buddhism has gained exclusive monopoly over the veneration of ancestors (except for a small number of sectarian Shintoists who conduct ancestral services according to Shinto rites), temples are assured of membership as long as Japanese maintain a belief in the value of ancestral veneration.

Kō

In addition to village Shintoism and Buddhism, there are a number of organizations of religious origin, though not necessarily wth religious concerns at present, which are generally known as *kō*. Some *kō* are organized on the basis of large nationally or regionally known shrines or temples. Members of such a *kō* worship the deity of the shrine or temple concerned, and aspire to visit it at least once in a lifetime. *Ise Kō,* named for Ise Shrine where the Sun Goddess is enshrined, is probably the most famous. In the traditional and more recent past, it was not economically possible for all members of a local *kō* organization of a given hamlet to travel to the shrine at once, and a certain number of them were chosen by lottery as representatives and took the trip, with the expense of the journey paid for by all members. The following year, representatives were chosen from among the remaining members, and so on until all members had a chance. Such a visit was both recreational and religious. As a religious act of representation, the representatives often held a ritual communion with other members prior to departure to secure the collective magical power to insure a safe trip. Upon returning, another communion would be held, this time to distribute among the remaining members the magical power obtained through the visit to the holy place. During the Depression and World War II this sort of religious trip or pilgrimage declined sharply because of economic recessions in rural areas and the consequent difficulty in raising funds. In the postwar years it has been revived to a marked degree, but primarily as a recreational activity. The recent affluence of rural folk has often made it possible for all members to take a trip together on a chartered bus instead of sending representatives. Group tours of rural folk on chartered buses are a common sight in Japan and are a boon to Japanese tourism.

In addition to the *kō* with national significance, there are locally based *kō*. Some of these are associated with a nearby shrine or temple, but others are completely independent of formally established religious organizations. These *kō* groups are often organized on the basis of a given sex or age group, and are sometimes part of the age grade organization of the community. Many of them worship particular deities with special functions. For example, the *Kannon Kō* is for married women of reproductive age and insures safe delivery of a child. *Tenjin Kō* is for children and insures growth and health. These *kō,* like those which carry out pilgrimages to distant holy places, hold periodic gatherings, at which time the guardian deity is worshipped at the house of one of the members, serving as the host on a rotational basis. This is, again, a time for feasting and recreation.

Finally, there are *kō* which, though they must have had a religious origin, have been organized purely for economic or recreational purposes in recent years. When people had no public financial institutions to borrow money from, the *kō* provided a convenient source of needed cash. The man in need borrowed the money contributed by all members and returned it with interest, the next year another member, usually selected by lottery, borrowed money and returned it with interest, and so on until the last person had his chance (Embree, 1939, pp. 138–147). With the increasing availability of public financing, e.g., through the agricultural cooperative, and with the rise in the income level of rural families, this type of economic $k\bar{o}$ has either died out, declined in importance, or shifted its major function to recreation.

Modern Associations

Besides these traditional organizations, there are a plethora of associations which came into existence in the modern period, mostly through the instigation of the central or local government. We have already mentioned the Greater Japan Youth Association. The Patriotic Women's Association, the National Defense Women's Association, and the National Veterans Association are some examples of organizations which played important part until the end of the war in bringing the otherwise parochial peasants into the fold of a nationalistic ideology. The Crime Prevention Association (working in close cooperation with the local police), the P.T.A. (the postwar successor of the Parents' Association connected with the local school), and the Tax Payment Association are some postwar examples.

There are three features common to most of these associations. One is that they utilize the local hamlet as the basic organizational unit. Above the hamlet, an association would have the former or the present administrative village as an intermediate level organization, followed by a higher, prefectural level below the national organization.

A second feature is that membership is, like the traditional associations, compulsory rather than voluntary. Even the P.T.A., which in American thinking should involve only parents of school children, in most rural Japan has as its membership all households of the community regardless of whether or not there are children currently enrolled in school.

Thirdly, membership in most of these associations, both traditional and modern, is on a family basis; that is, each family constitutes a member irrespective of how many there are in the family. (Some associations, such as age groups, are exceptions, and would include all those of proper category, even though there may be more than one in a family.)

These features, particularly the first two, serve to strengthen the solidarity of the community. Since the hamlet is the basic functioning unit for all these associations, activities carried out in their name tend to bolster the sense of its unity. However, there have been important trends breaking away from this hamlet-centered organization of associations. We have already mentioned the increasing number of nonfarmers living in rural communities. They often do not find any rationale for joining many of the associations, which are primarily oriented toward the benefit of farmers. Also, some newly created associations ignore the two basic featurs of older associations. For example, the 4-H may be a multihamlet organization without recognizing the hamlet as a constituent unit or level of its organization. Moreover, it may include only a small number of potentially eligible boys and girls rather than observing the time-worn compulsory membership system. Such associations are still few and relatively unimportant. But the very fact that rural communities tolerate such a nontraditional organization of associations is an indication of the degree to which the traditional community structure has broken down. These new associations are also a sign of what is to come. In the meantime, these strictly voluntary associations are a threat to the solidarity of the hamlet, which is already rapidly deteriorating without them, for this very reason, that conservative elements in the community are opposed to them. One important conclusion that we derive from the observation of traditional and modern associations in rural Japan is that the mushrooming of common-interest associations as such has little to do with the development of democracy or individualism (Norbeck, 1967).

Agricultural Cooperative

One association which grew phenomenally in importance in the postwar years is the agricultural cooperative, especially in areas where rice growing is the dominant form of economy. In areas where growing of other crops, such as vegetables or fruits, is dominant, the cooperative tends to be less important. Although the cooperative has its historical antecedents in the prewar period, its importance in contemporary rural Japan is far greater than before the war. While legally a voluntary association and presumably organized through the initiative of individual farmers, the cooperative is, like traditional associations, organized on the basis of virtually mandatory membership, with initiative coming from the national and local governments. (It is important to note, however, that there are sporadic instances of farmers who do not join the cooperative.) And like the Shinto guardian shrine of the community, there is only one cooperative in a given area, so that one has no choice as to which cooperative to join. The "territory" of a cooperative is usually coterminous with, or with a large segment of, an administrative village.

Because the cooperative is a multihamlet and multifunctional organization, through it the hamlet is brought into contact with a world outside itself in many crucial ways. For example, the cooperative is the principal agency through which members sell their products and buy both capital equipment and consumer goods. Capital equipment includes everything from farm machinery, tools, and chemicals to animal feeds and consumer goods ranging from work clothes, household furniture and utensils to canned foods. Moreover, the cooperative serves as a bank both for savings and loan. It

issues insurance policies both for business and personal property and provides guidance and educational services, for example, to introduce the
newest agronomical techniques. It also has auxiliary organizations for
youth and women. In short, it has become an all-encompassing organization, able to take care of more spheres of life than any other single organization outside the family.

Political Life

In the Tokugawa period, the hamlet community was a political corporation which handled internal affairs almost exclusively. Of course, the feudal
(han) government retained the ultimate authority to intervene and interfere
with the internal political affairs of the hamlet; but in fact the government
left hamlets alone unless matters pertaining to taxation, or to sedition or
other equally serious crimes came to the attention of the government.
Externally, hamlets as corporations made mutual pacts, borrowed money,
and sued each other (Befu, 1965).

The Hamlet Assembly

In the modern period, the hamlet lost its former legal status as a corporate political entity and became incorporated into the larger administrative
units of the village, town, or city. Nonetheless, on an informal basis, the
hamlet has remained to date—to be sure, with much reduced and ever
decreasing power. The hamlet assembly as the governing body is present in
just about every hamlet, and is composed of one person from each family,
no matter what the size of the family. Generally speaking, unanimity of
agreement is desired in reaching decisions, and every effort is made to
convince and persuade dissenters. (This unanimity requirement does not
imply, however, that a single dissenting vote constitutes a veto.) At the same
time, less influential members are no doubt more or less coerced into going
along with the more powerful members. There is evidence that by the end
of the Tokugawa period already the hamlet assembly was resorting to voting
as a decision making procedure, although there was no legalistic, strict
provision as to the number of votes necessary to decide any issue. But it is
evident that nothing like unanimity was required or expected in many
hamlet assemblies even in the Tokugawa period.

Functions of the Assembly

Although the hamlet assembly lost much of its former autonomy as the
central government and its prefectural and local branches began to exercise
more and more regulatory power in modern times, it has carried on a
number of functions of an internal nature, like road repair, maintenance of
irrigations systems, installation of street lights, etc. For these activities, the

assembly levies a tax upon member families both in labor and in cash, a custom carried on from the feudal days. Part of this tax goes to pay a token salary or rather an honorarium for hamlet officials. Many of these functions of the hamlet assembly have been forced upon it by the central or local government, in whose province these functions legally lie, only because the government does not have sufficient funds to carry out what is legally in its domain. Since these tasks, like road repair and irrigation-ditch cleaning, must be done if the community is to survive, the hamlet assembly is forced to take them upon itself to make up for the failure of the government.

Sanctioning Power

Decision making without sanctioning power is naturally ineffective. The hamlet assembly in former days had the power to levy fines and punish those who refused to conform to customs and comply with agreements. In those days, these sanctions ranged from verbal or written apologies and fines to banishment from the community. A concommitant of the gradual loss of hamlet autonomy was the loss of the more severe types of sanctioning power. One of the most powerful sanctions, which is still used occasionally, is *mura hachibu,* or village ostracism, whereby everyone agrees to refuse to associate with the culprit and his family for a specified or indefinite duration, which may continue for more than a generation (R. J. Smith, 1961).

This refusal may range through all spheres of social and economic life, including the refusal to render needed labor assistance in agricultural activities, or even greet the outcast in the street. Village ostracism refuses to recognize the social existence of the culprit. To the extent that economic cooperation has been essential for communal life, ostracism has been a fatal sanction and a powerful means of enforcing conformity. As agriculture has become more mechanized and hired labor available, it has become less necessary to depend on fellow villagers for economic life. These changes have weakened the sanctioning power of ostracism.

Increasing Involvement with the Outside World

It should not be thought that the political structure in the traditional hamlet was egalitarian. Although the assembly was represented by all families, the assembly was to a great extent controlled by a small number of elite families, whose criteria were, first, the genealogical depth of the family in the community, and second, wealth. These elite families held, in rotation or through mutual selection, all the key political positions in the village and exercised a great deal of power, although the precise relation of the assembly to the elite is not clear. These powerful positions are almost nonexistent now for two major reasons: (1) the central government has stripped the hamlet of any significant autonomy, and (2) the postwar land reform has stripped the elite families of the economic basis of their power. Since political positions in the hamlet nowadays have little if any power, they are euphemistically referred to as positions of honor (*meiyo-shoku*), and are held by relatively well-to-do families as a service to the community. In many hamlets they have ceased even to confer honor and prestige. As a result poor families have been induced to serve in compensation for a small salary.

With the amalgamation of hamlets into larger administrative bodies and with the declining autonomy of hamlets in modern times, the major political arena and the focus of political life in rural Japan began to shift from the hamlet to the administrative village. Until the very recent postwar years, however, politics still operated in the interest of constituent hamlets, each of which sent assemblymen to represent its interests. The elite of the hamlet who used to exercise power in the hamlet assembly were now active in the politics of the administrative village. It is important to remember that at this stage the hamlet was still an important political unit for the administrative village to contend with. After the drastic postwar amalgamations, however, the total number of villages shrank from 79,600 in the early Meiji to 1023 in 1960 and townships from 1930 to 620. When this happened, it became no longer possible for each hamlet to send its representatives to the assembly since there were not enough seats to go around. Several new processes of representation came into being. One was for several hamlets to band together and elect one representative, in which case the hamlet from which the representative came enjoyed special advantages while the others did not receive equal benefits. Interest groups such as the village youth association, irrigation cooperative, and agricultural cooperative, organized on the village-wide or nearly village-wide basis and having large memberships, began to send their representatives. Merchants in the village or township were now numerous enough to send their assemblymen. Lastly, as villages and townships attracted industries in order to benefit from the heavy tax they could levy, their governments found themselves contending with still another, and a powerful, interest group. In this heterogeneous and enlarged political arena the meaning of political life has drastically changed. As peasants became more and more aware of these new and different political processes, and began to play their role in them, they became de-peasantized. The basically closed corporate community of a hundred years ago now became open and lost its corporacy.

SUGGESTED READINGS

Beardsley, Richard K., et al.
  1959   *Village Japan.* Chicago: University of Chicago Press.
Dore, R. P.
  1959   *Land Reform in Japan.* London and New York: Oxford University Press.

Fukutake, Tadashi
1967   *Japanese Rural Society.* Tokyo: Oxford University Press.

Nakane, Chie
1967   *Kinship and Economic Organization in Rural Japan.* London: Athlone Press.

Smith, Robert J.
1961   "The Japanese rural community: Norms, sanctions, and ostracism." *American Anthropologist* 63: 522–533.

Smith, Robert J. and E. P. Reyes
1957   "Community interrelations with the outside world: The case of a Japanese agricultural community." *American Anthropologist* 59: 463–472.

Steiner, Kurt
1968   "Popular political participation and political development in Japan: The rural level," in Robert E. Ward, ed., *Political Development in Modern Japan.* Princeton: Princeton University Press.

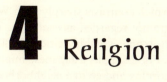

4 Religion

General Background

Among the various religions of Japan, Shinto (or Shintoism) is no doubt the oldest, and is in fact regarded as the indigenous religion of Japan. Unlike those of other religions, which were introduced into Japan in the late prehistoric or historic times, the origins of Shinto are concealed in the depths of prehistoric darkness. Although called by a single term, Shinto is scarcely one orderly system of beliefs; it is, rather, a conglomorate of primitive beliefs and practices surrounding spirits, souls, ghosts, and the like. In this respect, Shinto is somewhat like Taoism, which was introduced from China along with Confucianism, with its belief in mysterious forces inherent in nature. The two are alike also in that both are not so much established, organized religions as they are part of folk beliefs. Taoism, however, did not make as much inroad in Japan as Buddhism or Confucianism, possibly because it was functionally too much like Shintoism, which already had deep roots in Japanese soil.

Confucianism as practiced in China involves sacrificial offerings to Heaven and the veneration of ancestors, and is thus genuinely a religion as well as a moral philosophy. After it entered Japan, however, its religious elements were weakened to a great extent, and survived and spread in Japan by and large as a secular, ethical philosophy concerning human relations and the government of a nation. Also, until the Meiji Restoration, Confucianism was studied mostly by the *samurai* elite, who comprised only a small percentage of the Japanese population, and its widespread dissemination as a moral code for the general public did not come about until the samuraization process began in the early modern period.

Religious Attitudes

Before entering into a discussion of Japanese Shintoism, Buddhism, and Christianity, some general remarks concerning Japanese attitudes toward religion are in order. One important characteristic of Japanese religious orientation, and one which contrasts sharply with Western religious thinking, is that religions are not regarded as exclusive. This has several meanings. (1) The same person may worship deities of different religions without any feeling of conflict. For example, a Japanese might pray at the Buddhist altar at home in the morning and go to a neighborhood Shinto shrine in the afternoon. (2) Moreover, there are religious edifices which enshrine deities of different religions. For instance, there may be a Buddhist temple on the premises of a Shinto shrine, or vice versa. (3) A Japanese religious concept of a deity may combine elements derived from different religions. (4) A priest of one religion may officiate at ceremonies of another religion. The distinction between Shintoism and Buddhism especially is so blurred that sometimes it exists only in the mind of the scholar analyzing folk beliefs, ordinary people being quite oblivious of and unconcerned with the historical derivation of a religious concept. In fact, the relatively clear-cut distinction that the general public maintains now is an artifact of the Meiji government. Until modern times, the two religions were fused in popular religious practices in the above four senses. At the beginning of the modern period, the Meiji government insisted on the separation of the two religions in an effort to make Shintoism the national religion with the emperor as its highest priest. The separation, however, was never complete in the minds of the folk, and elements of Shinto-Buddhist fusion are still seen everywhere in Japan.

All this is not to deny, however, the existence of separate Buddhist and Shinto organizations. When we turn our attention from the folk level to formal ecclesia and doctrines preached by Buddhist and Shinto scholars, we can see that a distinction most certainly exists between them. Shintoism is generally divided into three different systems of belief: folk (otherwise called village or popular) Shinto, state (or national) Shinto, and sect Shinto. Folk Shinto will be treated in some detail later, and state and sectarian Shinto will be discussed briefly here.

State Shintoism

State Shintoism was an outgrowth of the concern of scholars of the late Tokugawa period who attempted to create a nationalistic ideology centering on the emperor. The movement, which began in the last years of the Tokugawa period, received official sanction from the Meiji government, which made the diffusion and inculcation of state Shintoism part of its national policy. Until the end of World War II, state Shintoism played an indispensable role in unifying the nation and bolstering Japan's nationalism. The emperor was officially regarded as semi-divine and as the direct and lineal descendant of the Sun Goddess, who, in the legend of Kojiki, the oldest document in the Japanese language, created the heaven and the earth

A Shinto shrine in Kyoto. Until modern times, Shintoism and
Buddhism were fused in popular religious practices.

out of chaos. Hence, the emperor and his nation had the divine right to rule
the world and be its center. The emperor served as the official priest in
ceremonies conducted on various occasions for the purpose of unifying the
nation and validating the imperial position. The state designation of various
ranks among thousands of Shinto shrines throughout the country also
aimed at the same nationalistic purpose by organizing and supporting individual shrines.

After the war, the new constitution separated state and religion, ending
state support of any religion. At the same time, the emperor publicly denied
any divine quality, and state Shintoism thus came to an abrupt end.

Sect Shinto

Sect Shinto is intermediate between the nationally organized and govern-
mentally controlled state Shinto and the communally based folk Shinto in
terms of its organization. Sect Shinto has as its center a sacred place such
as Mt. Fuji, with a shrine for the guardian deity, and attracts believers from
areas much wider than immediately surrounding communities. These sects
have an organized ecclesia of some complexity and a formal doctrine which
is Shinto in nature either in essence or by derivation. Their size varies
enormously, some having a membership of mere thousands and some hundreds of thousands. Except for the few large ones, including Tenrikyō,
Konkōkyō and Kurozumikyō, sect Shinto is of minor and declining importance today.

Buddhism

Aside from Shinto, Buddhism is no doubt the most important religion in Japan. Although Buddhism may have trickled into Japan in small doses in earlier periods, its first massive introduction to Japan took place in the sixth century. Buddhism has since then grown so enormously and become so deeply rooted in Japan that one may safely say it has largely lost its foreign flavor and become "naturalized". That is, Japanese feel just as at home in Buddhism as in Shinto and they would look puzzled if one were to call Buddhism a foreign religion in the same breath as Christianity. In terms of organization it is far more elaborate than any other religion in Japan. There are inumerable sects and splintering subsects and subsects of subsects. Each sect and subsect has a hierarchy of temples and priests with a headquarters at the pinnacle, located in Kyoto in most cases.

Higashi Honganji, the headquarters of the Ōtani branch of
the Jōdo Shinshū sect of Buddhism, in Kyoto.

Before the end of World War II, temples could rely on proceeds from their real estate, such as rented farm land in rural areas and, in cities, land rented for commercial purposes. The postwar land reform did away with farm land as a source of revenue for rural temples. Many temples in cities were destroyed during the war and had to bear the cost of reconstruction of the temple as well as the rising cost of maintenance. Temples must now depend for their financial needs on heavier regular dues and special contributions, such as from funeral and memorial services. Many famous temples have begun charging admission fees for visiting the temple grounds and viewing their gardens. Many of them also operate tea houses, restaurants, and gift shops to supplement their less than sufficient income.

In spite of considerable effort being made by leaders of various sects to modernize Buddhism it is still, by and large, regarded by the majority of Japanese as outmoded, a thing of the past, and of genuine interest only to the old. One major reason for this attitude is that Buddhism has not seriously turned its attention to contemporary problems, such as neglect of the aged, changing morality, juvenile delinquency, political corruption, a meaningless educational system and the psychological and psychosomatic problems arising from the individual's domestic, occupational, and social situations. The Buddhism of the established sects has stayed away from these worldly problems and concentrated on the question of salvation through faith. As we shall see, success of the so-called new religions of Japan has been partly because they have squarely faced the social and personal problems of the modern world.

Christianity

Christianity was first introduced into Japan in the sixteenth century by Spanish and Portuguese Jesuits, including Francis Xavier, during the period of internecine warfare. For a brief period of time, it received official support from a number of warlords, who wanted to take advantage of Western culture, especially military technology, in their struggle against neighboring lords. Only a century later it was banned and ruthlessly suppressed along with all other forms of Western contact, when the then military leader of Japan, the Tokugawa shōgun, saw the danger of military and political conquest by the West. Until the middle of the last century Christianity had virtually no influence in Japan except in small isolated areas, mostly rural, where a small number of Japanese continued to practice Christianity in secrecy. Known as *kakure-kirishitan* (Christians in hiding), they survive to date, some of them still maintaining a separate religious life from contemporary Christians. The situation is somewhat analogous, on a miniature scale, to Christianity in Ethiopia, which developed into a separate church after centuries of isolation.

Kakure-kirishitan aside, Christianity in modern Japan has its roots in the missionary activities begun in the middle of the last century. In spite of zealous apostolizing by practically all denominations of the Protestant and Catholic Church over the last one hundred years, the number of Christians still remains no more than a million, or less than one percent of the Japanese population. Reasons for the failure of Christianity to pread more rapidly are perhaps not hard to seek. For one thing, Christianity has not become "naturalized" in the way Buddhism has. Missionaries are still in large number foreigners. Christianity's saints bear distinctly foreign names. Its severe, uncompromising morality is unsuited to the Japanese temperament, in which sex, drinking, and other worldly desires are sanctioned if practiced in moderation and kept separate from other segments of life. Monotheism is also foreign to the Japanese conception of the supernatural world, for a single Japanese mind can encompass myriads of deities, even of different religions, without any feeling of conflict. Last, but not least, Christianity is par excellence a religion of the individual, while Japan has traditionally been a nation of families and communities, in which individuals have had to submerge their interests and desires for the sake of the groups to which they belonged. In this traditional world, Buddhism looked after family affairs and Shinto after community welfare. The spread of Christianity had to await the emergence of the urban individual in a modern industrial setting. It is thus in urban centers, where individuals tend to be neglected by the community and freed from traditional family constraints, that Christianity has its stronghold.

The small number of adherents, however, does not do justice to the social significance of Christianity in Japan. There are a disproportionate number of Christians who have held important political and social positions in Japan. Christian educational institutions from kindergarten through college are well known among Japanese, and are some of the best private schools in Japan. Christian welfare institutions, such as clinics and orphanages, too, have played a role far more significant in Japan than the small number of believers would suggest.

Folk Conceptions of Deities

Syncretism of Folk Beliefs

We shall now turn to a topic which is more central to anthropological interest: folk religious beliefs, the system of belief of the country folk as it has been practiced for centuries. One crucial consideration in the analysis of folk belief is that this "little tradition" is not simply a pale reflection or a simpler version of the great tradition as expressed in the organized religion of Buddhism or Shintoism. If this were the case, one might speak of, and analyze, "folk Buddhism" and "folk Shintoism". Instead, the system of folk belief cannot be meaningfully divided into its Buddhist, Shintoist, or Taoist components. To be sure, if one were to trace the historical development of present-day folk beliefs, it would be entirely possible to analyze them into their separate components and discover how and when the fusion took place. But as folk beliefs are practiced now, such academic concern as to how much is Buddhist and how much Shinto has no realistic meaning for the people. True, sometimes they are aware that given components derive from certain religions; but their knowledge concerning such matters as to why, how, and when the mixture of different elements occurred, and what

A shrine for the spirit of a small pine tree (hidden behind the
structure in the center). All natural phenomena are at least
potentially capable of spiritual manifestation.

such elements mean in the formal theology of the great tradition are of no
consequence to folk practitioners. Rather, folk beliefs constitute a system
of belief which makes sense to the natives only when seen as an integrated
whole, and that is how we shall view it.

Pervasive Supernatural Power

What kind of supernatural beings do Japanese think are capable of
influencing man and his natural surroundings (Ross, 1965, chap. 3)? In
general, it is safe to assume that all natural phenomena, animate or inanimate, and even man-made objects, are at least potentially capable of
spiritual manifestation. It should be noted that these phenomena and objects are simply abodes of supernatural beings—receptacles in which spirits
reside—and are not in themselves sacred or divine. While all phenomena
and objects are potential abodes of supernatural beings or forces, some are
more prone to spiritual manifestation than others. Also, some beings and
forces are quite potent, requiring careful attention, while others are relatively harmless and innocuous.

Fluid Role of Supernatural Beings

Another notable point is that the specific power, or function, of a spirit
or god may or may not have direct connection with the nature of the abode
itself. Related to this dissociation of a god's abode from his function is the

belief that a god of a given function can have different kinds of abodes and different functions can be assigned to the same kind of abode. An example of the former belief are the spirits who are often guardian gods of rice fields (*ta no kami*). Rice growing being traditionally the central subsistence activity among most Japanese farmers, it is quite understandable that a major role would be assigned to ancestors to look after the rice fields of their descendants. These gods of rice and the fields are often thought to reside in the nearby mountains and are called *yama no kami* ("mountain gods"). It is believed that ancestral deities reside in the mountains, away from human settlement. In the spring, at the time of the first tilling of the soil in preparation for rice transplantation, these gods are said to come to the rice fields, and in the fall, after the harvest is over, they are believed to go back to the mountains. The spring and fall ceremonies in connection with agriculture, which are almost universal in rural Japan, often include a symbolic welcoming to the gods of the mountains in the spring and a farewell in the fall. Further, the gods of mountains are often considered to be the same as fox spirits, because, some scholars theorize, the coming of ancestral gods from the mountains in the spring is heralded by foxes coming down from the mountains. Whatever the explanation, fox spirits are often identified as gods of rice fields. The shift in the role of the fox spirit from the guardian of the rice field to the god of good fortune and then to that of business success is a relatively easy one. Another example of the same sort would be the guardian spirit of a fishing boat, which might reside in a doll, a woman's hair, or a coin, whichever is the local belief.

Conversely, there can be a change in the god's function while the abode itself remains essentially the same. In many parts of rural Japan, ancestral gods of the family estate are often regarded as the guardian gods of the *dōzoku* group to which the family belongs. When regarded as guardian gods of the family estate, (*yashiki-gami*) they tend to be enshrined in a small shrine on the family property. As guardian gods of the *dōzoku*, they generally have a more elaborate and larger structure, and the shrine is likely to be outside the premises of any family. But these gods of the family and *dōzoku* are sometimes also guardian gods of the village in which the *dōzoku* is located. This last shift seems to have come about when the village community as a territorial corporate body began to supercede the *dōzoku* in its social importance. At this point the gods of the dominant *dōzoku* group of the village became the gods of the village. In some localities this evolution of the village shrine can be traced through historical documents. Another example of the same type would be the *Daikoku*, the black, corpulant smiling god who may be a god of the kitchen, good fortune, rice fields, or commerce, depending on where he is venerated.

I do not mean to imply that in any one locality one would find a god performing so many different functions or so many gods all performing the

Rice seedlings with rice balls placed on top to be offered
to the rice spirit just before transplantation.

same function. But it is very common in any village to equate two kinds of
gods for a given function or to have a given god perform two different
functions. This fluidity enables Japanese folk belief to adjust to changing
situations, since gods can readily change their functions as old needs die and
new ones arise. Another way of saying this is that Japanese readily impute
new functions to old deities and create new deities to suit the circumstance.
When the Japan Tennis Players Association was organized before the war,
a suggestion was made to create a guardian god, to be named "Heavenly
God of Speedy Ball" or *Ame-no-Hayadama-no-Mikoto* (Hori, 1962, p. 97).

The Abode of a Spirit

Another characteristic of Japanese folk deities which deserves mention-
ing is that most gods and spirits are associated with a particular locale and
identified with a unique abode, e.g., the spirit of *that* old pine tree which
is located at the north end of the village, or *the* ancestral spirits of a given
family for the protection of *its* rice fields. The guardian deities of trades or
occupations, to be sure, are not so restricted in their association, since they
may be venerated regardless of the locale, wherever the trade or occupation
is found. These deities are undoubtedly a result of adaptation to the rise of
economic specialization in Japan's historic past. At any rate, these conceptions of deity contrast with a belief in some universal deity like the Christian
God. The Sun Goddess, as the ancestress of the Japanese emperor and the
protector of the nation, is a very recent innovation which, along with state

Shintoism as the organized national religion of Japan, was popularized by political leaders of the modern period in their attempt to foster nationalism.

Kinds of Gods

As to different kinds of gods, first, there are mythological deities with human form, such as the Sun Goddess and her descendants, and historical figures, including founders of religious sects and religious leaders, like Minamoto no Yoshitsune, Nichiren, Shinran, etc. At a more humble level, deceased human beings all attain the status of a deity sooner or later. Customs require that the souls of deceased humans be cared for by their living relatives, who are in most cases their descendants; hence the term "ancestor worship." But as Plath (1964) has pointed out, both the terms "ancestor" and "worship" are misnomers. For deceased descendants and even collaterals are "worshipped" along with ancestors, although they are not so much "worshipped" as cared for, solicited, cajoled, and conversed with. Plants and animals, too, possess souls, or spirits. But there is a difference: all human souls are quite potent and must be taken seriously, whereas many species of plants and animals are, for all practical purposes, quite innocuous. Incidentally, as we shall see later when we consider retribution and possession phenomena, human souls and certain animal souls are capable of supernatural influence while the possessors of the souls are still alive. Among animals, certain species of mammals (foxes and dogs, for example) and reptiles (snakes) are considered particularly dangerous. Among plants, old trees are especially likely to be abodes of spirits. Then there are natural phenomena like the ocean, water falls, rocks of huge size and peculiar shape which harbor spirits. Lastly, there are man-made objects, like the mirror, the kitchen, the latrine, etc. where spirits reside.

In this analysis of Japanese folk beliefs, the theological distinctions often made among gods, deities, souls, and spirits is irrelevant: we are referring to an entity which resides in either natural or man-made phenomena, and has supernatural power of a benevolent or malevolent nature depending on the situation, much as the *mana* of Oceanic societies. The abode of this entity must be carefully attended to since an entity without an abode or with an unattended abode will do harm to man. Also an unnatural death of the abode, if it is an animate one, will cause the spirit to resent the death and take revenge.

Pollution and Purity

The concept of pollution in Japanese folk belief is not the same as "dirtiness" in the ordinary sense. Nor is it (and this is a more subtle point), as we shall see, the same as the Hindu or Buddhist concept of pollution. Another important consideration here is that pollution and purity are not dichotomous categories, but are ends of a continuum. In analyzing the concept, however, it is difficult to discuss it in terms of infinite gradations, and we shall recognize, perhaps somewhat arbitrarily, three initial points of demarcation.

Purified Beings and Purification

At the most purified end of the continuum, are most, but not all, gods, souls, and spirits. Souls of recently deceased human beings are polluted, since death itself is a defiling event, and must be treated with special care. Ordinarily, living humans are not as pure as most spirits of deceased beings, although they are capable of attaining a degree of purity equal to, or almost equal to gods. To do this, however, mortals must go through an appropriate purification ritual. Such a ritual is rather elaborate and arduous; for example an officiator at an important village ceremony is required to stay up all night in meditation and prayer, while pouring cold water over the body, and to abstain from women for a designated period of time. Such an individual can fully participate in the supernatural world. In the traditional past, there was a religious gathering known as *naorai*, in which gods and mortals joined in a communion by holding a banquet on sacred ground. To participate in this banquet, mortals were required to go through a rigorous purification ritual so that they would be as pure as gods. A simpler purification ritual might involve, as commonly observed even now at Shinto shrines, rinsing the mouth and washing the hands. Such an abbreviated purification, however, does not allow free trafficking with gods and spirits, but only allows the mortal to propitiate the gods, and to make his desires known or make reports to gods. Thus we already see that the "purified state" is a matter of degree.

Mortals

The second and intermediate category in the major tripartite division of the purity-pollution continuum includes most mortals. Men and women who are neither specially purified as described above nor specifically polluted as discussed below fall into this category. Because they are not completely pure, they must purify themselves to approach gods; at the same time, because they are not heavily polluted, it is possible for them to approach gods after purification. Also, their already somewhat polluted status makes them liable to become heavily polluted.

The Impurity of Women

Within this intermediate category, women are slightly more polluted than men. The reason is that blood is considered a potent source of pollution and women are capable of heavy pollution through menstruation and childbirth. For this reason, women were not allowed to officiate at important ceremonies in some areas of Japan, the assumption being that the pollution in womanhood is not removable even through the most rigorous purification ritual. By the same token, prepubescent girls were considered unpolluted, beyond the normal amount of pollution any mortal male has, and often served as attendants at Shinto shrines. The notion of female pollution was taken over by organized Buddhism, and some temples, such as the famous monastery of the Shingon sect at Mt. Kōya, forbade women from entering its premises. One may note here the difference between this Japanese notion of pollution and the Buddhist notion. In the latter, animal meat as such is a source of pollution, whereas in Japanese folk belief, it is blood and death which are polluting.

Polluting Conditions

The third, and the most polluted category includes men and women in special circumstances. With one exception as noted below, no one is permanently in this category, but on special occasions one becomes heavily polluted. A heavily polluted person is strictly barred from approaching gods. They must first remove the heavy pollution and attain the intermediate level of pollution and only then, with further purification, can they become pure enough to approach gods. A heavily polluted person, therefore, cannot become an officiator at religious ceremonies or even visit a shrine. A menstruating woman or a woman who has just given birth belongs to this category, being dangerously polluted because of her bleeding.

In many areas of Japan, a menstruating woman was required, in the past, to stay in a separate menstruation hut in a secluded section of the village. Where this was not the general custom for all women, special precautions were still taken by certain families or on certain occasions. For example, a family with special religious functions in the village would require menstruating women of the family to stay away from the house as the pollution of a menstruating woman might contaminate the sacredness of the religious functionary in the house. Or, on important religious holidays, such women might be required to observe certain taboos, lest they might pollute the sacredness of the holiday.

In childbirth, next to the mother herself, the new born baby, then other close relatives (especially the father) were, and still often are, also considered polluted and must observe requisite taboos and purification rites which, however, are less stringent than those for the mother. Local custom might require seventy-five days of seclusion for the mother and thirty-three days for the new born in a special childbirth hut, or at least in a special part of the house, and seven days of confinement in the house for the father. In some areas the whole village was required to abstain from work for a specified number of days after a birth in the village. It is believed that during the seclusion or abstention, the pollution would gradually dissipate so that by the end of the required period, the individuals involved would regain their normal state. Associated with the notion of pollution is the sacredness of the cooking fire and contagion through consumption of food cooked with the same fire. Food for a heavily polluted person, such as a menstruating or a post partum woman, therefore had to be cooked with separate fire.

Since death is a polluting event as dangerous as bleeding, close relatives of a deceased person were, and still are considered polluted, in degrees roughly in proportion to the genealogical closeness to the deceased. In some areas of Japan, close relatives, at least members of the family of the deceased, were required to live in seclusion, and villagers were not to share the food cooked by and for these relatives for the period of time specified by the local custom. Even attending a funeral would pollute a person, and an appropriate purification ritual had to be performed after returning home. Even now in cities, one sees a person throwing a pinch of salt over himself upon returning from a funeral, as an act of purification before entering his home.

Separate cooking for menstruating or post partum women is an indication of the strength of the belief in the power of food-sharing. There was a belief in the traditional past and until very recently in some parts of rural Japan that sharing of food was a way of sharing each other's magical power, health, etc. The custom of giving cooked adult food to the newborn, or the practice of a child with an eye disease begging food from neighbors and eating it as a cure is an example wherein the individual is believed to consume the growth power of adults or the health of others through consumption of food meant for adults or healthy persons. The custom of bringing a gift of food to a sick person is based on the same assumption. On such an occasion, the sick person does not give a token return gift, which is ordinarily required when one receives a gift, because he is liable to transmit his weakened health to the visitor through the gift.

Eta, the Ever-Polluted

While most mortals can relieve themselves of heavy pollution either through the passage of time or observance of proper rituals, there is one group of Japanese who are forever doomed to the status of being heavily polluted. This is the outcaste group known as the *eta*. The origin of the *eta* as a polluted outcaste group is obscure. It is probable that among their original occupations more than a thousand years ago were dealing with the care of dead human and animal bodies, slaughtering animals, and guarding graveyards, and that this had something to do with placing them in a polluted status. The beginning of the *eta* caste in the form we know it now, however, seems only a few hundred years old. Whatever their origin, the *eta* are so heavily polluted that ordinary Japanese feel repulsion at having physical contact with them. Many Japanese would throw salt about the house after a visit by an *eta,* if they would allow his visit, in order to purify the area which the *eta* polluted through his presence. Above all, marriage with an *eta* is a taboo which a normal Japanese would not think of violating.

The attitude toward the *eta* is much like the attitude of many white Americans, in both the northern and southern United States, toward the black. Among the many beliefs that whites espouse in order to justify their prejudice—such as that blacks are stupid, lazy, animal-like, shiftless, smelly, and dirty—is the belief that blacks are "polluted," that is, simply fundamentally unclean by nature, and that one should not come into physical contact with them. In this conception, marriage with a black is an ultimate form of damaging the purity of the white race. DeVos (1966, pp. 325–384) develops an extensive argument to demonstrate a close parallel between the caste segregation of the *eta* in Japan and that of the black in the United States. We shall return to the social problem of the *eta* in the following chapter.

The Nature of Ancestral Spirits

The Power of Spirits

Next to the notion of pollution and purity, the ways in which souls and spirits are conceptualized need elaboration. Here again one may conceive of a continuum from benevolent spiritual manifestations to malevolent manifestations. It should be understood that these spirits and souls are supernatural forces which are not immediately perceivable by human senses: only their manifestations are perceivable. In other words, the presence of spirits and souls must be inferred from various natural manifestations. In being invisible forces, Japanese spirits possess a quality akin to the *mana* of aboriginal societies of the Pacific and, although now somewhat differently conceived, the notion of Japanese spirits very likely was originally derived from the same source as the concept of *mana. Mana,* though potentially dangerous, is in itself a neutral force and could be channeled into benevolent or malevolent manifestations. Chiefs in some Polynesian societies were so full of *mana* and therefore ritually so dangerous that they had to be secluded from common people and carried in outings lest their presence or contact with the ground cause danger to commoners. The Japanese conception of the emperor, until he secularized himself with an official proclamation after World War II, is strikingly similar. Frazer astutely saw this sacred quality of the emperor and noted it in his *Golden Bough.* At a more mundane level, too, the Japanese hold the notion of a potentially dangerous force which must be approached with care. For example, for a human being to approach and manipulate the force, he must go through an appropriate purification ritual. At the same time, some of the Japanese spirits or souls are inherently more dangerous and prone to malevolent manifestations than others which are less inclined to harm mortals. The more dangerous ones, obviously, must be approached with greater care than the less dangerous ones.

The Recently Deceased

Souls of the recently deceased, or "the departed" (Plath, 1964b), are quite dangerous because of their association with the polluted dead bodies from which they have just been separated. These souls, and especially those of individuals who died unnatural deaths, need particular attention. If failure to provide needed attention—in adequate daily offerings and prayers—is followed by a family misfortune, it is a sure sign that the spirits are displeased. Proper attention is also necessary to graduate spirits of the recently departed into a more purified, less dangerous state. Misfortune can occur when spirits are resentful of the fact that they are still polluted and are having difficulty joining the more purified spirits because their living relatives do not properly care for them with offerings and prayers.

In this connection, the practice of dual graves, known throughout most of traditional Japan, is significant. In the dual grave system, the dead body is first buried, immediately after the death, in a graveyard which is usually maintained by the village or by the kin group. This graveyard is located some distance from the settlement, perhaps at the village border, or in the mountains. After the burial, no one visits this graveyard; hence the name *sute-baka,* or "abandoned grave." It is considered to be haunted by dangerous spirits and contaminated with the pollution of the dead bodies buried there. Some time after the initial burial, a new grave is constructed near or even within the residence of the family of the deceased, and periodic memorial rituals are henceforth conducted there. In this dual grave system, the body of the deceased, and the pollution of the dead body, remain at the first grave and are not brought to the second grave. The new grave is for his soul, which is cleansed of death pollution.

Gradual Purification of the Deceased

This still does not mean that the spirit is now completely purified. As we said above, pollution and purity are a matter of degree, and a spirit does not suddenly pass from a polluted state to a purified one. Instead, it gradually becomes less and less polluted and correspondingly more and more purified. It is often believed that a spirit becomes completely purified and harmless after the thirty-third, or some such, anniversary. Until then, as Plath (1964b) has noted, spirits of deceased relatives have individuality: they are remembered intimately as former members of the family. Their likes and dislikes, their hopes and aspirations are to be taken seriously. Thus a morsel a man liked when alive should be offered whenever the opportunity presents itself. If he disliked a crying child, a young member of the family

A graveyard in Kyoto.
In traditional Japan, the
graveyard was
considered to be haunted
by dangerous spirits.

will be reminded of the fact and told to heed the desires of the deceased even though he is dead, or rather especially because he is dead and is capable of supernatural punishment. A son who had passed the entrance examination to a college would not forget to report the result to his deceased mother, who had wished him success. In short, positively and negatively, recently departed ancestors provide moral guidance to the living. They are very much of the family as they were before their death. It is highly important that when a family member dies, he does not suddenly and abruptly disappear and sever his psychological ties with the survivors. Instead, emotional bonds still remain and are expressed in the way the living remember and treat the dead. This provides emotional satisfaction to the living, in whose life the recently departed once occupied an important place. The import of this conception of ancestors should become further clarified later when we discuss the emotional patterning of Japanese.

As the memory of the living begins to fade, the dead begin to join the

A home Buddhist altar. The spirits of deceased relative are remembered intimately and their likes and dislikes, their hopes and aspirations are taken seriously.

more abstract, anonymous collectivity of "ancestors" who lack individual personality but still retain a generalized supernatural power able to affect the living. In many locales, the thirty-third anniversary of the death marks this final rite of passage. The personal tablet in the family altar is abandoned and the ancestor is incorporated into the one collective tablet marked "generations of ancestors." At the grave yard, too, for one reason or another, such as lack of space, older graves of less remembered and more innocuous souls are collectivized in the tomb marked "the Grave for Generations of Ancestors of Such-and-Such Family."

Nonhuman Souls

Although we have mainly discussed human souls so far, nonhuman beings are also considered to have souls. But they are not all equally dangerous. There are some, like the snake and the fox, which must be treated with care because of the great potential supernatural danger, and there are others which are of no serious concern for man. Human souls are venerated at the family altar and graveyard, and are thus distinguished from nonhuman souls. But in terms of the potential effects on the living and in causing fortune and misfortune for man, human and nonhuman souls constitute a single category.

One interesting characteristic of the Japanese folk beliefs we have examined is the fluidity of supernatural concepts; continua, rather than well-demarcated categories, constitute the supernatural world. For example, while all living beings have spirits, there is a great range in their potential power or manifestation from innocuous flowers and insects to very dangerous animals. In the pollution-purity continuum, we saw that a person can move from the most polluted to the most purified state. Interestingly, deceased beings, too, migrate from the most polluted to the most purified stages in their careers.

Possession and Retribution

Possession

One way in which spirits are capable of affecting mortals is through possession *(tsukimono)*. Among various species of animals capable of possession are human beings (living or dead), foxes, dogs, and snakes. Distribution of possession phenomena is heavily concentrated in the southern half of Japan. In the north, the number of occurrences per community or per year is far less than in the south, and possession in the north is generally caused by an outsider and not by a fellow villager, as is generally the case in the south. For this reason possession in the north does not pose a major threat to the community integration, and it is not a major concern of the people. Our discussion will be concerned with the phenomena in the south.

Animal spirits which are capable of possession do not wander around in the countryside. They are, instead, maintained in certain family lines from generation to generation. These families have no way of ridding themselves of the spirits. Since these spirits can be transmitted through both sexes, marriage with these families is carefully avoided by ordinary families.

Possession is manifested in a variety of illnesses, including some psychosomatic ones, and in injuries and accidents. When one suspects such a manifestation to be due to possession, he tries to find out whether it is in fact due to possession, and if so who is the holder of the spirit which has caused the misfortune, by resorting to one or another of various methods locally available. Some diagnoses require a professional diviner. Some methods are simple home diagnoses, such as placing by the victim an object which the spirit is known to dislike. If the victim is indeed victimized by this spirit, he will manifest dislike of the object, even though ordinarily he might have a passion for it. Once it is determined that a spirit possesses the victim, the spirit is driven out of the victim by one of the locally prescribed methods. Again, some are "home remedies," such as tying up the patient and beating him until the spirit supposedly runs out, or smoking the spirit out of the patient by burning green leaves in the patient's enclosed room. Some remedies require professionals, like the diviner, Shinto or Buddhist priest, or shaman, who drive the spirit out through incantation, prayer, rituals, sympathetic magic, or in the case of the shaman, by going into a trance.

Possession seems to occur when the culprit is jealous or envious of the victim, for example of the latter's success, wealth, etc. But the culprit himself may or may not be aware of having caused the possession: his spirit can leave him without his awareness and possess another, causing injury. In such a case, it is up to the injured party, possibly with the help of a diviner, to make inferences as to who the culprit is. The fact that the culprit has in the past shown signs of jealousy would serve as an important clue in the divination. The social function of such a diagnosis is obvious: it serves to maintain harmonious community relations by discouraging the expression of jealousy. It is significant, seen in this functional perspective, that possession should be common in areas of Japan characterized by the presence of groups and associations which crosscut and partially overlap, providing grounds for conflicting interests and allegiances (Yoshida, 1967).

Retribution

Similar to possession is retribution *(tatari)*, or supernatural punishment. Such punishment can occur under a number of circumstances (T. Seki, 1954, p. 885), of which there are seven major kinds: (1) when a shrine is moved and the god enshrined there is displeased with the move; (2) when two or more gods who do not get along are enshrined together; (3) when a god is neglected or not properly cared for; (4) when a mortal actively curses or intentionally neglects the care of a god he is supposed to care for; (5) when a taboo is violated, such as opening a forbidden door of a shrine or a menstruating woman going to a sacred place; (6) when a person dies an unnatural death, like suicide, drowning, being murdered, etc; (7) when a man kills or injures animals of certain species, such as a dog, fox, snake, or cat.

Misfortune arising from retribution may range from damage to property (through fire, crop failure, etc.) to illness or injury to the culprit or his relatives. As in other cases of supernatural acts, the discovery of supernatural punishment is made through backward reasoning: since we cannot know the god's or spirit's displeasure directly, it is inferred from the observed misfortune. That is, when a misfortune strikes, one suspects retribution, and tries to think of some "wrong-doing" of the sort listed above for which he might be responsible. Usually it is not difficult to find some such god-displeasing act, it being human to err. Once the specific cause for the retribution is discovered, it is necessary to restore normalcy by performing a proper ritual or otherwise removing the cause of the supernatural displeasure.

The Social Significance of Folk Beliefs

The Community

We have so far examined Japanese folk beliefs in relation to individuals. By way of concluding this chapter, a few words may be said of the importance on folk beliefs to social groups, such as the village, the household, and the family. As noted in the chapter of rural life, the village community in Japan has always been more or less a corporate unit, more so in the premodern past than subsequently. As a corporate unit, it generally has economic and political bases for the maintenance of the community as a unit. A corporate group, particularly when its political and economic functions are crucial for the group, must have some symbolic means of validating the importance of the unit. It is for this reason that Japanese village communities have always had a tutelary deity which is believed to look after the welfare of the villagers and the village. This deity may be of any nature. Sometimes it is an ancestral figure of one of the kin groups of the village. He might be a fox god, who, as we saw, is identified also as the deity for the protection of rice fields. Whatever its nature, its function as the guardian of the village and the villagers is the same everywhere in Japan. He looks after agriculture in general, but particularly rice cultivation, and is also the guardian of the health and fortune of villagers. In sickness villagers go to the shrine and pray for speedy recovery. For the academic success of the son, the mother solicits the aid of the village god.

In connection with the corporate function of the village guardian god it is interesting to note that in the past hundred years, as villages of the Tokugawa period have become amalgamated into larger and larger political units for administrative efficiency, a corresponding process has been observed in the celestial world. That is, as the amalgamation of two or more village communities takes place, the shrine of one or the other of these villages becomes the guardian shrine of the new, amalgamated unit. How the decision is reached as to which shrine will assume this dominant role is not always a smooth process and often reflects the problems and conflicts in the terrestrial process of administrative amalgamation. This shrine, then, would be honored by all members of the newly created, larger village. The

A Shinto structure on a sedan being carried
around the community on a festival day.

other shrines, however, do not disappear at once, or become incorporated
into the official village shrine. Instead, they remain and continue to be
celebrated by the local residents of the former villages—usually on a smaller
scale than the official village shrine. This again reflects the degree of self-
identity which peasants retain with their old village community even after
the amalgamation.

The Family

The village guardian deity is generally conceived of by the rural folk as
Shinto in nature, although close analysis will show that non-Shinto (Buddhist, Taoist, etc.) elements are often mixed in. Beliefs surrounding family
deities, on the other hand, are by and large Buddhist, although these beliefs
are heavily colored by folk Shinto beliefs. We have already seen how ancestral spirits are regarded by living descendants at various stages from death
to eternity. It only remains to add that by continuing to have an intimate
relationship with and deep concern about living members of the family,
deceased members assist in keeping the family together. To the extent that
the living believe that dead members are still spiritually alive in the family
and continue to be moral guardians of the traditional values of the family,
ancestors play a powerful role in the corporate perpetuity of the family unit.

The Household

As the family is looked after by deceased members, the household is taken care of by household gods, who are generally not former members of the family. One exception is the *yashiki-gami,* who is often an ancestral figure. His shrine is located outside the house, but within its premises at some corner judged to be strategic by divination. But this "estate god", too, is occasionally a deity with no family connection. Other household deities have limited functions and are located at strategic places: the kitchen god in the kitchen, the latrine god in the latrine, the hearth god by the hearth, etc. These deities help keep the household in order: they do not so much look after the kitchen, hearth, etc. as "reside" at these locations, from which they look after the welfare of the household members. It is believed that certain illnesses or misfortunes can be traced to the neglect of specific household gods by household members, whereas proper attention given them will bring about beneficial results.

To conclude, folk beliefs in Japan have an indigenous origin, but have been influenced by the practices and beliefs of religious systems of the great tradition. They are thus a composite system, and make sense to common people only as such. The importance of this belief system to individuals is quite obvious, but it also affects group life—the family, the village, etc. It would be a mistake to think that such a belief system is a thing of the past or that it is relevant only for rural Japan. On the contrary, it is practiced daily in urban centers as well, although urbanites are more reluctant to admit such practices. In modern business firms and large department stores one almost invariably finds a shrine for a god of business success. Dore has reported of Tokyo residents (1958, pp. 291–373) that their belief in the efficacy of supernatural beings is still quite strong.

New Religions*

While traditional beliefs concerning supernatural forces continue to be observed in urban as well as rural areas, these beliefs no longer adequately meet the spiritual needs of city people. Urban dwellers, scientifically somewhat more sophisticated than their rural brethren, are no longer convinced of the concrete details of the supernaturalism which their forefathers believed in. Moreover, the social nexus of the city is so different from the village that the social functions of rural folk beliefs are effective only to a much reduced degree in cities. Also, as we have seen, established religions are in no better position to help the modern urban man, for state Shinto has ceased to exist, and sect Shinto and Buddhism as an established church have

*The author would like to acknowledge a special debt to Edward Norbeck for providing much of the material presented in this section.

by and large held to traditional practices. In the changing modern world, in which traditional forms of belief have failed to change correspondingly and have become neglected by a large number of city people, new forms of religion have begun to rise in large numbers, especially since World War II.

The formation of new religions in Japan is not something unique to the recent decades. Long before the modern period, new religious sects have been established by discontented individuals from time to time. Among them, Nichiren, who organized a militant, nationalistic Buddhist faith in the thirteenth century at the time of the Mongol attack on western Japan, is one of the earliest and best known. More recently, during the Tokugawa period, Tenrikyō and Konkōkyō were founded in 1833 and 1855 respectively, both stemming from Shinto. While relatively new, these sects may now be regarded as established religions which have gone through a period of trial and proved themselves to be viable religious faiths.

Postwar Developments

In the modern period, especially since the late 1930s, a plethora of new religious sects began to emerge. Until the end of the Second World War, however, the Japanese government, acting under the wartime measure to keep a tight control over all types of organization, made formal registration of new sects difficult. When the war ended and the government lifted its control of religious organizations, a large number of new sects—upwards of 700—were registered with the government, compared to less than fifty religious organizations of any type recognized during the war. This increase was only in part due to the post war removal of control of religion; it was also significantly due to the turmoil and confusion which swept the country in the wake of a complete military defeat and unconditional surrender.

The general public has regarded the new and religious splinter groups that have arisen in the past several decades with contempt and ridicule. Many of them were in fact involved in rather shady commercial or political activities at one time or another which were widely publicized through the mass media. Also, their founders have often made what seem to outsiders as simply fantastic supernatural claims. While most of them have remained small—a few thousand members or less—some of them have grown in importance to a degree not to be overlooked. For example, Sōka Gakkai, Risshō Kōseikai, and P L (for Perfect Liberty) Kyōdan have claimed memberships, respectively, of fifteen million, two million and one million (as of 1965), although the actual membership, while not precisely known, is definitely much smaller.

Simple Doctrinal Base

The doctrinal basis of most of these new sects is very simple. They derive their tenets from Shinto, Buddhism, Christianity, and other religions in varying combinations and in different proportions. Depending on how strongly the leaders of a sect feels its tenets are derived from a given religion, they register their religion as Shinto, Buddhist, etc., as the case may be. Perhaps the strength of the new sects lies in part in their simplicity, in contrast to the complex and esoteric philosophy of traditional Buddhist sects. Simple tenets make the doctrine understandable to all followers and helps prevent the development of a special elite class within the faith who possess special knowledge unavailable to others. The principal tenet of the new sects stresses the salvation of believers simply through their belief or the recitation of religious formulas. Above all, they emphasize this-worldly happiness, the importance of getting along with one's fellow men, achieving peace of mind, and in some sects, curing illnesses through faith. Emphasis is also placed on universal humanitarianism, brotherhood of mankind, and peace in the world.

Organization

The original founders of the larger sects have a common social background of psychological suffering and economic deprivation. Some of them in addition manifested pathological tendencies, which were curiously brought under control after they received the call to religious duty. The leaders' charisma played a vital role in the early stages of these sects, attracting new members and helping to maintain the sects' solidarity. However, when membership increases to tens of thousands, the founders' charisma plays a less and less important role, and the group depends for its maintenance on its own organizational momentum and ingenuity. Above all, there is a vertical, hierarchical line of organization, coupled with a horizontal bond of members. Members find themselves in a social nexus which strongly binds them and which at the same time make them feel important and valued. As a technique of organizing, members are placed in small intimate groups in which, at frequent meetings, such things as family problems and difficulties at work are unloaded to sympathetic ears, and troubled members receive psychological support and practical suggestions for solving their personal problems. Individual members thus gain a sense of importance in a way they never do outside the group.

The larger sects correctly recognize the importance of youth for the viability of the sect and accord them a special place, for example, by organizing athletic and other club activities for them. Health is also a central concern for many of the new sects. Some, such as P. L. Kyōdan, run modern hospitals where Western scientific medicine is practiced. Others rely more heavily on faith healing in which psychosomatic components play a major part. Faith healing does not rely on the presence of a great charismatic leader. Instead, it typically takes place in small groups like those mentioned above, in which mutual support and encouragement are an important element.

The rank and file membership of a new sect are typically drawn from lower class urbanites, especially those who have domestic problems, illness, and trouble at work, and also to a less extent, from those who have just left their rural home and come to an unfamiliar urban environment. These individuals are drawn into the new sects as a way of relieving personal difficulties and loneliness; the large and increasing membership of these sects attests to their success in meeting the needs of troubled urbanites.

The leadership of these sects, however, does not by and large consist of ill-educated, troubled industrial workers, but comes from the more sophisticated, well-educated, urban middle class. Like other middle-class individuals, they are achievement-oriented and strive to move up the organizational hierarchy of their sect. Larger sects have been able to reward these leaders because of the rapid increase in organizational size. Leaders of a large new sect are keenly aware of the competition which their sect faces with other religious bodies, and strive to achieve an advantageous position in recruiting members and providing a favorable public image. In these respects, these leaders are little different from business executives.

Many of the so-called new religious sects are not new any more. Just as Tenrikyō and Konkōkyō have become established and joined the ranks of "old religions," many of the new sects have also become well established. There is the danger that these sects may become conventionalized and maintain themselves through inertia, and that the leaders may become satisfied with what they have, as in the established, older Buddhist sects. Will the new sects maintain their present hold on the society and continue to be a viable force in this changing world? This will depend on whether they remain active in developing new devices to continue to meet the needs of the people.

SUGGESTED READINGS

Anesaki, Masaharu
   1963   *History of Japanese Religion, with Special Reference to the Social and Moral Life of the Nation.* Rutland: Charles E. Tuttle Co., Inc.

Bellah, Robert
   1957   *Tokugawa Religion.* Glencoe: The Free Press.

Embre, John F.
   1941   "Some social functions of religion in rural Japan." *American Journal of Sociology* 47: 184–189.

Hori, Ichiro
   1968   *Folk Religion of Japan.* Chicago: University of Chicago Press.

McFarland, H. Neill
1967   *The Rush Hour of the Gods: A Study of New Religious Movements in Japan.*
New York: The Macmillan Company.

Norbeck, Edward
1970   *Religion and Society in Japan.* Houston: Tourmaline Press.

Plath, David W.
1964   "Where the family of God is the family." *American Anthropologist* 66:
300–317.

Smith, Robert J.
1966   "*Ihai:* Mortuary tablets, the household, and kin in Japanese ancestor
worship." *Transactions of the Asiatic Society of Japan* 9: 83–102.

5 Class, Work, and Education

The Stratification System in Traditional Japan

As we saw earlier, the official class system of the Tokugawa period set warriors as rulers, below whom came peasants, then artisans, and finally merchants. Merchants were despised by the Confucian-oriented warrior-rulers for not creating anything, as peasants and artisans did, but making profit simply by passing goods from one hand to another. To these four, frozen, endogamous classes—in effect, castes—should be added two more, one on top and one at the bottom. The Imperial family and the nobility surrounding the Emperor constituted a class superior to the warriors at least in prestige, in spite of lack of power or a significant amount of wealth. Although their prestige declined considerably toward the end of the Tokugawa period, this class could not be dismissed or ignored even by the Tokugawa shogunate. The elaborate court rituals and etiquette surrounding the Emperor and nobles symbolized their high position—"above the cloud" as the Japanese expression goes. At the bottom of the social hierarchy were the *eta,* the polluted outcaste group who were thoroughly despised and feared. They were not even considered human, and in official censuses they were omitted from the count of human population and included among chattel.

Thus in the traditional stratification system, prestige-holding court nobles, along with the Imperial family, had the highest position, followed by power-holding warriors. Below the warriors, officially speaking, came producers—peasants and artisans. But in fact, toward the end of the Tokugawa period wealthy merchants were gaining more and more respectable positions in the society. Thus it may be said that next to prestige and power, wealth served as a criterion of stratification. This does not mean that power-holding warriors had no wealth. Indeed, high-ranking warriors received a considerable stipend; but it was power which put them above merchants.

Early Modern Changes

With the inauguration of the modern era, the Meiji government did away with the feudal caste structure and permitted, at least in theory, free occupational mobility among the classes. This of course facilitated Japan's modernization, for its rapid modernization required the most rational allocation of human resources—recruitment of personnel according to talent and skill. A caste system which froze occupations obviously impeded this objective and had to give way to a more efficient system, although an entirely new class structure did not suddenly come into being in early modern Japan. Transformation took place slowly.

We might start with the new legal arrangement of social classes in early modern Japan. The emperor of course occupied the pinnacle of the society. Below him were recognized the imperial family *(kōzoku)*, nobility *(kazoku)* —with several ranks—, former warriors and their descendants *(shizoku)*, and commoners *(heimin)*.

The Imperial Family and the Nobility

The imperial family and the nobles were given a special status and stipend to maintain their social position. The nobility, a hereditary status, included distant members of the imperial family, court nobles, former high ranking warriors like the *daimyō,* and finally others, such as notable statesmen, industrialists, and military leaders, who did not have a respected family history, but who had demonstrated great ability. There was a fairly sharper line drawn between the last category of "instant" nobles and others with a time-honored, respected family history (Fujishima, 1965). It is this sense of history which has conferred on the latter group of nobles their prestige and the rationale for their position. Their pride comes from the fact that such a rationale cannot be bought or replaced by power or wealth. That the possibility of "instant nobility" opened up to commoners, however, was important as an indication of the extent to which the government recognized and rewarded individual merit and talent.

Former Warriors and Commoners

Because former warriors had been trained as administrators and were experienced in exercising authority, their talents were widely used in the newly created modern government. They by and large monopolized the government bureaucracy at first. As industrial enterprises began to assume an important role in Japan's modernization, both former high-ranking warriors and wealthy merchants began to go into industry. Warriors entered business for two reasons: because of the close connection between industry and the government, which heavily subsidized it, and because of their wealth, which could be converted into capital. Merchants, on the other hand, entered business because of their access to both know-how and capital. Thus in the modern period both power and wealth began to have more or less equal value in the stratification system. Peasants, artisans, and small merchants—who had neither power nor wealth—remained at the bottom of the hierarchy. They were nonetheless above the outcaste *eta,* who, though legally freed and granted a status of equality with ordinary Japanese, remained socially despised and discriminated against. It may be mentioned here that universal conscription, which was instituted to build up Japan's military power, opened an avenue for non-samurai descendants to raise their status through a military career.

Another new avenue of success developed in the modern period as formal education, especially at the college level, began to be an important criterion for employment in government bureaucracy and in private businesses. Of course, education requires financial resources, and sons of wealthy families had a distinct advantage. But gradually men of less privileged classes also began to receive college educations in larger and larger number. At the same time, the number of positions requiring advanced education, both in the public and private sectors, increased, further opening up avenues of success to the middle and lower classes.

Postwar Changes

Continuity and change are both evident in the overall picture of the stratification structure after World War II. The military as a source of power and an avenue of success has disappeared almost completely, although the Defense Force, while still a minor element in society, has been gaining prestige. While the imperial family has remained, the nobility was legally abolished. Also discontinued was the legal distinction between "descendant of warrior" and "commoner". Such legal abolition, however, did not totally eliminate the sense of class distinction between them. The former nobility still gather around the imperial family and continue to enjoy high prestige despite the economic decline which many of them have suffered because of the elimination of an annual stipend and because of the formidable taxes levied against them. They still maintain a tightly knit organization and do not readily admit outsiders. Marriage, for example, is strictly limited to their own group. By now, even the "instant nobles" of the Meiji era have acquired enough lustre to have a vested interest in their social status, in spite of the fact that it is now stripped of legal sanction. The more recent industrialists, especially the *nouveaux riches* of the postwar period, remain distinctly below the social elite, no matter how much wealth they may accumulate.

The descendants of warriors and commoners had intermarried so much by the end of World War II that the legal removal of their class distinction simply more or less confirmed the social reality, although the *shizoku* designation still carries some prestige.

Minority Groups

Although the *eta* are the best known, there are many other minority groups in Japan toward whom the majority expresses prejudice and exercises discrimination (Norbeck, 1966). Parenthetically, this minority phenomenon should be distinguished from the kind of prejudices which Japanese have toward those from other regions or prefectures, somewhat akin to the American Northerner's stereotyped notions of the Southerner. As a result of these prejudices, those who move away from their home are likely to encounter stereotyped reactions. For example people from Kōchi are expected to be heavy drinkers, people from Osaka are expected to be shrewd and businessmanlike in their dealings with others, etc. Okinawans, among others, coming to large cities like Tokyo and Osaka to work, also encounter such prejudice and discrimination.

The minority groups, some of which are to be discussed below, differ from these above groups in that they are considered less desirable people, lacking in a sufficient amount of certain qualities necessary to be fully-fledged human beings, or at least upstanding Japanese, and this lack is considered to be biologically inherent.

The Eta

The *eta* still remain a distinct caste group of at least a million distributed throughout western Japan. Marriage across the caste line is strongly opposed to both the *eta* and non-*eta* Japanese. Various social and psychological barriers set up by both sides prevent the *eta* from "passing" as non-*eta*. Although the *eta* have organized themselves into political associations in order to bring about equality, the government has not done enough to remove the caste barrier. To make it worse, ordinary Japanese are either naively ignorant of the *eta's* situation or underestimate its gravity.

Atom Bomb Victims

As we saw, one basic reason for the *eta's* segregation is the inherently polluted nature of the *eta*. Curiously, a similar attitude has developed toward the victims of the atom bombs which were dropped over Hiroshima and Nagasaki near the end of World War II. In spite of scientific demonstration to the contrary, the Japanese have come to believe that exposure to heavy atomic radiation has made the victims capable of producing human monstrosities and susceptible to rare diseases. For these reasons ordinary Japanese are careful to avoid marriage with such victims or with their children. As a consequence, atom bomb victims have become the victims of social discrimination as well. Along with the *eta,* they have become another polluted pariah (Lifton, 1967).

Why did this happen? From time immemorial, Japan has had a number of minority groups besides the *eta* whom ordinary Japanese have despised and discriminated against and refused to intermarry with, such as the boat-dwellers known as the *ebune* (Norbeck, 1966). In short, the notion of pollution and attendant discrimination and refusal to marry are indigenous to Japanese culture. It is therefore no surprise to see another group like atom bomb victims being added to the list of such groups.

The Ainu

Another indigenous minority group discriminated against in Japan is the Ainu of Hokkaido. The *eta* of Japan are to the Negro of the United States as the Ainu are to the Indians. As the Negroes have been part and parcel of the social and economic history of the United States, *eta* have been an integral part of Japan's social and economic development. As Indians were the aboriginal group pushed off to undersirable parts of the land by force and inequitable "treaties," so were the Ainu. The attitude of ritual pollution which surrounds white-black relationships in the United States is clearly evident in the Japanese attitude toward the *eta,* while such an attitude is absent in their relation to the Ainu, as it is in the white attitude toward Indians.

Foreigners

Japanese sharply distinguish between themselves and foreigners. Unlike residents of the United States, who believe that everyone living in the country is more or less an American, regardless of his length of residence or whether or not he is native born, the Japanese believe that only the descendants of Japanese can be truly Japanese. Non-Japanese, no matter how long they live in Japan, even though they may be born in Japan, and however well they may adopt Japanese cutoms, habits of thought, and speech, are still foreigners. A sharp line is drawn between them, which cannot be justified objectively on behavioral grounds.

. Among foreigners, a distinction is made between Orientals—mostly Koreans and Chinese—and Caucasians. Orientals, particularly Koreans, are accorded a lower status than Japanese, while Caucasians are given a higher status. Since other foreigners, such as southeast Asians, the Hindu, and Africans, are so few in Japan, they are not of social consequence. It may be safely assumed, however, that Japanese have a low esteem for all these groups, and a particularly low one for the Negro.

Children of mixed parentage, i.e., of a Japanese and a foreign parent also have a special but unenviable status. They are referred to as *ainoko,* which means a child of mixed blood but has a derogatory connotation. Those who were born to Japanese girls and G.I.s in the postwar Occupation period suffer additionally the social stigma of being illegitimate. Many of them have grown up in orphanages because their mother would not or could not bear the stigma and the economic burden of raising the child. Of late, the entertainment world has begun to exploit the now adolescent boys and girls of mixed parentage. For if they have any talent, their exotic looks certainly make them worthy of exhibit.

The origin and development of these minority groups are of course in part due to historical accidents. One can trace the history of any minority group in Japan back to its point of origin, some, like the *eta,* going back more than a thousand years, others, like the A-bomb victims, going no further back than a generation. Yet all of them share the common problem of prejudice and discrimination from the majority. As an ultimate proof of his prejudice, a normal Japanese would not marry a member of a minority group. What is unfortunate is that the majority of Japanese tend to minimize the gravity of minority problems. They are apt to think that minority problems are disappearing and that nothing in particular need be done. They consequently lend little support to various social movements to ameliorate minority conditions. The gravity of the problem lies in the fact that it is not a passing event in history, but deeply rooted in the structure of society and the attitudes of the people. The persistence of the *eta* in Japan for centuries and into the modern era can be understood only by taking account of the institutional arrangement in which an outcaste group plays a role and in the disposition of the majority of Japanese to feel superior to the outcaste and therefore justified in their acts of discrimination. It is on these social and psychological bases that new minority groups like the A-bomb victims and the *ainoko* are created and given a definite place in society.

Occupational Mobility and Ranking

The great bulk of Japanese lie between the two extremes of the social elite and the outcaste. How this group is to be divided into social classes depends on the theory and methods one uses. Japanese sociologists have used various questionaire survey methods for determining the class system in Japan. Table 5:1, obtained from the 1955 national survey referred to above and from a 1964 survey (Nishihira, 1964), shows the ranking of occupations by Tokyo male samples. One can note in this table the rise during the nine-year period of certain occupations which modern technology has put in the limelight, such as civil engineers and garage mechanics. Some others, such as charcoal makers and independent farmers, which have declined in national importance as the nation has moved away from dependence on primary industries, have gone down in their ranking.

It should be noted that Table 5:1 does not include many occupational

Poorer people living on boats in Kobe.
Note also the cluster of waterside shacks.

types, such as industrialists, lawyers, artists, and grocers. Within this limited list, however, it is interesting that the general pattern of ranking of various occupations is similar to what we might expect in the United States (Inkeles and Rossi, 1956). At the same time, certain peculiarities in the ranking also stand out. The high position which the university professor occupies is an indication of the high prestige he enjoys, even though his income is by no means commensurate with his prestige. We see here at work the traditional Japanese stratification theory in which prestige, power, and wealth were separate and somewhat independent criteria of ranking. The disproportionately high place of the independent farmer as an unskilled laborer also echoes the relatively high status he enjoyed in the official theory of social classes in the feudal past.

These occupations may be grouped into a smaller number of categories, such as "professional," "managerial," etc. It is then possible to estimate the proportions of Japanese belonging to each such category. According to Nishihira (1968), 1.9% of Japanese in 1960 belonged to the top category of "top administrator and researcher"; 5.5% belonged to the next, "professional, service specialist, and middle-managerial" category; 31.9% belonged to the third category of "white collar worker in large company, small enterpriser, and artisan"; 32.3% belonged to the next "skilled and semi-skilled worker and store clerk" category; and finally 28.4% to the lowest,

TABLE 5:1. OCCUPATIONAL RANKING (1955 AND 1964)
(TOKYO MALE SAMPLE)

Ranking		Occupation
1964	1955	
1	1	University professor
2	2	Physician
3	6	Civil engineer
4	4	Mechanical engineer
5	4	Section head of a company
5	3	Section head of a city government
7	7	Grade-school teacher
8	7	Buddhist priest
9	9	Accountant
10	10	Policeman
11	11	Small retail store owner
12	15	Cabinet maker
13	14	Barber
13	15	Garage mechanic
13	13	Railway station attendant
13	18	Carpenter
17	12	Independent farmer
18	15	Truck driver
19	18	Lathe operator
20	25	Textile operator
20	20	Typesetter
22	23	Store clerk
23	26	Porter
24	20	Insurance salesman
24	23	Baker
26	22	Fisherman
26	27	Tenant farmer
28	32	Coolie
28	29	Road-construction worker
28	29	Itinerant trader
31	28	Coal miner
32	29	Charcoal maker

(Occupations with the same ranking were given an equal rating by the respondents.)

"manual laborer" category. Although no data are available for the recent years, in all likelihood the percentages of the top categories have increased and the bottom categories have shrunk. For with increasing technological advancement, the demand for service specialists as well as for highly trained managerial and professional specialists has greatly increased. At the same time, labor-saving devices have forced a considerable number of workers out of the unskilled and semiskilled occupations. (Next to the United States, Japan owns the largest number of computers in the free world.)

While occupational mobility, that is, a shift in occupation from father to son or within one's own career, has been increasing, it is not uniform throughout all occupational groups and categories. The 1955 survey shows that among nonagricultural occupations, professional occupations tend to be taken over by sons of professionals, while clerical, managerial, and semiskilled occupations tend to be assumed by those whose fathers had an occupation in a different category (Nihon Shakai Gakkai Chōsa Iinkai ed., 1958, p. 65). According to later surveys, occupational mobility continues to increase, reflecting Japan's rapid industrial growth. Agriculture is taking a definitely secondary place in the nation's economy and is losing workers at the highest rate of all occupational categories. On the other hand, young people are moving into semiskilled industrial occupations at a faster rate than into any other occupational category.

The 1955 survey also shows that in Tokyo 17% of the respondents indicated upward mobility in their own occupational career, 9% downward mobility, 10% a fluctuating trend, and 64% an immobile career pattern (Nihon Shakai Gakkai Chōsa Iinkai ed. 1958, p. 55). Although it may seem odd, across the nation, as in Tokyo, there is more upward than downward mobility; the former is not balanced by the latter to produce an over-all equilibrium in the occupational structure. This trend is also seen in inter-generational occupational mobility, as shown in Table 5:2. One see, for example, that only 2.9% of the respondents had a paternal grandfather who had a professional occupation, whereas 6.7% of them are professional themselves. On the other hand, agricultural workers have decreased from 61.9% to 35.6% in three generations. This fact reflects the continuing industrial growth of the nation; the labor forces employed in agriculture and at unskilled labor are diminishing in size, or at best growing at a slower rate than semiskilled and white collar occupations.

The Middle Class, New and Old

The New Middle Class

The middle-class wage earner, commonly known in Japan as the "salary man," has a style of life distinct from other urban dwellers (Vogel, 1963). The salary man phenomenon is not entirely new in postwar Japan. Its history goes back to the early modern days when the government bureaucracy, the school system, and industrial organizations were established and manned with officials, teachers, and managerial workers with regular salaries. The postwar situation is a continuation of the prewar phenomenon, whose social significance has been augmented by the much increased and ever increasing scale of operations in the political, economic, and social spheres of life, which require bureaucratized management with salaried, white collar personnel. The white collar job is becoming increasingly reserved for college graduates. Most college graduates hold some kind of white collar job; and at the same time more and more white collar jobs

A government housing project in Nara prefecture. The families living
in these projects tend to have homogeneous social backgrounds and
be more "modern" than their counterparts in the older parts of the city.

require a college education. At the present, however, a large minority of
white collar workers, especially in medium-sized and small enterprises, are
only high-school graduates. There is also some indication that there are now
so many college graduates that some are forced to take jobs which require
only high-school training.

The salary man typically works for a regular salary in a medium to large
size enterprise (Hayashi, Suri, and Suzuki, 1964). His job is secure because
he has tenure from the beginning of his employment and is on the whole
satisfied with his work. The employer, especially in a large company, provides generous fringe benefits, including a twice-a-year bonus of two to three
months's pay, discount sales of company products, recreational facilities,
paid vacation and sick leave, company-run resort facilities made available
at cost, etc. The salary man tends to be relatively young because of the rapid
increase in the number of white-collar jobs in recent years, which have had
to be filled by new graduates from colleges. What is important about the
salary man, in addition to the quantitative increase in white-collar jobs, is
the fact that the salary man status has high prestige and is considered to
be the most desirable and at the same time realistically attainable goal for
most young Japanese preparing for occupational careers.

The majority of salary men live in rented housing, such as the new
apartment projects which mushroomed in the postwar years, and the family
tends to be of the conjugal type. Since most of the dwellers in postwar

TABLE 5:2. INTERGENERATIONAL OCCUPATIONAL MOBILITY
(NATIONAL SAMPLE)*

	Ego		Father		Father's Father	
	n	%	n	%	n	%
Professional	133	6.65	90	4.50	57	2.85
Managerial	87	4.35	142	7.10	71	3.55
Clerical	221	11.50	95	4.75	43	2.15
Retail	240	12.00	222	11.10	137	6.85
Skilled labor	229	11.45	169	8.45	104	5.20
Semiskilled labor	146	7.30	81	4.05	34	1.70
Unskilled labor	121	6.05	144	7.20	87	4.35
Agriculture	711	35.55	1031	51.55	1237	61.85
Other	112	5.60	26	1.30	230	11.50
Total	2000		2000		2000	

*Nihon Shakai Gakkai Chōsa Iinkai, ed. 1958, p. 160, p. 161, p. 163 (compiled from Tables II-9, II-10, and II-12).

housing projects built by the Japan Housing Corporation are white-collar workers, it may be well to say a word about life in the housing projects.

The income needed and the other requirements for renting apartments built by the Japan Housing Corporation are such that in a given housing project families tend to have a homogeneous social background. Typically the family head is between twenty-eight and forty-five years of age, a college graduate working for a company on a regular salary basis with at least several years of service, married, and has two or three young children. While he spends most of his waking hours at work away from home (hence the term "bed town" to refer to housing projects) and tends to remain aloof from local social activities, wives generally stay home and dominate the social scene. The wives' association with one another is most commonly initiated by the friendship of their children. Apartment dwellers tend to be more "modern" than their counterparts in the older parts of the city. Their family is smaller and tends to be conjugal-nuclear. Their preference is toward birthday parties, Christmas, wedding anniversaries and the like, rather than memorial services and visits to the ancestral graveyard. Apartment life is far from idyllic, however. Lack of privacy, poor construction, small size, poor service and maintenance, etc., are sources of constant complaints from the dwellers. On the other hand, the very reasonable rent is an attraction which surmounts disadvantages. This does not mean, however, that residents plan on staying in apartments for the rest of their lives. Of all the things apartment dwellers would like to do if they had a large sum of money, building their own single dwelling is by far the first choice for both men and women. As their career advances and savings accumulate, they plan to build their own houses and move out of the apartment (Seikatsu Kagaki Chōsakai, 1963).

The Old Middle Class

One significant effect of the rise of the white-collar worker as the new middle class has been to push small independent enterprisers—the old middle class—into the background of the social and economic scene. They are not only decreasing in number, but are taking a position subordinate to white-collar workers in the economic structure of Japan. In the Tokugawa and early Meiji periods, the Japanese economy was by and large carried on in family enterprises or at a scale only slightly larger than the family, which were, as we mentioned in the chapter on kinship, run on semikinship basis. In those days, these small enterprises constituted the bulwark of Japanese economy, there being few large- or medium-scale establishments. As modern industrialism required larger and larger enterprises for efficiency's sake, and as large-scale non-industrial organizations such as the school and government bureaucracy began to develop, they assumed a more and more important role in the nation, and reduced smaller enterprises to a position of minor importance. Also, large manufacturers could make products more cheaply and better than small ones; and large retailers like department stores could offer the advantages of convenient, centralized shopping, the prestige of the store, and various services which smaller retailers could not provide.

This is not to say that large and small businesses are always competing. Far from it. Large enterprises and smaller ones are often in symbiotic relationship. For example, some small manufacturers make products which, given the present Japanese economic structure, cannot be made as economically by large enterprises. This is true of many traditional crafts like lacquer work, folding fans, religious objects, *tatami* mats, *sake* and the like; some "modern" products like match boxes, pencils, clothing, books with Western binding, etc., are also made in small shops.

In addition, there are small enterprisers who subcontract work from large manufacturers. This subcontracting arrangement plays a crucial role in Japan's economy. For, as will be explained, larger companies are obligated to keep their regular employees even in business recessions, and they cope with recessions in part by reducing the amount of contract work. If all work is done in the company without subcontracting, present employment practices in Japan make it difficult for the company to survive during a recession. Thus, the brunt of economic insecurity is shoved off to small, subcontracting enterprises which have little margin of safety to play with. This means that the rate of bankruptcy among smaller businesses is necessarily much higher than among larger ones.

A *tatami* maker. In the Tokugawa and early Meiji periods, small enterprises constituted the bulwark of Japanese economy.

Japanese economists refer to the "dual" structure of the Japanese economy in reference to this economic arrangement in which the upper level is characterized by streamlined, large-scale modern organization equipped with the latest technological innovations, while the lower level has features of traditional, small businesses and operates on the smallest of margins and with substandard working conditions. The differences between the two, however, go further than relative economic wellbeing and relate to social aspects as well.

The organizational pattern of the small business can be traced back to the Tokugawa period, with of course a considerable amount of transformation. As we saw earlier, the distinction between family members and others working in the shop was only a vague one. In the early modern period, partly due to the sharp legal distinction then created in the civil code, a clear line began to be drawn between kin and non-kin, and non-kin gradually lost their kinshiplike quality in the family enterprise vis-a-vis the core members.

One expression of this conceptual distinction was seen in the physical separation of the shop, located in the front part of the house, from the family, situated in the back of the house. At the same time, the branch stores which were set up by the main store for capable, long-time employees began to be regarded purely as branches of the main store, and not as branches of the main family. In keeping with this change, non-kin employees, who in the Tokugawa period received either no salary or only spending money, now received a genuine, regular salary. This led to the period in early modern Japan in which non-kin employees were treated as ritual kin (or ritual children). At present, the paternalistic elements in small enterprises, though not completely gone, are quite attenuated.

The employees of smaller enterprises must work harder and longer hours in small, dirty, ill-lighted work shops because the margin of profit in smaller business is so small. With the boss, they also must work long hours under substandard conditions in disregard of labor regulations established by the government. When paternalistic relationships prevail in these smaller enterprises, they in part compensate for or substitute for the more impersonal fringe benefits of larger companies. But bosses of the *"oyabun"* type, that is, ones who take personal interest in the welfare of the employees, are becoming rare in Japan. At the same time, the disparity in working conditions and compensations between the large and small enterprises is growing. Consequently most young workers prefer large companies for employment, and small businesses are finding it more and more difficult to find competent workers.

A small enterpriser, whether a manufacturer or a retailer, often has his shop in the front part of his house. It is quite common for the wife and older children to help out. In the sense that the whole family is involved both in the production of income and in consumption as well, these small enterprises are an urban counterpart of farm families. The similarity is more than just economic. As in the farm family, a high value is placed on the shop, which is regarded as a family property as much as the property of the family head. Such a family, though it may be structurally nuclear, tends to be corporate or stem, rather than conjugal. The owner regards the family and the family business as integral, and desires to have an heir succeed him in the family business. This is becoming more and more difficult, since young people do not see—and rightly—much future in small independent enterprises. It is illuminating in this connection that a significantly greater number of the eldest sons of independent enterprisers suffer from psychosis than do the other sons (Caudill, 1964). This results most probably from the ambivalence which develops out of the eldest son's sense of obligation to take over the family business and his desire to fulfill his personal ambitions by pursuing other goals.

Industrial Relations and Employment Patterns

After graduating from college or high school, practically all men and an increasing number of women seek employment. Japanese prefer to be hired by a large, well established company which offers high wages, security, fringe benefits, opportunities for promotion to high positions, as well as the prestige of being affiliated with a well-known company. Since we have already seen briefly the development of small independent enterprises out of the traditional context, it remains to outline the development of the management-labor relation of large enterprises.

In the early days of industrialization, most plants in Japan were still relatively small, even the largest ones employing only a few hundred workers (Hazama, 1963). It was not impossible then for the employer to keep in close touch with his employees and try to meet their individual needs as they arose—particularly the expressive needs for emotional satisfaction. Moreover, the employer took seriously the norm which compelled him to take care of his employees; workers, on the other hand, by and large accepted whatever work conditions and wages were set by the employer.

In some industries, such as mining and construction, workers were organized into small but well defined ritual kinship groups in which the ritual parent controlled recruitment, the work schedule, and wages, as well as the off-the-job aspects of the workers' lives. This system began to die out or become attenuated early in this century in mines, but continued to operate in construction work until much later.

In short, during Japan's early industrialization some form or another of paternalistic human relationship was employed. It is well to remember that paternalism implies unequal status and that acceptance of inequality depends on the implicit agreement between the superior and inferior that what each receives is more or less equal to what each gives. When the superior demands more without what is felt to be adequate compensation, the feeling of mutual trust begins to break down. Then we may justly speak of exploitation. Even before the turn of the century, employers were often making demands on workers which were even then considered inhuman, without making compensations either materially by means of pay increases, or psychologically in terms of greater personal attention to workers' needs, the fostering of camaraderie, etc. As early as in the 1880s the problem caught the attention of the government and caused it to consider legislation to protect industrial workers. The labor laws which were enacted from time to time well into the early part of this century, however, did not improve labor conditions sufficiently to eliminate labor disputes. The rising socialist movements, of course, helped to create a feeling of discontent with the existing situation among workers. These facts of exploitation and labor disputes should be remembered since some Western observers have hastily suggested that Japan's industrial relationships have been characterized by benevolent paternalism.

With continuing economic growth after World War I, Japan began to feel an acute labor shortage. To retain workers, companies introduced a system of on-the-job training, which would not be immediately useful in another company, and of rewarding workers, among others, on the basis of length of service. This reward system practically precluded securing exceptionally talented workers from other companies at a special salary, since employees' wages were strictly determined by a rigid pay scale worked out on the basis of education, age, and years of service. If a man advanced in age were to shift employment, he would have had to take a drastic cut in his salary. The system of lifetime employment which developed as a result worked in favor of those who came into the company early in life and stayed on. The system was an innovation without roots in tradition, in spite of the fact that some Western observers have regarded it as "traditional." The system was nonetheless successful precisely because it utilized the traditional pattern of favoring stable, long-lasting, face-to-face relationships and of loyal service expressed in the lifetime committment of the workers. It is thus that this system became incorporated into the pattern of managerial paternalism.

Another development in Japanese industrial organization about this time is the introduction of a category called "temporary workers" as against permanent workers. While the latter have tenured positions in the company, temporary workers do not. Although many temporary workers do work for a company for many years, the company has the right to lay off temporary workers any time and reduce the amount of work. Thus large companies have at least two ways of coping with business recessions: reducing the amount of subcontracting with the enterprises of the lower level in the dual economic structure and laying off their own temporary workers.

The notion of managerial paternalism, then, applies only to its own permanent workers. Paternalistic benevolence does not apply to subcontractors and temporary workers. In fact it is at the expense of the latter that large companies manage to dispense largesse to its own workers. To be sure, subcontractors often have a relation to large companies which in some sense resembles paternalism, but the feeling is quite attenuated and is not strong enough to controvert the basic economic considerations governing the relationship between large companies and their subcontractors. That is, although the relationship may be quasi-paternalistic, in times of economic hardship, large contracting companies readily respond to economic demands and dispense with paternalistic considerations by dropping the contract and letting the subcontractors starve.

It should be remembered that the ritual kinship system was defined in Chapter Two cannot operate effectively and without modification in large business concerns employing thousands of workers. A company president cannot possibly have warm personal relationships with and personal knowledge about each of them. The modification brought about may be called *managerial paternalism (onjō shugi)*. In managerial paternalism, the true personal concern and care of the management for employees is no longer present, but the material effects which supposedly result from paternalistic relationship are observed. For example, in addition to the regular pay, employees are given special pay for sickness, weddings, funerals of close kin, a childbirth in the family, etc. Paid leaves are also given for some of these occasions, and a retirement fund is provided for. Another essential component of managerial paternalism is the notion that the company president is to a feudal lord as employees are to vassals. This idea was indoctrinated into employees and used to justify the policy of lifelong commitment to a company and of rewarding employees on the basis of particularistic criteria. This managerial paternalism was given further ideological support by being couched in the framework of the time-honored concept of *on*. That is, the employer dispenses *on* when he provides employees with resources (jobs) which they have no other way of obtaining and gives them material support on particularistic and functionally diffuse bases, e.g., salary scaled according to length of service and number of dependents and other factors, among which the employee's skill plays only a small part. Much of this compensation was a "favor," or *on* in the sense that it was not required by law, but provided simply by the employer's graciousness. This favor creates indebtedness which has to be repaid in such intangible forms as loyalty and dedication, over-time without pay, providing services to the employer over and beyond the labor and skill required by the terms of employment.

This was at least the rationale on the basis of which employers operated their business. It is fair to say that many employers genuinely believed in the principles of managerial paternalism. Their attempts to suppress labor protection bills introduced in the Diet from time to time were often based on the argument that such laws, common in Western countries, were unnecessary in the context of Japanese managerial paternalism. To a certain extent, managerial paternalism did successfully operate to the satisfaction of both management and workers. But since paternalism is among other things a power relation, the power could be, and often was, malevolently used to exploit workers, while at the same time employers tried to justify their exploitation in traditional terms, i.e., workers owed *on* which had to be repaid in unquestioned loyalty to the management.

Within a plant, workers were often organized into small units headed by a foreman, who more or less acted like the leader of a ritual kinship group and in fact was commonly called *oyakata* or *oyabun*. But the relationship of the leader to workers was by and large confined to the work situation, although the leader often had some knowledge of and in certain cases personal familiarity with the family situation of his subordinates. Still the relation was not the same as what we saw in the traditional period, when the household and the work were for all practical purposes inseparable. In short, a ritual kinship institution became established, in which there was clear understanding that the relationship was not genuine kinship but only simulated. Again, we must not assume that ritual kinship always worked to the advantage of both sides. The leader's use of power was often ill-conceived and exploitive rather than benevolent and considerate of the needs and desires of subordinates.

In spite of some degree of attenuation and malfunctioning, this paternalistic ideology largely governed the management-labor relationship of large businesses until the Second World War. As the war progressed and demands for production rose while at the same time an acute labor shortage ensued because of military conscription, major changes began to take place. Workers who were actually engaged in production began to receive higher wages, and as overtime work increased, young workers, who would ordinarily receive the lowest wages, could now take advantage of their stamina and work longer hours and earn proportionately better wages than older and more experienced workers. As a large number of "permanent" employees were conscripted into the military, the number of "temporary" workers, who were outside the system of paternalistic management, had to be increased. As a result, a smaller and smaller percentage of employees began to come under paternalistic treatment. As the war went on and conscripted employees did not return from military service, the concept of lifetime employment began to lose meaning even for permanent employees. At the same time, many of the fringe benefits which management used to dispense as largesse were now required by law and thus ceased to be the management's "favor" or *on*. In addition, the government began to ration subsistence goods, many of which used to be sold at cost or given by the management to its employees as part of paternalistic largesse. These goods were now distributed by the government, robbing companies of another basis of paternalism.

After the war, many of the material elements of the prewar managerial paternalism were revived. The reward system now, as before, favors those who remain with the company rather than shift employment. There is the expectation on the part of management that one will remain with the company until retirement. And a variety of fringe benefits not required by law are offered in large companies. (Abegglen, 1958). However, a crucial change in the postwar management-labor relation is that these features of employment are no longer considered by the majority of employees as a special "favor" *(on),* for which they have to feel indebted and repay over and beyond the contracted work. Instead, they consider these benefits now rightful compensations for their work (Whitehill and Takezawa, 1961, p. 106). In fact, many of them were gained through union demands. In short, while the material manifestations are there, the ideological underpinning of managerial paternalism has all but disappeared. To be sure, employers still often describe and rationalize their management policy as being derived from the praiseworthy traditional pattern of Japanese paternalism, with the suggestion that the ideological component is also still present. In all fairness, it should be admitted that many employers of large companies do genuinely believe in the ideology of managerial paternalism, or at least in some modification of it. But often the management's public pronouncement of adherence to managerial paternalism is based on a rational calculation that the traditional system offers economic advantages to the management. The same pattern of "rational" paternalism seems to be manifested among workers; that is, they show a preference for the traditional paternalistic arrangements only insofar as they are advantageous to the self-interest of the workers themselves.

For example, when 55% of the workers in a sample studied by Whitehill and Takezawa (1961, p. 43) favored the traditional reward system of family allowance with extra compensation for all family members, this preference was quite likely motivated by economic considerations rather than by their commitment to the ideology of paternalism. This may be constrasted with their finding that 55% of the managers were opposed to the family allowance. Similarly, in the same study (Whitehill and Takezawa, 1961, p. 88) almost three-fourths of the managers responded that if the company is operating at a loss, "the union should either be satisfied with what the company states it can afford to pay or at least feel reluctant to make new wage demands." At the same time, only about one-third of the workers shared the same view (Whitehill and Takezawa, 1961, p. 31). These and other findings show that managerial paternalism as an ideology has become weakened to the extent that only a small fraction of managers or workers genuinely believe in it. Most of them are openly opposed to managerial paternalism or support it only if it advances their self-interest.

This is not to deny the retention of traditional Japanese patterns of social organization in employment situations, whether of a paternalistic nature or otherwise. For example, subjective identification with one's employment and the sense of pride and ego-involvement with one's company, are much stronger among Japanese workers than American workers. (It should be remembered that in the United States, because of the relatively high occupational and employment mobility, an American cannot afford, so to speak, to have a strong emotional identification with any one place of employment; for such an attachment would be detrimental to his psychological adjustment later on when he changed his job.) As Nakane (1965) has said, a Westerner is likely to ask a newly introduced person what his occupation is rather than where he works, whereas a Japanese is more likely to ask where he works. In this pattern of discourse Japanese manifest their primary concern with where one works, i.e., identification with a group. Whether one is a truck-driver or an executive in a company becomes of secondary importance.

Another traditional pattern prevalent in Japanese employment situations is the relative lack of sharply defined job specifications and the corresponding looseness of the job assignment for an individual or a segment of the organization. As a result, an employee is often asked to perform a job which is entirely outside his competence, or a section of a company may collect heterogeneous duties not originally having much to do with the purpose for which the section was established. The most extreme example of the latter is the department called *sōmu-bu,* which is found in practically all large public and private bureaucracies. It is sometimes translated the "general department" for want of any appropriate term. This department handles anything that has no specific assignment to other departments, which may range from taking care of office supplies to entertaining guests.

Lifetime employment is still the practice for most companies, where permanent workers cannot be fired. This often necessitates the inefficiency of having to create useless positions in the company in order to keep incompetent workers on the payroll. This is, as it were, the price the company has to pay for having made a mistake in hiring them to begin with. Firing incompetent "permanent" workers would cause drastic repercussions throughout the company and would eventually cost the company more than retaining a few incompetent workers; for firing permanent workers would constitute a breach of normative expectation and at the same time demoralize the entire rank and file of the work force.

As demands for efficiency increase in the Japanese industrial world, it will be more and more difficult to maintain some of these traditional features of Japanese business organizations. Changes are bound to take place, as they have in the past one hundred years. But it is not likely that any changes in the near future will completely obliterate peculiarly Japanese features from industrial organizations.

Poverty

A large modern industrial society based on capitalism like Japan cannot escape having in its large cities its share of people living in what the majority of "upstanding" and "respectable" citizens consider substandard and shameful conditions. There is inevitably a shady borderline between the respectable and unrespectable strata of society; but there is no doubt who is at the very bottom. There, people scarcely have enough to eat, and live in crowded, dirty housing, if it could be called housing. Many, if they have a job, collect waste materials like rags, metal scraps, waste paper, and broken pieces of glass, thrown away in garbage cans. These materials are

The central business district of
Nagoya, Aichi Prefecture.

sold for reclamation through industrial processing (Taira, 1968). A disproportionately large number of the urban poor are unemployed and do not
even have the minimum education required by law. Illegal activities like
prostitution and pickpocketing are also found in this stratum.

Family life in the sense of both spouses living together with their children
under one roof is not very common. Many urban poor live alone, although
in their past many have been married. Some of them are still legally married
but for one reason or another do not wish to lead a married life. Many are
social failures by their own admission. They loathe to talk about their past
precisely because they feel their past is shameful. Starting out their life in
the "respectable" stratum of society, they could not compete successfully
and drifted down to their present shameful existence. Perhaps because they
do not have the perspective to analyze their situation objectively, there is
on the whole a marked lack of the feeling that they have been victims of
the social system. Instead, they individually account for their failure as
being due to certain unfortunate accidents in their past, such as wartime
dislocation, a long illness which has drained the family resources, the early
death of the father (which meant a lack of economic support for training
and education), etc. Also partly because they see their present circumstances as a result of their own failure rather than the fault of the system,
many of them do not feel right in accepting public assistance, even though

Congested city dwelling in Kyoto.

they may be forced to accept it. There is a deep-seated feeling that it is shameful to accept government money—like beggars, as they would say. In this personal pride one sees that though downtrodden and poverty stricken, they are perhaps not completely lost in despair and hopelessness.

The Japanese government provides financial assistance to households which it regards as being "needy of livelihood protection." In 1968, 660,000 households involving 1,450,000 individuals, or 14.3 persons per 1000, were classified as needy and received government subsidies (Ministry of Welfare ed., 1969, p. 330). The highest rate of needy households is found in northern Kyūshū, where a recent decline in the coal-mining industry has resulted in loss of employment for a large number of miners. In Fukuoka prefecture, in northern Kyūshū, for example, the rate of needy households was 52.4 per 1000 in 1968. The predominantly rural, southern Kyūshū and Shikoku have the next highest rates of needy households. In contrast, central Japan—the area of the greatest amount of industrial and commercial activities and the areas adjacent to it—has the lowest rate (less than 10 per 1000). In Tokyo it is as low as 6.8 per 1000.

Oscar Lewis (1966) has characterized the culture of poverty in terms of the relation of the slum subculture to the larger society, the internal features of the slum community, the nature of the family, and attitudes, values, and character of the individual. We do not yet have an adequate description of the Japanese culture of poverty, although there are a great number of reports, some of a sociological nature and others merely of a descriptive sort. In these reports, we recognize the disengagement of the poor from the majority of society caused by segregation, discrimination, suspicion and the like which Lewis describes. Chronic unemployment and underemployment, low wages, lack of savings for emergencies, which are characteristic of the Latin American culture of poverty are also features of the Japanese counterpart. The sense of despair and the attitude of fatalism which also characterize Lewis' culture of poverty may not be as strong in Japan as in Latin America, but as Plath (1966) has suggested, the concept of fatalism needs refinement before we can make a final judgement.

Lewis points out the emphasis people in the Latin American culture of poverty place on sex as a compensation for their poverty, and the consequent development of consensual, as opposed to legally or religiously sanctioned marriage and of female-centered households. In Japan, there is little evidence that people in slums are as concerned with sex as their Latin American brothers. Evidence does show that a fair number of households lacking the father-husband are receiving government assistance (Mitsukawa, 1966, pp. 215–218; Seki, 1966, pp. 231–257). In Tokyo in 1964, 26.9% of households on government relief lacked the father-husband. However, only a negligible percentage of these households without the father-husband has resulted from illegitimacy or desertion by the male, or even legal divorce. A great majority of them are the results of widowhood, especially of women who lost their husbands in the World War II (Isomura, 1956, p. 164).

The cultural stigma attached to once-married females, especially those with children, makes it far more difficult for them to remarry than once-married males. In addition, since women are not as well trained for high-income occupations, they tend to take low income jobs after losing their husbands. This often reduces a woman to the lowest social level. Thus the whole handling of sex and the genesis of female-centered households in the Japanese culture of poverty seems quite different from its Latin American counterpart.

Education

No matter what social stratum one belongs to or what style of life one leads, education is accorded prime importance in Japan. One does not see in Japan strong anti-intellectualism, the attitude that education is not important or necessary, which one sees particularly strongly expressed in the United States among the lower classes and in the rural hinterlands. Education, especially college education for boys, is a highly desirable goal, in spite of the fact that very often graduates of small unknown colleges nowadays do not obtain jobs any more easily than some high school graduates because of the tremendous increase in the number of colleges and college graduates.

Emphasis on education goes back to the Tokugawa period. Warriors received a considerable amount of education by attending, in most cases, state-supported· schools. Merchants in cities and wealthier peasants also sent their children to schools—mostly private—so that they could read and write at least simple materials. The spread of popular literature primarily intended for commoners rather than warriors was naturally possible in the

Rural school boys on the way home. No matter what social stratum one belongs to or what style of life one leads, education is accorded prime importance in Japan.

Tokugawa period because of relatively widespread literacy. Dore estimates that something like 40% of the Japanese at the close of the Tokugawa period had attended school and gained some degree of literacy. What is more important, according to Dore, are the specific values emphasized by the Tokugawa educational tradition, such as "the training in abstract analysis, and the application of evaluating principles to policy, the development of a respect for merit rather than status, the stimulation of personal ambition, and the strengthening of a collective ideology" (Dore, 1965, p. 131). In important ways, the Tokugawa tradition prepared Japan for rapid modernization, for which a large literate population was urgently needed, ready to take advantage of the advanced knowledge of the West, create an industrial capitalism, and press forward nationalistic goals.

From the beginning of the modern period, formal educational institutions in Japan served to spread the great tradition of the ruling class to the masses and also to disseminate a nationalistic ideology. The Japanese educational system until the end of the World War II was based on the Imperial Rescript on Education, which, promulgated in 1890, outlined the broad guidelines for educational policies. In Hall's word, the rescript "fused elements of Shinto statism, Confucian Ethics, and a modern attitude toward learning into a comprehensive statement on the purpose of education and the responsibilities of the citizen in the new state." (Hall, 1965, p. 397). The rescript and the educational policies resulting from it were thus both traditional and modern at the same time. To foster nationalism, for example, the policies emphasized traditional values such as loyalty to the Emperor, at the same time exhorting the Japanese to achieve a place in the modern world community.

The facts that the public school system spread rapidly throughout the country and that 90% of school-age children were attending schools by the early part of this century were crucial in the rapid diffusion and acceptance of nationalism and in the preparation of a disciplined citizenry.

From the beginning of the establishment of the modern educational program, the government played the major role, with private schools playing a minor though growing part. Private institutions lacked, and to this day still lack, the financial base which government schools have had. More importantly, they lack the prestige of government institutions. Consequently, public schools in general and government-financed universities in particular have better faculties as well as research facilities and attract better students.

In the prewar period, college education was for a small number of students and had a definite elitist quality from which the masses were excluded. Reflecting this was the intermediate educational system (beyond the required six years but below college level), which was sharply divided into academic and technical tracks. Academic intermediate schools were preparatory for college education, whereas technical (commercial and industrial) intermediate schools were terminal for most students, only a very few going to advanced technical schools.

Another important sharp line was drawn in prewar Japan between the education of boys and girls beyond the compulsory level. After graduating from the coeducational grammar school, boys and girls attended separate schools. Keeping in line with the inferior social status accorded women, education in girls' intermediate schools was generally inferior in quality to education in boys' schools, and far fewer girls received education beyond grammar school. College education was available to an infinitesimal number of girls.

Grammar-school children doing morning exercises.

Postwar education did away with the "meritocratic" system of prewar education, removed the sex barrier, and lengthened compulsory education from six to nine years. These changes were accompanied by a mushrooming of colleges and universities, both public and private, making possible higher education for a phenomenal number of high school graduates. Although the sex barrier was removed and coeducation was started in the intermediate and higher levels, integration of sexes was incomplete from the beginning of the postwar education reform. Since girls had not been given academic training comparable to boys, they immediately faced difficulty moving into a coeducational system and competing with boys successfully. Moreover, the legal adoption of equal sexual status did not automatically change social attitudes toward different sexes. While legal changes enormously enhanced women's status, women still remain considerably socially inferior to men. This discriminatory social attitude was responsible for the incomplete equalization of sexes in school. At present, the tendency is toward less coeducation, especially at higher levels.

The Japanese educational system, especially at the college level, is currently facing serious problems. These problems are rooted in the historical past and interrelated with a complex set of social and cultural factors, only a few of which will be mentioned here. One source of problems is that the ladder for success in the world is found by entering and obtaining a degree from a university with high prestige, rather than in actual performance in the various courses taken in colleges. Employers, for example, typically favor hiring graduates of prestigious colleges and universities. Also, universities and colleges have tended to recruit their own graduates into their own faculty, though this practice is now somewhat declining. The faculty of a reputable school has a great deal of prestige and the advantages of better research facilities and greater opportunities for publication. These factors have led to the establishment of the institution known as *gakubatsu,* or the practice of favoritism among graduates of the same school in employment, promotion, and advancement.

Motivated toward worldly success, high-school students engage in an intense competition to enter good universities. Because attendance at a good

High-school girls returning home. Postwar educational reforms did not fully alleviate the inferior status accorded women.

high school increases one's chance of entering a good university, there is intense competition to enter a good high school. The same competition is repeated at successively lower levels, even down to kindergarten. This competition takes the form of an entrance examination, the passing of which has become a goal in itself for a great majority of students, especially for high-school seniors applying for admission to various colleges (Vogel, 1962). Preparation for this entrance examination consumes an inordinate amount of the time and psychic energy of the applicants, their parents, and their teachers, all of whom coordinate and cooperate in achieving one goal. One unfortunate consequence of this "examination hell" is that education ceases to have much meaning except as a means for passing the entrance examination. The consequences can best be seen at the college level, where, having passed the last hurdle, students lose much of their motivation and incentive to study.

To make the situation worse, once a student enters a university he is virtually assured of graduating even without studying. Many students, therefore, take courses just to accumulate required credits but seldom attend classes. In addition, many private schools, lacking sufficient operating funds, have greatly increased enrollment, often admitting students far beyond their capacity or admitting borderline students on the condition that they make a huge contribution, amounting to thousands of dollars, to the school. At public schools where such practices do not occur there are still serious problems. For one, the faculty find themselves too busy in research and other activities to be mentioned presently to devote enough time to students. The mushrooming of colleges after the war without a corresponding increase in trained faculty to fill the newly created faculty positions has resulted in the majority of Japanese professors having to teach at two or more schools in order for all schools to offer all the required courses. The poor pay of the faculty in Japan has encouraged them to take on a second or a third job, and also to engage in lucrative writing for the general public in newspapers and popular magazines. While such writing does serve to communicate scholarly knowledge to the public, most of it is of little research value. The principal reason for writing for public consumption, in the professors' own admission, is financial. Research, teaching at two or more schools, and writing for financial gain leave little time for the faculty to have contact with students and to innovate more creative and meaningful ways of imparting knowledge to them. Instead they tend to give dry lectures, reading from yellowed notes, and thus driving students away from classrooms rather than attracting them to study and research.

Another serious problem in higher education has to do with the organization of the faculty, especially at old, established and prestigious universities. In these schools, the faculty are ranked on the basis of seniority. A full professor has under him an associate professor, an assistant professor, and assistants, who can move up the ladder only through the retirement of the full professor. The associate and assistant professors and the assistants are expected to show respect to the full professor, run errands for him, and carry out his research projects. Yet, some of the lower level faculty receive no pay. It has been reported that one professor in the medical school of a reputable national university published in one year over 150 papers in professional journals. It is quite obvious that his subordinates did most of the work, and that he simply attached his name to the research papers they wrote.

In the past, the senior faculty member was a benevolent paternalist in the traditional ritual kinship sense, dispensing largesse as required by custom. And his subordinates willingly accepted their role, expecting one day to move up the ranks to full professorship. There was a subjective feeling in those days on both sides that the give-and-take between the professor and his subordinates was more or less balanced. Now, in the postwar period, the ideology of the society has greatly changed; it has become more egalitarian and no longer supports the hierarchical, authoritarian structure of university departments. Senior professors, however, have too much to gain in the traditional system to yield their powerful role, while the junior faculty and students have become increasingly dissatisfied with the existing arrangement, in which they feel they are being exploited.

As if these internal problems were not enough, students, who are by and large Marxist-oriented, have been critical of Japan's capitalistic economic system and Japan's friendly relations with the United States. They demand the termination of the security treaty with the United States, which allows her to maintain numerous military installations and training grounds in Japan and in its territorial waters. They also demanded immediate and unconditional return of Okinawa, which was held by the United States as a strategic military base in the Far East for over twenty-five years.

These internal and external problems have exploded in the last few years into widespread and violent demonstrations which have become endemic throughout Japan. Radical students have shut down school operation, barricaded entrances to schools with desks and chairs, and imprisoned university presidents and faculty, subjecting them to the most humiliating experiences. As a result, in no time in Japan's history have so many university presidents and other administrators resigned because of ill health and because of their inability to solve university problems, some of them even committing suicide. Students have snake danced and fought riot-police both on the campus and in the streets. This student unrest is likely to continue in Japan until international tension eases and internal university problems are at least partially solved.

SUGGESTED READINGS

Abegglen, James C.
1957   "Subordination and autonomy attitudes of Japanese workers." *American Journal of Sociology* 63: 181–189.

DeVos, George and Hiroshi Wagatsuma
1966   *Japan's Invisible Race: Caste in Culture and Personality.* Berkeley and Los Angeles: University of California Press.

Dore, Ronald P.
1958   *City Life in Japan: A Study of a Tokyo Ward.* Berkeley and Los Angeles: University of California Press.
1967   "Mobility, equality and individuation in modern Japan," in R. P. Dore, ed., *Aspects of Social Change in Modern Japan.* Princeton: Princeton University Press, pp. 113–150.

Levine, Solomon B.
1967   "Postwar trade unionism, collective bargaining, and Japanese social structure," in R. P. Dore, ed., *Aspects of Social Change in Modern Japan.* Princeton: Princeton University Press, pp. 245–285.

Nakane, Chie
1965   "Towards a theory of Japanese social structure: an unilateral society." Economic Weekly, Bombay. 17: 197–201; 203–207; 209–211; 213; 215–216.

Olson, Lawrence
1963   "A Japanese Small Industry," in Lawrence Olson, ed., *Dimensions of Japan.* New York: American Universities Field Staff, Inc. pp. 13–33.

Passin, Herbert
1965   *Society and Education in Japan.* New York: Bureau of Publications, Teachers College, Columbia University.

Taira, Kōji
1962   "The dynamics of industrial relations in early Japanese development." *Labor Law Journal* 13:483–492.

Whitehill, Arthur M. and Shin'ichi Takezawa
1968   *The Other Worker: A Comparative Study of Industrial Relations in the United States and Japan.* Honolulu: East-West Center Press.

6 Ethos

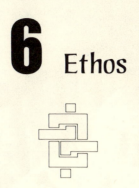

Emotional Patterning

Modern middle-class mothers in Japan, now mostly living in nuclear households, away from their parents and parents-in-law, often do not know the traditional Japanese ways of child rearing. And even if they do, they are apt to dismiss the traditional methods as old-fashioned or "feudalistic" and therefore not to be followed. As a result, publications on child-raising practices have mushroomed into a major industry, with conflicting methods being recommended to bewildered mothers by different experts, each claiming to be the most modern and scientific. Mass-communication media, such as newspapers, weekly and monthly magazines, and radio and television programs are all ready outlets of experts' advice, which is eagerly sought by parents. Proliferation of professional advice has resulted in diverse child-rearing practices throughout Japan, or even in a small neighborhood area, some preferring bottle- to breast-feeding, some using a play-pen and others frowning on its use, some favoring early weaning and others not, etc. In spite of all the variations, as Vogel has noted, we can still discern salient, systematic patterns of child rearing which hold generally for most Japanese, and these patterns sharply contrast with practices observed in the United States. These patterns provide a basis for the formulation of Japanese personality. Within the complex structure of personality, we shall single out for our analysis here the handling of emotion in interacting with others because it constitutes an important component of the Japanese character.

By "emotional patterns" is meant here conventionalized ways of handling one's affect and managing one's mood in relationship to other human beings. Our concern is not so much with violent expressions of emotion, such as anger and fear, as with day to day handling of one's feelings toward other persons. The position taken here is that a consistent patterning of emotion develops, not simply because of a certain feeding practice or a specific weaning method, but through an accumulation of a large number

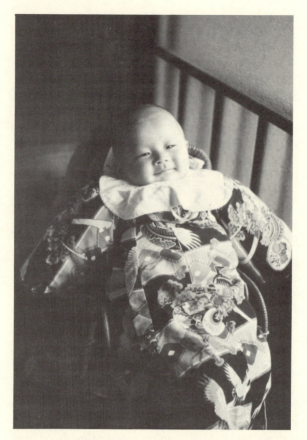

A specially dressed baby
ready to visit a shrine.

of behavior patterns in which parents relate themselves to their children and
which taken together tend to produce a clearly recognizable mode of handling emotion. For this reason, we shall examine various practices of child
rearing from infancy on, rather than concentrate on one or two kinds of
practices.

Quiet, Soothing Infancy

An appropriate starting point is the behavior of young infants—the way
in which a few months-old infant's behavior is already culturally condi-
tioned. In Caudill and Weinstein's (1969) comparative study of mother-
infant interaction in middle-class families in Japan and in the United States,
they discovered that at the early age of three to four months, Japanese and
American babies already behave differently and also that mothers in these
cultures interact with their babies somewhat differently.

Their findings show among other things that infants in the United States
tend to be left alone, be much more active (in bodily movements), and

express vocally either to themselves or toward the mother significantly more than Japanese infants, statistically speaking. Japanese infants, on the other hand, tend to make more frequent protests or complaints to be satisfied by the mother than American infants do. American mothers tend to talk to their infants more, physically stimulate them by patting and positioning them, and show overt affection toward them oftener than Japanese mothers. Japanese mothers, more than American mothers, tend to quietly rock the infants rather than provide vigorous physical stimulation.

These differences in infant behavior and maternal care at so young an age already point to the later personality differences between Japanese and Americans. For example, because they are often left alone, American infants must learn to handle the problem of emotional security by themselves, whereas Japanese infants tend to rely on the physical presence of their mothers for emotional security. We shall have more to say about this difference later. Another important difference is that the mother-child interaction in the American sample tends to stimulate the infant's physical activity as well as verbal responses, whereas in the Japanese sample interaction tends to be less active and less verbal and instead tends to have a soothing and quieting effect on the infant. Again, this difference points to the general direction of the development of adult personality among Americans and Japanese. That is, Americans tend to emphasize verbal ability a great deal more than Japanese. Although the emphasis has been slowly changing, the ideal Japanese has been a man of few words, one who would show his character through action rather than through verbal promises of what he would do and one who would persevere without complaint. In short, this nonverbal emphasis in the Japanese character seems to start very early in infancy. The Japanese mother's effort to soothe the child by quietly rocking him on her lap without much verbal interaction relates to the Japanese emphasis on seeking emotional comfort in direct physical contact with and in the presence of the mother and other individuals with whom one has a close, intimate relationship.

Punishment and Separation Are Minimized

In the above patterns of mother-child interaction, we are seeing the beginnings of a strong emotional dependence. How does such a strong positive affect toward his mother develop in the Japanese infant? It develops to a great extent through a pattern of mother-child relationships in which the withdrawal of maternal affection, or to put it another way, anxiety-provoking situations in the mother-infant relationship are kept at a minimum. This is in turn accomplished through avoidance, as much as possible, of (1) punishment as a means of social control and (2) physical separation of the infant from the mother and forced contact of the infant with strangers. In comparison, American child-rearing patterns, which incorporate these techniques, tend to create anxiety in the child. As a result, American children quickly learn to depend less on parents for emotional security—since they are sources of anxiety—and instead to handle their emotional problems on their own. Let us elaborate on Japanese child-rearing techniques. The explicit or implicit comparison with American techniques will substantiate the contrast mentioned above.

Emotional Dependence through Demand Feeding

Dr. Michio Matsuda, a pediatrician who is fast acquiring in Japan the fame that Benjamin Spock has in the United States, is impressed with the rationality of traditional Japanese child-rearing methods, developed over centuries of experience. According to him, (1964, pp. 61–72), for example, the best way to stop an infant from crying is to feed him, even in the middle of the night if the baby cries. He is thus advocating the traditional Japanese practice of feeding on demand in contrast to scheduled feeding, which was introduced from the West in the early modern period (although it did not gain much popularity until recently). Scheduled feeding forces the infant to keep crying and to learn somehow to manage by himself the emotional tension with develops through hunger. If left alone in a room, as an infant often is in the United States, he must learn in addition to cope with the insecurity of being alone. It is important to note that an American develops the capacity to deal with his emotional problems alone and that this emotional independence serves as the psychological underpinning for the social independence expressed in the ideology of individualism. The on-demand feeding, on the other hand, tends to create the opposite effect, not only eliminating opportunities for developing emotional independence, but creating further opportunities for reinforcing emotional dependence on the mother.

Sleeping Arrangements

The same type of indulgent approach is taken in Japan at bedtime. In the United States, relatively fixed bedtime and nap schedules are worked out and more or less enforced, quite often over the crying protests of the infant. In this situation, the American infant is early thrown into a situation in which he learns to cope with the tension arising from being left alone in a crib in a separate room. In Japan infants and children generally do not have fixed schedules for taking a nap or going to sleep at night. If there is a schedule of a sort, it is usually worked out by the infant rather than the parents, and even then it is not very closely followed. At night, for example, children tend to stay up as late as they wish until they fall asleep from exhaustion. When infants are put to bed, the mother usually lies down beside the infant until he falls asleep—a practice the pediatrician Matsuda recommends (1964, pp. 98–99)—often breast-feeding at the same time.

Also, when the parents retire at night, at least one of them normally sleeps in the same quilt in the child's infancy and in an adjoining one later on. Thus Japanese infants and children tend not to experience the sense of insecurity arising from being left alone, and the Japanese mother is a much more reliable source of emotional satisfaction and less a cause of potential insecurity (by leaving him alone) than the American mother.

Babysitting is Rare

Another example pointing to the same pattern of the handling of emotions is the baby-sitting arrangement. American parents as a matter of course leave their children from early infancy with baby sitters who may be complete strangers to the children. Whether or not they are complete strangers, they certainly are not sources of emotional security in the sense and to the degree their parents are. For many American children, being left with a baby sitter is a painful experience, accompanied by crying and even tantrums; but somehow, they learn to adapt to this situation and cope with the temporary absence of the sources of security and the intrusion of strangers.

Baby-sitting arrangements of this sort are rare indeed in Japan. Although a married woman without a child leaves home for outings quite often, once she has a child she generally becomes home-bound, and her life revolves around the child much more than an American mother's life. If someone like her mother or sister lives with her, she can leave her child with her relative; but a Japanese mother would generally not think of leaving her child with a stranger or even with a neighbor. The child thus tends not to experience the fear of separation from parents, but instead regards parents as a dependable source of positive affect.

Isolation

It is highly significant in this context that in Japan isolation, for example in a toolshed or closet, i.e., physical separation from parents, is a very powerful method of punishment, precisely because physical separation from parents provokes heightened fear in Japanese children. When an American child is isolated for punishment—in his room, for example—the punishment consists primarily in a deprivation of freedom rather than in provoking fear of isolation.

Solicitude

When a child becomes old enough to understand verbal communication, Japanese parents show a great deal more tolerance toward his failure to obey parental commands than American parents. Japanese parents, especially the mother, tend to be much less authoritarian vis-a-vis children than American parents. American parents, especially the mother, believe that

A boy old enough to walk
enjoys being carried.

they must be firm in their approach to children and impress them with who
is boss when children become too demanding or disobedient. Punishments
of various sorts meted out by American parents are both a way of teaching
what is right and what is wrong and also a method of demonstrating who
the authority figures are in the parent-child relationship. An unintended
consequence is that children learn that parents are sources of threat and
cannot always be depended upon for emotional security. In contrast, socialization techniques used by Japanese parents tend to involve less authoritari-
anism and direct punishment.

The Japanese mother typically approaches a demanding or disobedient
child with solicitude rather than with authority, with as much reasoning
and explaining as the child is capable of understanding. Both Lanham
(1956, p.234) and Vogel (1963, p.245) emphasize the importance in the
Japanese child-rearing pattern of not going head-on against a child, not

directly saying "no," but instead inducing the child to behave properly. Their views concur with results of national opinion surveys taken in 1953 and 1958 in both of which the majority of respondents preferred "explaining thoroughly the reason why the child must do what he is told to do" to other methods, such as giving him a bribe or a mild threat. (Tōkei Sūri Kenkyūjo. Kokuminsei Chōsa Iinkai ed., 1961 pp. 482–483). Failing this, a Japanese mother might even plead and beg the child to do as told, rather than resort to physical punishment or other authoritarian methods of making the child behave. In extreme cases, if the mother fails in all other methods, she is prone to give sweets to the child as a method of appeasing him—even minutes before mealtime. In a comparable situation, an American mother is more likely to stand firm, let the child know who the authority is, and make the child behave. And she is not averse to punishing the child, if necessary. Giving sweets to appease the child in the American context would ordinarily be interpreted as bribing and generally avoided. If sweets are given, they are given as part of a disciplinary technique (as a reward for good behavior), rather than as a bribe—as a method of avoiding a scene that a child might create. An American mother who begs and pleads with her three- or five-year old child would simply look ridiculous to bystanders, as a Japanese mother who took an authoritarian approach toward her child would be regarded as lacking in human feeling. Neither mother would receive the sympathy of onlookers because both are acting contrary to the cultural norm.

I do not imply that Japanese mothers are always bribing their children with sweets any more than American mothers are always punishing their children to make them behave. What I do mean is that in Japan and in the United States there is a range of behavior patterns, for example with respect to the method of handling a difficult child, which are accepted as expectable, although perhaps not quite normal or normative, and beyond which people would generally express disapproval. And this range of expectable behavior is different enough in the two countries that what the Japanese regard as expectable behavior—such as readily giving sweets to quiet a child—may be totally abhorrent to Americans, and what Americans consider expectable—spanking a misbehaving child even in public—may be shocking to Japanese. Since most members of a society tend to remain within the expectable range of behavior, resultant parent-child relationship and the consequent emotional patterning manifest differences.

To sum up, the effects of these contrasting approaches between Japanese and American parents are to avoid stressful experiences in the Japanese child's relations with his mother on the one hand, and to subject the American child, relatively speaking, to stressful situations on the other. As a result, Japanese children tend to develop stronger positive affect toward their mothers, relatively unhampered by any negative affect discharged by their mothers, whereas American children tend to develop an ambivalence because their mothers discharge both positive and negative affect toward them.

When a Japanese mother of a grade-school child is unable to enforce obedience upon the child even after repeated attempts, she often asks the child's school teacher to admonish the child. When the mother comes to the teacher to request admonition of her child, the teacher quite well understands that it is his role to help the mother by giving a talking-to to the child. The effect of this recourse is that the mother succeeds in avoiding discharge of a great amount of negative affect upon the child through scolding, punishment, etc. And the effectiveness of this recourse lies in the fact that the teacher is an outsider, relatively distant, emotionally speaking, from the child, and therefore can discharge negative affect without endangering the teacher-pupil relationship; and at the same time, the authoritative position he has vis-a-vis the pupil forces the child to listen to his admonition.

When children do not behave, Japanese parents often resort to threat of supernatural sanction, saying for example, that ghosts, ogres, demons, etc., will appear and frighten misbehaving children, or that a deity will punish them (Lanham, 1956, p.576). Another common technique is the use of shame. Parents would tell their children that neighbors or friends would ridicule or laugh at them for their misbehavior. A third method widely used in the past, though not much now, is to threaten that that the police will come and get a misbehaving chld. The significance of these techniques, in contrast to direct punishment by parents, is that the sources of punishment and anxiety rest somewhere other than in the parents themselves, who are simply informing the children how the world is constituted, precisely in the same sense that American parents who warn their children of speeding cars are simply reporting how the world outside is. In neither case it is the parents' fault if the outside world is dangerously constituted: just as American parents are not causes of speeding cars, Japanese parents are not causes of fear-provoking ghosts, etc. However, an American parent who sees his child run into the street is likely to resort to swift punishment, thus becoming a focus for the child's anxiety. A Japanese parent, on the other hand, is likely to repeat the stories of scary deeds of supernatural beings to a misbehaving child.

Moxa, a highly inflammable dried herb burned on the skin for therapeutic purposes in the traditional Japanese medicine, has been often administered to a recalcitrant child. But as the Norbecks note (1956, p. 660), even the application of moxa was considered by most mothers as a cure for fretfulness rather than as a punishment.

Thus one sees in Japanese child-rearing practices the consistent avoid-

ance of outright and severe punishment as a method of discipline, which has
the effect of removing some of the positive affect from parents and of making
them into potential sources of anxiety. As a result, Japanese children, much
more than American children, tend to associate positive affect with their
parents, and seek and find emotional security in them.

Over-protected Children

Of late, one of the primary concerns of Japanese parents has been the
parents' excessively protective attitude. With the highly successful application of population control measures, most families in Japan now have only
one or two children. Each child thus has much greater importance for the
parents than a generation ago in the days of overpopulation. Parents concentrate their affection on their one or two children and attend to every little
problem they detect. As a result, parents show an obsessive concern over
children's illnesses, often making children unnecessarily fretful and demanding. For children quickly learn that they can get parental attention by
being ill. Also with so much importance attached to education, Japanese
mothers, especially of the middle classes, have turned themselves into dedi-
cated servants of their school-aged children. Again, children quickly learn
that they can get what they want from their parents if they can couch their
demands in terms of education. A tearful mother once wrote in a newspaper
that her son acts as though he is studying solely to please her and that he
demands expensive cakes and cookies for snacks, the warmest room in the
house in winter, etc. All this spoiling of children is quite intelligible when
seen in the light of the Japanese pattern of indulgent child-rearing, which
permits children to be unbearably demanding. This is not to say that all or
even most Japanese children are impossibly fretful, demanding, and spoiled,
but that one often sees such children and when we do, we have no difficulty
understanding the genesis of such behavior.

Amae

We have said enough to make intelligible the rather complex Japanese
concept of *amae,* which, according to Doi (1962) is the tendency to depend
and presume on another's love, or to seek and bask in another's indulgence.
Any child is considered to have a natural tendency to seek and depend on
parental affection. It is this indulgence in parental love that is the genesis
of the behavior labeled *amae.* This behavior is manifested, for example, by
a child who makes excessive demands of parental affection—to a degree
embarrassing to the parents or even to the child himself. For example, a
three-year old boy who still wants to suckle his mother's breast now and
then is manifesting a behavior which is best described as *amae;* and charac-
teristically, one finds the mother, while teasing, allowing the child to suckle.
In making such a demand, and having the demand met, the child finds

Families walking in a park. The young woman is carrying her
child in what is still a common way in Japan.

warmth, comfort, and satisfaction in spite of embarrassment. The significant point about this concept is that Japanese adults too have the same need
to indulge in affective relationships with others. That is, even in adulthood
Japanese seek affective satisfaction through emotional dependence on other
individuals with whom the ego is in intimate relationship, although such
behavior is not always identified as being *amae*.

It is worth repeating the reminder stated at the beginning of this chapter:

namely, that not all parent-child relationships in Japan manifest all the patterns described above to an equal degree. And to the extent that there are variations in the relationship, one can expect variations in the adult personality with respect to the ways in which a Japanese handles his emotion and to the extent which he becomes emotionally dependent on those around him.

On, Psychologically Seen

The normative concept of *on* that we discussed in earlier chapters has a psychological meaning seen in this whole complex of dependency need which is nurtured in Japanese from infancy (Doi, 1962, p. 137). *On* was defined earlier as indebtedness resulting from a gift of resources which a person needs but lacks. One important resource which parents control and a child lacks but vitally needs is affection. This affective resource, unlike economic or political resources, cannot be dispensed to just anyone and in a single act. Only through years of intimate contact does an effective discharge of affect take place. In contexts other than the parent-child relationship, too, indulgence by the socially inferior in the superior's affective discharge—the element of *amae,* if you like—is an essential ingredient of the *on*-relationship. Looking at this *on*-relationship from a slightly different angle, we can see that while indebtedness to parents is normatively specified as being based on the parents' gift of life to the child and their provision of sustenance and other material necessities to him, the child's ready acceptance of this definition is in part due to his psychological dependence on his parents. The motivation to repay this debt, seen in this context, derives from his desire to repay the emotional satisfaction which parents or parents-surrogate have provided.

Mother's Dependence on Child

In addition to the child's dependence on the parents, especially the mother, another related facet in this complex relationship is the mother's dependence on the child. As the child develops dependence on the mother's discharge of affect, the mother in turn begins to seek satisfaction of *her* emotional needs through her child's dependence on her. The child's attempt to act contrary to the mother's desire (and thus act independently) tends to provoke anxiety in the mother, since she is thus no longer needed and can no longer satisfy her emotional needs. The mother's anxiety and consequent suffering in turn, when communicated to the child through the devious means through which emotion is communicated, is likely to cause the child to feel guilty and attempt to correct the situation. It may be recalled that in Japanese folk belief a spirit's anger is recognized by natural calamities or misfortunes in those areas in which the spirit is supposed to have

A mother and her child. Sweets are a common means of keeping a child contented.

control. Similarly, the child interprets his deviant behavior as causing parental suffering. That is, the child's behavior which goes contrary to parental wishes tends to produce anxiety in parents, which in turn, when perceived by the child, tends to create a feeling of guilt. In other words, parental suffering tends to be interpreted by the child as a result of his failure, and because the child does not like to see his parents—the sources of his emotional gratification—suffer, he tries to relieve parental suffering by conforming to parental wishes. To the extent that parents wish for their children's success and achievement in his world, these parental wishes serve as a powerful source of motivation to achieve success. Herein DeVos (1960) finds the psychodynamic source of guilt, social control by parents, and achievement motivation among Japanese.

The validity of DeVos' finding is in part attested to in the popularity of motion pictures of the genre known as *hahamono,* or that which deals with motherhood. In most "motherhood" movies, the basic structure is the same. A devoted and loving mother is the heroine of the story, and she is the key to the reform or success of her child. She achieves this end through what DeVos has called "quiet suffering," blaming herself for the child's failure and making heroic, though not always instrumentally effective effort to change the child's behavior and perhaps becoming ill, injuring herself, or even dying in the process. The child, perceiving the mother's suffering and feeling guilty for causing her suffering, reforms, albeit sometimes too late to save the mother's life.

In addition to the psychodynamic processes depicted, however, there is another point of interest in the "motherhood" and similar movies in Japan. That is, scenes of deep and moving human relations such as those in "motherhood" movies readily provoke tears in the audience. This shedding of tears results from the audience's close identification with the hero or heroine. The degree of fusion, or emotional interpenetration of the audience with the hero in this movie situation is much greater in Japan than in the United States. American audiences, of course, identify with the hero or heroine of a movie, but manage to retain their identity and sense of emotional aloofness. Japanese movie producers profitably take advantage of the Japanese capacity not only to readily and deeply empathize, but even to enjoy this emphatetic emotional interpenetration in which sadness is the principal emotional ingredient.

Affective Interdependence in Adulthood

That Japanese in adult life manifest affective interdependence and moreover that they indulge in such interdependence is clearly seen in various studies, notably those carried out by Caudill and his colleagues. For example, Thematic Apperception Test responses which Caudill analyzed indicate that Japanese, both children and adults, enjoy "gratification of simple physical pleasures in situations of close contact with other persons—as in bathing, sleeping arrangements, nursing care, child rearing, and so on." (Caudill, 1962, p.129). This gratification is not specifically sexual in nature. On the contrary, it is a much more diffuse sort of emotional satisfaction which is achieved precisely through deep repression of sexual interest.

Sleeping Together

In another study, with the intriguing title "Who Sleeps by Whom?", Caudill and Plath (1966) found that Japanese family members tend to sleep in groups of two or more in the same room, rather than spreading themselves throughout the house and sleeping one person per room, even when there are enough rooms to accomodate all members in separate rooms. In the United States solitary sleeping starts only a few weeks after birth in many cases, and as we saw is a method of training a child to manage his emotional security by himself. Japanese sleeping arrangements emphasize the opposite: mutual dependence for emotional security. Japanese, indeed, find it deeply satisfying to sleep in the company of others. Again, as in the TAT responses above, there is little sexual interest manifested during this co-sleeping, even when individuals of different sexes, other than husband and wife, share a sleeping room. Instead, overt interest in each other's sexuality is repressed. Here again, one sees the primacy in Japanese emotional life of sharing each other, as it were, over the idea of privacy, so much cherished in the United States. As Plath puts it (1964a, p.175), among Japanese the very desire to sleep alone raises suspicions of deviancy.

Hospitalized patients in Japan often have an attendant called *tsukisoi* (Caudill, 1961). Such an attendant is not a registered nurse, but a person with a modicum of training or none. She (as the attendant is invariably a woman) used to be, and still often is, the patient's relative, although nowadays she is generally a hired "professional" attendant. A *tsukisoi* is, as Caudill puts it, an "around-the-clock" attendant. She is hired to look after one patient, and attends to his needs and usually stays with him day and night, often cooking for him, dressing his wounds if any, writing letters for him, consoling and comforting him when in pain, acting as his confidant when he has personal problems to discuss, etc. Caudill finds that the nurturing or expressive role which the attendant plays for the patient in satisfying his emotional needs to depend on another person, especially in time of stress like illness—his need to *amaeru,* if you will—is very akin to the role which a mother plays vis-a-vis her own child.

Drinking Party

The last example of the Japanese pattern of affect-management will deal with behavior patterns in drinking parties. Although Western style cocktail parties are becoming more and more common in cities, still the traditional party pattern is widely observed both in cities and in the countryside. The Western type of cocktail party assumes that anyone invited to the party is on his own, save for but a few erratic introductions he might have. Anyone is free to, and will, go up to strangers and introduce himself to them and start a conversation. In addition, the cocktail party pattern assumes that if someone should get left out and is standing by himself, say looking at a painting, he is psychologically able to manage this solitude in the crowd. In the Japanese drinking party, these two assumptions do not hold and are not made. On the contrary, parties are organized so as to avoid such situations. Unless the party is attended by hundreds of guests, all guests are seated in a circle, or in a rectangle around a large room with their back toward the wall. This arrangement assures that everyone is equally included in the party: no one will be in a situation where he is left out. Such solitude in a crowd would be emotionally particularly painful to Japanese since they derive security through interaction with others. Moreover their facility for "emotional interpenetration" enables them, in drinking situations, with very little alcohol to reach quickly a level of euphoria where they "loosen up" and start talking in loud voices, singing, and generally manifesting "drunk" though not drunken behavior patterns. That it is not the amount of alcohol alone which causes euphoria is obvious from the fact that the same person, drinking the same amount of alcohol alone, would remain quite sober.

The Japanese custom of pouring *sake* out of the same container among members of a party is also a way of expressing their emotional solidarity. Of course in the West, too, two martinis may be made from liquor out of the same bottle; but we attach no significance to this fact. In Japanese parties the sharing of liquor out of the same bottle is ritualized. First, the sharing is public, since pouring it is done in front of the party guests, rather than behind the scenes—say in the kitchen. Second, one does not pour one's own drink; pouring is done for each other. This is true even when serving beer, a liquor introduced from the West. Several years ago individually-sized beer containers were introduced in Japan but did not gain much popularity. Psychologically, this failure can be traced to the fact that individual size containers cannot be shared, and when used in the company of others fail to help produce the emotional interpenetration which drinkers seek.

In the above discussion I have not characterized the totality of Japanese personality by any means. I have tried to delineate one aspect of it—an aspect, however, which is extremely important in the personality make-up of Japanese and helps explain much of Japanese social behavior.

To summarize the first section of this chapter, Japanese child-rearing practices have the effect of creating an environment in which the child associates a minimum of anxiety and tension with his parents, especially his mother. This effect is achieved by eliminating as much as possible severe punishment as a means of disciplining and avoiding situations where a child is forced to handle alone the problems of his emotional security. As a result, the child learns close human relationships to be warm and comforting ones. In contrast, American child-rearing practices, which involve a considerable amount of punishment, firm disciplining, and physical separation from parents, tend to create an environment which involves a considerable amount of anxiety, with the result that the child becomes somewhat ambivalent about close human relationships and learns not to accept parents as an unvarying source of emotional satisfaction.

Childhood Indulgence and Adult Authoritarianism

It is a curious reversal that the indulgent, non-authoritarian child-rearing practices of Japanese lead to an adult personality in which submission to authority is a salient characteristic, while the relatively authoritarian practices of American parents result in an adult personality which emphasizes fierce independence and resistance to authoritarian control. American adults seem to be revolting, symbolically, against their authoritarian parents and dramatizing the anxiety and tension which were first implanted in them through child-rearing.

It is often said that Japanese lack a sense of individualism, self-identity, or the concept of self, implying that one's decision is heavily affected or colored by considerations of how others socially around him might feel about his decision and its consequences. Decisions a Japanese man makes are affected by these considerations because his anticipation of how the others will feel in turn affects his own emotional state of mind. Thus an ethical decision tends not to be made strictly on the basis of abstract or universalistic principles, but rather on the basis of his anticipation of the feelings of others.

The American sense of individualism and independence, in which one is to act on his own accord and on the basis of his own conscience, in which one can openly disagree with his closest associates, requires an emotional independence from "meaningful" others, so that one's actions are not influenced, basically, by considerations of whether the actions would please or displease them, but is determined by one's own conviction as to what is right or wrong. At the psychological level, individualism and independence result from not having developed deep, positive emotional ties with one's parents and therefore not being able to transfer them to others, or to put it positively, from one's ability to manage his own emotional security without relying on others.

Many Western observers have commented on the difference between Japanese "democracy" and that of the West, pointing to the absence of individualism in Japan, and wondered whether Japan's democracy would someday be like the West's. The desirability of such simulation entirely aside, the above analysis points to the psychodynamic basis of the difference between Japan and the West in the application of democracy based on individualism.

Normative Values: *On*, *Giri*, and *Ninjō*

In the preceding section of this chapter, we have analyzed the processes whereby emotional patterning takes shape through a variety of experiences during socialization. In this section we shall examine three major normative concepts of traditional Japan: *on, giri,* and *ninjō*. Although many Japanese nowadays disclaim the significance of these traditional values, calling them by the epithet "feudalistic," their own behavior patterns betray social relations which can best be described in terms of these concepts.

On

We shall start with the concept of *on* because the other concepts can be analyzed in relation to it. *On* is, first of all, indebtedness, which arises, as was noted earlier, from receiving some resource which one needs but does not have. Second, dispensation of this resource is clearly institutionalized. That is, there are socially expected relationships which demand dispensation of resources, for example, parents providing nurturance to children and *oyabun* looking after the welfare of his *kobun*. Such dispensation, however, need not be required by law; in fact, the sense of indebtedness is strengthened because the resource is given without external legal compulsion forced upon the dispensing agent. In the early feudal period, when the concept of *on* was beginning to be institutionalized, the most critical resource to be dispensed was land, which vassals received as a reward for their loyalty to their lord. Third, the giver and receiver of the debt are in a particularistic relationship—one which is meaningful only because the giver is a particular individual to the receiver and vice versa. However, two individuals who are not in such a relationship to begin with may become an *on*-giver and an *on*-receiver, e.g., when a stranger saves another's life. In such a case, a particularistic relationship is expected to develop between the two.

Fourth, as noted before, the *on*-giver and *on*-receiver are in hierarchical relation. A hierarchical relationship is built on power and authority. The person in the superordinate position has the right to demand that his subordinate carry out his orders. It is because of the primacy of this power ingredient in the *on* relationship that it became the central ideological basis for the feudal political order among warriors. In the *on* relationship there is no legalistically defined area in which power can be exercised or other areas in which it cannot be, i.e., since the relationship is functionally diffuse, the *on*-giver *can* exercise power indiscriminately. To curb this tendency, however, there is a normative definition of the limits of the superior's power. When this norm is not observed, as it often is not, it is legitimate to speak of "exploitation".

Fifth, the *on* relationship assumes that the debt created by dispensation of the *on* will be returned. Now, since an *on* relationship is created by the dispensation of resources which the subordinate lacks, he cannot return in kind. His return must be in some other form, such as labor or military service. But the two resources, one dispensed by the *on*-giver and the other returned by the receiver, are qualitatively different and non-comparable. One cannot know how much military service, for example, is equal to how much land. Secondly, since the relationship between the giver and the receiver is functionally diffuse, the receiver is required to provide his repayment whenever it is needed. For these reasons, the repayment of *on* is never complete, no matter how hard one tries, and gives rise to the norm of lifelong loyalty and service by the subordinate and to such expressions as "returning of one-ten-thousandth of one's debt" (Benedict, 1946, pp. 114–132).

Although *on* is a normative concept, it has a psychological basis which should not be difficult to understand from the above analysis of emotional patterning among Japanese. The genesis of the *on* relationship is found in the parent-child relationship, where parents give life to the child, provide nurturance, and socialize him. The child is then forever indebted to the parents, and the child's behavior patterns, which are directed toward returning this debt, are what is indicated by the concept of filial piety *(oya kōkō)*. The child's motivational basis for striving to return the debt comes, however, not simply from his intellectual awareness of his debt nor from the inculcation of the normative expectation to return it, but also from the deep, psychological security he has received from his parents and from his desire to maintain an emotional bond with them, and from the anxiety aroused by the thought of their disappointment. Insofar as parents expect the child to repay the debt in socially accepted forms, the child must behave accordingly if he is not to hurt the parents' feelings and consequently alienate himself from them. This pattern of relationships is then transferred later in life to other persons than parents. And to the extent that a similar psychological bond and mutual dependence develop between the two individuals, one feels compelled to repay the debt.

It is at this juncture that the concept of loyalty *(chū)* enters. At the normative level, loyalty is an expression of returning *on* to one's master, lord, or the emperor, and is essentially the same as filial piety in quality. It is important to note that these two normative concepts, filial piety and loyalty, imply the same thing in substance. The readiness with which Japanese can move from the kinship context to other social contexts has had crucial implications for Japan's modernization. Ideally, in loyalty situations, as in parent-child relations, there should be, as there generally was in the traditional period, a particularistic relationship between the superior and the subordinate, so that a psychological bond which had developed in the parent-child relationship could be transferred. In short, loyalty was not a generalized concept that involved being loyal to a principle or to the nation or state, but a relationship holding between two specific individuals. In the modern period, however, Japanese political leaders extended the concept to apply to one's relation to the nation and the emperor—abstract entities to which one did not have any psychological ties. That is, the psychological underpinning for the concept of *on* was almost entirely lacking in this situation.

Although such traditional concepts as *on* and repayment of debts are often said to be dying out and no longer important, a nation-wide survey conducted as late as 1968 indicated that these concepts are far from being dead. Respondents were asked to choose two important items out of the following four: *oya-kōkō,* repaying debt *(on),* respect for individual rights, and respect for freedom. The largest percentage chose *oya-kōkō.* The other three were chosen in about the same proportion. Thus one can say that filial piety is still a very powerful concept and that the concept of *on* is no less important than the more modern concepts of individual rights and freedom (T. Suzuki, 1970).

Giri

There remain two more concepts of traditional Japan to be discussed: *giri* and *ninjō. Giri,* which may be translated as "social obligation," is a normative or ethical imperative requiring Japanese to behave as expected by the society in relation to another individual with whom one is in some meaningful, or particularistic realtion. It is, if you like, an instance of Durkheim's collective representation. It is important to note that as in the case of *on* and loyalty, the concept of *giri* is applicable to particular persons, not to just any individual. In this respect, *giri* goes hand in hand with indebtedness, filial piety, and loyalty in that it was the normative force which compelled or obliged a person to repay his debt through filial piety or loyalty.

But *giri* is a broader concept in that it also applies to egalitarian social relations where individuals are not in a hierarchical relationship, e.g., between friends, neighbors, and relatives. Behaving properly in an egalitarian context—observing gift-giving etiquette, providing labor services in an agricultural community when expected, etc.—is regarded as observing one's obligation, or *giri*. A breach of this obligation is a breach of the moral codes of society and results in sanctions of various kinds and degrees. People will lose trust and confidence in such a person as a moral individual. Although *giri* is a concept which became institutionalized in the feudal past, it can be applied to modern Japanese society and still serves as an important motivational force in social interaction. In short, *giri* is the normative force which attempts to maintain social institutions in a smooth-running condition, irrespective of how an individual might feel about the social order or about other persons with whom he must interact.

The crucial substance of this concept is its moral compulsion to force people into behaving properly even though they personally may not wish to do so. One may find it a nuisance to have to pay visits to a relative or give a gift to a neighbor; but it is imperative to do so lest one's reputation as a social and moral being suffer impairment. There is a pragmatic side to this imperative. Since social life in Japan is based, much more so than in the United States, on social exchange, the observance of *giri*—the governing principle in reciprocal social relations—is a way of assuring needed assistance in the future. Conversely, disregard of *giri* can cause normal reciprocations from kith and kin to cease.

Ninjō

The moral compulsion implied by *giri* is important also in contrasting it with the concept of *ninjō,* a person's "natural" inclinations, feelings, and desires. Whereas *giri* is social and moral, *ninjō* is psychological and personal. It is entirely possible for a person's private feelings to be in complete accord with what the society dictates. One may truly wish, for example, to marry the person selected by one's parents and be happy with the marriage. But it is not likely that the private feelings of all members of a society, no matter how well integrated, are in harmony with social demands. The discrepancy between what is expected of individuals by the society and what one wishes to do is the dilemma between *giri* and *ninjō* which has been made so often the theme of *belle-lettres* in traditional and modern Japan. There is no satisfactory resolution of this dilemma. To honor the society's ethical codes requires suppression of one's feelings; but succumbing to *ninjō* will cause social censure. Caught in this dilemma, there are three alternatives: one, to suppress one's private feelings and honor moral principles; two, to close one's eyes from moral obligations and follow the dictates of one's feeling; and three, to annihilate oneself through committing suicide, being able neither to ignore the society's moral obligations nor suppress one's personal desires. It is this third alternative which many Japanese have chosen and which has been dealt with in modern and traditional stories, attesting to the power of moral compulsion in Japanese society.

Value Orientations

Kluckhohn and Strodtbeck (1961, p.4) have defined value orientations as "complex but definitely patterned (rank-ordered) principles, resulting from the transactional interplay of three analytically distinguishable elements of the evaluative process—the cognitive, the affective, and the directive elements—which give order and direction to the ever-flowing stream of human acts and thoughts as these relate to the solution of 'common human problems' ". They have selected five areas of "common human problems" for close analysis. They are as follows (Kluckhohn and Strodtbeck 1961, p.11):

(1) *Human nature* orientation, or what is the character of innate human nature?

(2) *Man-nature* orientation, or what is the relation of man to nature and supernature?

(3) *Time* orientation, or what is the temporal focus of human life?

(4) *Activity* orientation, or what is the modality of human activity?

(5) *Relational* orientation, or what is the modality of man's relationship to other men?

What are the Japanese patterns of these values? We shall attempt to answer this question below, using as our major bases the findings of Caudill and Scarr (1962) and of Japanese national opinion surveys.

Human nature orientation

Caudill and Scarr's published data do not include materials on the human nature orientation. According to the 1953 public-opinion survey which used a stratified sample of the entire nation, 30.7% responded that human nature was basically good, 2.4% basically bad, 24.7% both good and bad, and 35.0% neither good nor bad, the remaining percentage not answering (Hayashi, 1954, p.38). Thus the dominant orientation—the highest percentage group—assumes human nature to be a *tabula rasa* as far as its moral substance is concerned. This is closely followed by a variant orientation which views human nature as basically good, and then by another variant orientation which admits both good and bad qualities. Conspicuously absent is the orientation which assumes original evil in man, an orientation which is very strong in the Puritan heritage of the American value system. If one can trace the roots of the incessant industry of Americans to their vigorous attempt at repentance, it is clear that no such motivational basis is evident among Japanese.

Man-nature orientation

Caudill and Scarr find that the dominant Japanese orientation in man's relation to nature is the idea that man must have mastery over nature, which is followed by the view that man must maintain harmonious relationship with nature. Trailing far behind is the notion that man is subjugated by nature. These findings are essentially in accord with those of national surveys, results of which are summarized below (T. Suzuki, 1970, p.53).

TABLE 6:1.   MAN'S RELATION TO NATURE

| | In order to be happy, man must: | | | | |
	adapt to nature	make use of nature	conquer nature	other	no response	total
1953 Survey	27%	41%	23%	1%	8%	100%
1963 Survey	19%	40%	30%	1%	9%	99%
1968 Survey	19%	40%	34%	1%	6%	100%

Caudill and Scarr's notion of "mastery over nature" would correspond to the two categories of "make use of nature" and "conquer nature" in the national surveys, and their "harmony with nature" to "adaptation to nature". Since the "subjugation" category of Caudill and Scarr's study is absent in the national surveys, comparison is somewhat misleading; but the national surveys do show, as in the Caudill and Scarr study, the dominance of the "mastery" orientation over the "harmony" orientation.

Many a Japanese scholar, notably Tetsurō Watsuji (1961), has argued that the inhospitable environment in which Japanese live has had profound effects in shaping Japanese value orientations. They have argued for the overwhelming power of the nature which Japanese were incapable of overcoming. While the empirical findings above, coming from postwar Japan, demonstrate that such a view is hardly in keeping with the view of present-day Japanese, it is probable that in the traditional past there was a stronger orientation toward "subjugation by nature" than at present. This is suggested by the fact that in the mere ten years from 1953 to 1963, the national surveys have revealed a considerable (8%) reduction in the preference for the "adaptation" orientation, which in terms of the continuum on man-nature orientation stands in between "subjugation" and "mastery", and an almost equal amount of increase in the "conquest" orientation. Moreover, the spectacular technological success in modern Japan, having profoundly affected the life of Japanese, is very likely the basis for the preference of present-day Japanese for the "mastery" position. If so, in the traditional past, when technological advance was at a snail's pace in comparison with recent times, the "subjugation by nature" position must have been held by a much greater proportion of the population than now. At any rate, what determines value orientations seems not so much the physical environment as the technological basis of the culture.

At the same time, as Plath's analysis (1966) of the Japanese concept of fatalism shows, within the Japanese folk conception of fatalism, the folk view of the "law of nature", there is still room for planning, optimism, and moral responsibility, and because of which "mastery over nature" in Japan need not be seen simply as an incongruous Western transplant, but may be regarded as an outgrowth of more traditional orientation in response to modern technological progress.

Time Orientation

Caudill and Scarr found that Japanese show the primary preference for orientation toward the future insofar as technological issues are involved in the questions asked. However, in the area of everyday life—child-rearing, weddings, funerals, etc.—they show the first choice for the present orienta-tion. That is, they do not obsessively hang on to things of the past, but take things (changes) as they come, without being overly anxious about change.

In a 1953 national survey, people were asked whether they thought more about the future than the past, or vice versa, or about the same. Since a choice for the "present" orientation was lacking in this questionnaire, we cannot claim strict comparability with the Caudill-Scarr findings; but in general the results are confirmative. 61% of the respondents showed prefer-ence for future orientation, 27% equal preference for future and past, and 9% for past orientation. In 1968, as one would expect, there was a slight increase in the future orientation to 69%, the past/future orientation and the past orientation both decreasing to 22% and 7%, respectively (T. Suzuki, 1970, p.54).

Activity orientation

Neither Caudill and Scarr nor Japanese national opinion surveys present data on the activity orientation. Kluckhohn and Strodtbeck suggest, on intuitive, rather than empirical grounds, that in traditional Japan the "be-ing-in-becoming" orientation, characterized by "that kind of *activity* which has as its goal the development of all aspects of the self as an integrated whole" (italics original 1961, p. 17) was a central focus and was expressed in the intellectual-aesthetic behavior sphere. This orientation toward a "whole man" is seen, for one, in the philosophy of Zen Buddhism, but is also evident in the traditional Japanese conception of the great man, who is expected not only to demonstrate technical excellence in his chosen field, but to manifest the highest human virtues in all spheres of life.

Along with this orientation, the "doing" orientation, so strong in the United States, was probably also quite important in the traditional past. The "doing" orientation implies "the kind of *activity* which results in accomplishments that are measurable by standards conceived to be external to the acting individual" (italics original, Kluckhohn and Strodtbeck, 1961, p. 17). Whereas the "doing" orientation allows a quantitative measure, as in the amount of accumulated wealth, and is therefore strongly manifested in the economic sphere of life, the "being-in-becoming" orientation is not manifested in quantities, but is instead expressed in political, intellectual, and aesthetic activities. There is not doubt that in Modern Japan, the "doing" orientation is the dominant one, although the "being-in-becoming" orientation probably still retains a significant place.

Relational orientation

In the relational sphere, Caudill and Scarr's findings show a dominant orientation toward "collaterality," i.e., working together, and cooperating with others more or less on an egalitarian basis in the family, the community, and at work. This orientation is followed in preference by "individualism," and then finally by "lineality," i.e., organization of persons in a hierarchy. These findings are unexpected in view of the strong and clear-cut "lineality" emphasis in traditional Japan, as we have seen in previous chapters. Pelzel, in direct reference to Kluckhohn's scheme of value orientations, noted the emphasis on lineality in traditional Japan, without, however, ignoring a variant, collateral orientation (Pelzel and Kluckhohn, 1957). As Caudill and Scarr state, the rejection of the "lineality" orientation is probably "an expression of the post-war Japanese reaction against traditional pseudo-familial work relations, often characterized by the epithet 'feudalistic' " (Caudill and Scarr, 1962, p. 69). However, rejection of lineality at the conscious attitudinal level does not immediately imply its absence in actual life. As these authors note, hierarchical human relations continue in various forms in modern Japan. Nakane (1965) has recently forcefully argued for the lineal structure of modern Japanese society.

It is difficult to guess how much change has taken place in these value orientations since we do not have any comparable empirical data from the traditional or even from the more recent prewar past. At the same time, it is probably safe to assume that some changes are taking place in these regards. But changes in value orientations most likely do not mean that a new orientation, entirely absent in the past, suddenly assumes dominance, or that a dominant orientation will suddenly disappear altogether. Rather, what has become dominant of late was probably adhered to by a sizeable, if minority, segment of the population in the past. Insofar as we are measuring attitudes of individuals, it is reasonable to expect quantitative shifts, rather than quantum jumps.

Cultural Style

Every culture has its peculiar style—a complex of cultural patterns which more or less make that culture unique and different from any other. Such a cultural style is, in one sense, "superorganic," that is, it is a quality of culture *qua* culture. But at the same time a cultural style is expressed in individual behavior and is more or less part of individual personality make-up. But in stylistic analysis we are not so much concerned with emotional moods or interpersonal patterns of behavior as with that which is felt to be intrinsically valuable—"good, right, beautiful, pleasing, or desirable in itself." (Kroeber, 1952, p. 402).

Subtlety

One such stylistic emphasis in Japan has been the refinement of form, combined with unverbalized subtlety as seen in the Japanese esthetic concepts expressed in such words as *shibusa, sabi,* and *wabi.* While the Japanese may have not manifested a propensity toward inventiveness, they have directed their energy toward refining and perfecting what they have acquired. This cultural style is seen, for example, in making a cult out of such ordinary affairs as drinking tea and enjoying flowers. The Japanese have turned these activities into fine arts, with many contending masters and schools and much discussion not only on the art but also on the philosophy of these arts.

One of the important esthetic styles in Japanese art reflects a notion which can be expressed in a cluster of English words such as subtlety, simplicity, and indirection. Subtlety implies lack of obviousness, and requires a careful study for appreciation. Japanese gardens are made to look "natural," as if no human effort has gone into their creation. One does not see the geometric formalism of some Western gardens, which immediately impress the viewer with the unmistakable fact of human creation. Rather, one is drawn into nature in viewing or walking through a Japanese garden, where maximum human effort is made to minimize the impression of artificial creation. It is this studied naturalness which is appreciated not only in landscape architecture, but in other forms of art as well. American cultural style, in contrast, emphasizes obviousness, that which can be immediately perceived and appreciated. A flashy car, bright pastel colors, the beaming smile of a salesgirl, etc., play a vital part in American daily life, where interpersonal relations very much remain on the "surface," each person carefully guarding his privacy.

The element of subtlety probably reaches its peak in the Noh play where the actors' movements are on the whole slow and restricted, and do not follow "natural" gestures. The difficulty of playing Noh lies precisely in the fact that the actor's movements are limited and that he must convey his dramatic artistry and express a variety of meanings with highly restricted movements.

Another expression of subtlety is seen in folk ceramics, in which appreciation comes from the subdued beauty expressed in relatively somber colors and in the simplicity of form. Folk pottery even gives the appearance of crudeness, until one learns to see the sophistication and mastery behind the obvious. It is this refined simplicity which is characteristic of much of Japanese art. One sees it, to take another example, in the black-and-white brush painting which uses a few strokes to represent objects and lets the blank space speak almost as much as painted areas.

Indirection

The studied naturalness, refined simplicity, and sophisticated subtlety discussed above all imply indirection. Rather than directly perceiving that which is to be appreciated, one mentally "goes behind" what is immediately perceived to get at the essence of Japanese art. This indirection is most clearly manifested in the poetry of the thirty-one syllable *tanka* and the seventeen syllable *haiku*. Particularly in the latter, the maximum number of words that can be used in one poem is so restricted that one is forced to let the expressed words suggest as much as possible what one is unable to express in words because of the formal restriction. Emphasis here is on what is unsaid and unverbalized rather than in what is expressed. Here, for example, is a haiku by Buson, and eighteenth-century master of poetry:

> *Yomizu toru*
> *Satobito no koe ya*
> *Natsu no tsuki*

Blyth (1952, p. 39) gives the following direct translation of this poem:

> The voices of village people
> Irrigating the fields;
> The summer moon.

To this Blyth adds the following commentary, which may be regarded as a translation of the full meaning of the poem, saying the unsaid and making obvious the subtle points. It demonstrates how much is packed into the short poem and how much imagery a reader is expected to conjure up from it.

"It is so common and yet so strange, the fact that the absence of something is more moving than its presence. Regulating the level of the water in the fields, the people of the village are making their rounds, talking to one another in the bright moonlight. The poet can see the moon and hear the voices; he cannot see the people themselves, nor the quick silver water that falls into the indigo depth."

Expressions of Cultural Style

Suppression of verbalism, indirection, and emphasis on that which is hidden and can only be intuited are well exemplified in Zen Buddhism, which virtually denies to language the role of communication of information and logical reasoning. In Zen, no amount of verbal instruction and reasoning is directly helpful in attaining enlightenment, or *satori*. As if to emphasize the inutility of linguistic communication, a Zen master is likely to engage in a dialogue with his disciples which defies logical understanding and is completely absurd if taken literally. One may recall the findings of Caudill and Weinstein that Japanese infants are significantly less verbal than American infants. There is a good deal more emphasis placed on the nonverbal communication of emotion between mother and child in Japan, and this emphasis continues into adulthood. Zen may be seen as an ultimate expression of nonverbal communication. But there are other expressions of nonverbal emphasis in Japan.

Pedagogical procedure in traditional arts and crafts in Japan calls for many years of disciplehood during which learning is expected to take place as much through informal observation, intuitive understanding, and "absorption" of the master's techniques as through formal, verbalized instruction. This learning, in traditional days, took place in the context of the stem family, where the father was the master and the son the disciple, or in a similar context in which the master and the disciple were in a ritual kinship relation, either in the formal institutionalized or in a less formal sense. In such social contexts as these, a great deal of nonverbal communication takes place between the master and the disciple. While certain obvious aspects of arts and crafts can be and are taught through verbal instruction, it is believed that certain essentials cannot be so taught and must be learned somehow through an intuitive grasp of the method. And this intuitive learning comes about only through a long and intimate relationship with the master. Through prolonged, personal contact, the disciple learns the master's personality and his idiosyncrasies. He learns them so well that he can predict the master's behavior and respond to his demands without verbal cues. In short, he incorporates the master's personality, and by thus "becoming" the master, as it were, the disciple learns to execute the master's skills without so much verbal instruction.

Thus one sees how traditional arts and crafts and the paternalistic social system of traditional Japan are integrated. The basic assumption that technical skills can be mastered only through a long association with the master and only intuitively is widely held even today in many other contexts than traditional arts and crafts. According to Whitehill and Takezawa's findings, 53% of the machine operators interviewed believed that industrial skills are best learned through observation of senior workers in the shop, and only 6% thought that such skills can be best learned formally in technical or trade schools (Whitehill and Takezawa, 1961, p. 50). Even in the university setting, graduate students, especially in the humanities and the medicine, learn their professor's theoretical stance through their long association with him. It is important to note that whenever technical skills are imparted through long and intimate association and nonverbal communication, the interpersonal side of the relationship manifests the sort of emotional interpenetration which we discussed earlier.

Melancholy

Another cluster of Japanese esthetic styles may be termed the esthetics of melancholy, sadness, and suffering. Minami (1953), writing on Japanese personality, practically dismisses the Japanese conception of happiness in a mere two sections and eighteen pages. According to Minami, the Japanese terms for happiness, such as *kōfuku* and *shiawase* lack realism in Japanese life and instead have a certain artificiality about them. Minami thinks that the Japanese are basically unhappy people, and elaborates on Japanese conceptions of unhappiness in thirteen sections and fifty-six pages. We have had occasions to mention Japanese attitudes toward nature and Watsuji's theory about fatalism in Japanese. All these seem to be consistent with one another.

In the context of the present discussion of cultural styles, however, my point does not so much concern unhappiness as such as it does the esthetic of this feeling. The term unhappiness conveys too violent an emotional disposition. Perhaps a mixture of melancholy, a small amount of sadness and some suffering is a more accurate characterization of this feeling. The feeling of melancholy, combined with some sadness is best expressed in the Japanese term *monono aware* (Ōnishi, 1939). We are referring not to the psychological state as such but to the esthetic appreciation of this mood. Being an esthetic concept, it is best expressed in the arts, particularly in literature, and the concept can be traced back to early Japanese literature, such as the *Tale of Genji*. We should remember that this mood is appreciated as an esthetic concept because the general populace in Japan enjoy it. I have mentioned the popularity of "motherhood" movies, which the audience cries while watching.

The concept is expressed in such diverse areas of life as the Tokugawa plebian literature on unfulfilled romance and love suicide, in the philosophy of contentment with one's station no matter how wretched, in the Buddhist notion of contentment in the midst of this-worldy uncertainties, and in the attitude that suffering is a necessary part of life, at least at present, for the attainment of a future goal.

This concept is reflected in the training methods of traditional arts and crafts, to which we may also add trades. In these occupations, a long period of apprenticeship is required, during which one must work hard and long hours with little compensation and much abuse—verbal and sometimes physical—by the master. It is believed that one must undergo such hardship and taste the bitterness of life in order to become a "whole person," to become a respectable human being who, beneath the ruggedness on the surface, has a quality of inner attainment, and to perfect the skill one desires to have. This philosophy is deeply engrained in the traditional Japanese thinking and is still widely accepted. In college club activities, such as athletics, mountain climbing, etc., training of club members involves harsh treatment for no apparent reason other than to subject junior members to hardship. And senior members often quite frankly state that hardship as such is a necessary part of training.

It is not difficult to see how some of the cultural styles discussed here are interrelated. For example, the emphasis on subtlety, indirection, and implicitness requires an unverbalized, intuitive approach which can be mastered only through personal, tutorial apprenticeship in which one depends on non-verbal communication more critically than verbal instructions. Appreciation of the subdued and somber beauty in ceramics and of the quiet serenity of the tea ceremony are in harmony with the esthetic of melancholy, even though the former do not have necessary or logical connections with the latter.

SUGGESTED READINGS

Benedict, Ruth
1946   *The Chrysanthemum and the Sword*. Boston: Houghton Mifflin.

Caudill, W. and L. Takeo Doi
1963   "Interrelations of psychiatry, culture and emotion in Japan," in Iago Galston, ed., *Man's Image in Medicine and Anthropology*. New York: International University Press, pp. 374–421.

DeVos, George and Hiroshi Wagatsuma
1959 "Psycho-cultural significance of concern over death and illness among rural Japanese." *International Journal of Social Psychiatry* 5: 5–19.

Iga, Mamoru
1961 "Cultural factors in suicide of Japanese youth with focus on personality." *Sociology and Social Research* 46: 75–90.

Lanham, Betty B.
1956 "Aspects of child care in Japan: preliminary report," in Douglas G. Haring, ed., *Personal Character and Cultural Milieu.* Syracuse: Syracuse University Press, pp. 565–583.

Plath, David W.
1964 *The After Hours: Modern Japan and the Search for Enjoyment.* Berkeley and Los Angeles: University of California Press.

Suzuki, Daisetz
1959 *Zen and Japanese Culture.* New York: Pantheon Books.

Vogel, Ezra F. and Suzanne H.
1961 "Family Security, personal immaturity, and emotional health in a Japanese sample." *Marriage and Family Living* 23: 161–166.

7 Modernization

The Theoretical Background

The rapid transformation of feudal Japan into a modern nation, in fact into the first non-Western nation to join the ranks of the world powers, has been a topic of much discussion among Western observers. Leaving the feudal past a hundred years ago, in three-quarters of a century Japan already rivaled Western powers and took issue with them in World War II. Soundly defeated, she made a remarkable recovery and continues to make rapid progress. This overall development has been labeled "modernization." Before we go into the substantive discussion as to the whys and hows of Japan's rapid modernization, a few words of conceptual clarification are in order.

Concept of Modernization

First, it should be made clear that modernization is not synonymous with westernization, Europeanization, or industrialization. Westernization or Europeanization refers to the process of assimilating Western or European culture in the broadest sense, from the bikini to Christianity. Modernization is a generalized process which does not necessarily imply the assimilation of Western culture, although in effect it does involve, for practical reasons, taking over portions of Western culture since it is in the West that the features of modern society first developed, affording a ready model to borrow, although to be sure such borrowing invariably involves modification of the model in varying degrees. Industrialization is a narrower concept than modernization, and is primarily concerned with the process by which a nation takes over industrial technology.

Modernization, on the other hand, directly involves several issues at once. The most obvious of these are economic and political. In the broadest sense, modernization implies the preponderant use of inanimate sources of energy converted into productive power, especially through chemical changes rather than mechanical conversion. At the same time, it implies development of a government which aims to encourage this economic process, work out political integration, e.g., through fostering nationalism, and disseminate economic, educational, political, and other benefits to most of the population, rather than limit these benefits to the small ruling elite. Although the economic and political processes of modernization are somewhat separate, historically they have been extremely closely related in most parts of the world, particularly where modernization has been successfully carried out. This is in large part because the economic development which accompanies industrialization, if it is to be successful, requires vast planning and massive capitalization of the degree and kind only the government of a nation is capable of providing.

It is important to distinguish between indices of modernization on the one hand, and causes and processes of modernization on the other.

For example, the proportion of literacy, degree of urbanization, level of personal income, rate of increase in gross national product, and extent of mass communication, are themselves indicators of modernization. Hence the more of them there are in greater quantities, by definition the more modernized the nation is. A progressive increase in these traits is what we expect if modernization is continuing. In our analysis, rather than discuss these indices of modernization, we wish to focus our attention on the underlying causal or contributing factors and processes of modernization.

Anthropological Approaches to Modernization

Anthropology has not shown a major interest in the conceptual problems of modernization as such, which have been by and large the domain of political science and economics. Anthropologists, however, have concerned themselves with various problems related to or similar to the process of modernization under the rubric of cultural evolution, culture change, etc. Modernization can be conceived of as the latest stage in the evolutionary development of culture. Cultural evolution is a process which effects the increasingly efficient organization of culture for harnessing and utilizing the thermodynamic energy available in the environment. At the latest stage of cultural evolution, the sources of energy to be harnessed and utilized have been found in the inanimate environment and converted for human use through chemical changes such as internal combustion and atomic fission, rather than through mechanical means such as the horse-drawn plow and windmill. This chemical conversion is, as we have just noted, the very basis of industrialization. Now, in order for industrial technology to operate effectively, the culture incorporating it must have other facets supporting it. For example, the motivational problems of creating enough drive in man to want to work according to the required industrial schedule must be solved. Social and economic systems must be organized so that they are suitable to industrial technology.

In the West, where industrial technology originated, there was a gradual (not to say painless) development of social, political, and psychological concomitants to increasing industrialization. Elsewhere in the world, including Japan, when industrial technology is adopted from the West, other aspects of the culture must be modified to bring about a new adjustment with the technology, unless the traditional culture is in certain respects "ready" and "preadapted" to it. Success in modernization thus in large part depends on how well and to what extent a culture can mobilize its social and cultural resources in maximizing the borrowed technological potentials. Let us now consider Japan's modernization in the light of this general background.

Japan's Early Modernization

Historical and Geographical Background

Numerous factors of different kinds have been suggested as having caused, accelerated, or otherwise been responsible in some sense for Japan's rapid modernization, particularly in its early days. There are the historical "accidents," e.g., the arrival of European powers in Japan in the middle of the last century, demanding the opening of her ports just at the time when Japan was internally "ready" for a major change because the feudal regime was then facing major economic and political crises, making introduction of drastic changes relatively easy. There are aslo the geographical factors, such as the isolation afforded an island nation, which made foreign invasion and colonization relatively difficult compared, e.g., with a country like Korea. Similarly, the small size of the nation made tight control and planned change easier than they would be in a vast country like China.

Social and Economic Factors

It should also be remembered that Japan had already developed a civilization with many of the qualities necessary for modernization, such as the presence of a well-developed political organization, complete with a taxation system, a stratified society, urban centers, and a minimum of literacy and educational institutions. In the economic sphere, there was already in the late Tokugawa period the development of mercantile capitalism, manifested in a complex system of money, banking, and bank notes, in investment in manufacturing enterprises, in a wholesale and retail distribution systems of goods, and even in stock exchanges. Although the industrial technology to be imported from the West was too advanced to be "grafted" directly on the existing economic system, the Japanese were familiar with many of the facets of industrial capitalism and the Tokugawa economic system provided a ready context into which Western industrialism could be adopted without major disruption either in the economic system itself or in the patterns of thought and the attitudes of people toward economic affairs.

Role of the Government

We cannot ignore the role of the government in planning the course of Japan's modernization, stimulating economic development, and fostering nationalism. Like most other non-Western modernizers, the Japanese government took the major initiative in developing an industrial economy and higher education, as well as inculcating nationalistic ideology and making Japan into a strong military power. To these ends, the Japanese government invited and hired a large number of foreign teachers and technicians to teach at Japanese universities and to provide technical assistance at newly established industrial plants, sent Japanese citizens to Western countries for education and technical training, and made direct investments in industries. Details of these processes have been the concern of political scientists and economists, to whom we shall leave this subject.

Aside from the historical accidents, geographical factors, an antecedent economic base, and the role of the governments, we are as anthropologists interested in generalized cultural patterns, social practices, and personality traits which have contributed to Japan's modernization. We have already examined a number of such factors in the preceding chapters from slightly different angles. It remains to re-examine these factors from the perspective of modernization.

Japan as a Borrower

From time immemorial, Japan has been by and large a borrower rather than an innovator, most of the basic cultural innovations having been introduced from outside. As the Japanese anthropologist Masuda (1967) has argued in detail and with cogency, this willingness, and indeed eagerness to borrow has gone hand in hand with the "inferiority complex" of the Japanese, which at the psychological level has facilitated the cultural process of extensive borrowing. This feeling of inferiority and the desire to rid herself of the inferior position, psychologically underpinned by the motivation to achieve, were largely responsible for Japan's eagerness to take over the industrial technology and to adopt the political concepts of nationalism and imperialism to her advantage in the early days of modernization. Without this feeling of inferiority, Japan might have resisted the encroachment of Western technology and ideology, as China did during the early stages of her contact with the west.

Japan, however, has not been simply a copier, an imitator. As we noted earlier, Japan has devoted her energy to making refinements—technical improvements, subtle changes, and added precision. We have seen some examples of these in the consideration of the esthetic styles of Japanese culture. Essentially the same stylistic character is manifested in the handling of borrowed technical innovations. That is, the success in the adaptation of Western technology in Japan can be in part attributed to the cultural pattern of making innovations to fit the borrowed elements to Japanese culture and making the products attractive to foreign buyers. Since Japan has had to rely on foreign trade for executing its economic development, this cultural pattern has paid off and played a crucial role in Japan's modernization.

Kinship System

The kinship system of Japan has traditionally been a fairly flexible institution which can be "manipulated" to fit the exigencies of a situation, in sharp contrast to, say, traditional China, where the patrilineal system was a relatively rigid structure. The frequent adoptions in Japan are a case in point, in which the adoptee may be male or female, infant or adult, a blood-relative or unrelated individual. What is important in the Japanese kinship system has been the perpetuity of the corporate household, for which purpose kinship may be, and has been manipulated. Perpetuating a corporation implies carrying out its instrumental activities, the "business" the group is engaged in. Adoption practices in Japan are adapted to recruiting the most competent personnel. Seen thus, the emphasis on the instrumental goals of a group and the relatively flexible kinship system, which permits maximum opportunity for attaining such goals, are yet another set of contributing factors to Japan's rapid modernization. For a nation's economy is built upon the economic activities of individual families; to the extent that each family is concerned with economic success and is given "a chance" through a flexible kinship system, the cumulative effect for the whole nation can be impressive. Particularly at the early stages of economic development, as Benedict (1968) has pointed out, the economic activities of individual families play a major part. Japan was fortunate in having a kinship system which could immediately respond to the needs of modern economic development.

The Japanese kinship system was important for Japan's modernization in still another way. I refer here to the absence of a sharp distinction between kin and non-kin in traditional Japan. Instead, the dominant consideration was the role one played in the family not simply as a kinship group but as a business organization. Along the same line, we also saw that the dōzoku was never strictly defined as a kinship group, and that non-kin were given status within the dōzoku structure. We have just noted above that adoption of non-kin was and still is a common phenomenon. Lastly, we have examined the widespread phenomena of ritual kinship (oyabun-kobun) groups and ritual kinship-like groups and relations in the form which I have called institutional paternalism. All these examples attest to the rather ready transfer of the "true" kinship relations, attitudes, roles, values, etc., into social contexts in which kinship is not the basic structural feature. When a society undergoes a rapid change in which the society's non-kinship institutions play an increasingly dominant role, as happens under modernization, a society which can utilize the resources available in the kinship institution in the process of change is in a more advantageous position than another society in which the kinship institution simply breaks down without serving any major adaptive role. Thus Japan's early modernization owed at least in part to the adaptability of its kinship institution to the changing environment.

We have already mentioned the role of ideological paternalism in the early period of Japan's modernization. That is, while the interpersonal aspects of the kinship institution are absent in the emperor's relation to subjects, in the ideological sense the emperor was looked upon figuratively as a parent, if not explicitly as the father, at least as one to whom subjects owed an immense amount of *on,* as one does to parents, which had to be repaid in the form of loyalty to the state, and devotion to one's assigned duties for the promotion of the national well-being. For otherwise, it was said, the emperor would be concerned and worried about the state of the nation and the welfare of the people; and it is imperative to ease the emperor's mind. Thus the paternalistic ideology served as a basis for developing a political focus, became a symbolic rallying point and thus fostered a nationalistic attitude which was essential for Japan in its competition with Western nations in the second half of the last century.

On

We have already elaborated on the concept of *on* and the related notion of personal loyalty, but it is worth reiterating the importance of these normative values in Japan's modernization. To review, *on* implies a hierarchical relationship and compels the *on*-receiver to repay. An important difference between *on* and the concept of filial piety, emphasized in traditional China so much, is that filial piety is a concept bound in the kinship context, outside which it has no application, whereas *on* has no such boundary, in spite of the fact that psychologically *on* has its origin in the family context, as we saw in the last chapter. Since in traditional Japan the concept of *on* took precedence over filial piety, and since kinship as a category imperceptibly merged with nonkinship, for the Japanese leaving the kinship context and moving into non-kinship groups did not pose major psychological problems. Whatever group into which one moved, a hierarchical structure and the attendant *on*-relationship prevailed. Thus in the early modern period of Japan, when non-kinship institutions increased in size and number and more and more Japanese were recruited into them, the familiar concepts of *on* and personal loyalty derived from the *on* concept served as a ready institutional framework which was at once both meaningful to people and efficient for the society.

Achievement Motivation

In the section on the patterning of emotional moods among the Japanese, we touched on the relation of personality formation to achievement motivation. The close affective interdependence between mother and child which develops as a result of the relatively lenient child-rearing practices is turned into a mechanism for social control. That is, the child interprets parental suffering as the result of his misconduct and becomes motivated to alleviate his parents' suffering. Because parents desire the child's success, the child is motivated to achieve it. To be sure, evidence for this process of achievement motivation comes exclusively from postwar investigations. We have no empirical studies to demonstrate that in traditional Japan the same configuration of socialization patterns existed which would cause achievement motivation in the manner found in the postwar studies. On the other hand, there is no positive evidence to show that the patterns of child-rearing which are responsible for achievement motivation in contemporary Japanese are recent innovations and that in the traditional period child-rearing was carried out in substantially different forms. On this basis, then, we may assume as a working hypothesis that the same configuration of socialization patterns did exist in traditional and early modern Japan and that it was responsible for motivating Japanese to achieve success in their chosen fields.

I do not pretend to have exhausted all the major reasons for Japan's success in modernization. Rather, the ones I have discussed are illustrative of the different kinds of causal agents, operating at normative, social, and psychological levels. Obviously all these factors and many others were operating simultaneously for the accomplishment of Japan's rapid modernization. How important or necessary each of these was for Japan's modernization is another question. An assessment of the relative importance of each factor would take us deep into methodological issues, which are not our concern here. Suffice it to say in this context that the availability of a large number of relatively important causal factors in the early period of Japan's modernization—in short, the fact that traditional Japan was predisposed toward, or pre-adapted to rapid modernization—permitted Japan's spectacular success and development.

Contemporary Problems and Prospects for the Future

Japan in the modern period should not be regarded as homogeneous. Nor should it be assumed that the modernization process has been uniform for the last hundred years and that the same causal factors responsible for

Japan's early modernization are still operating and still fostering its modernization now. Such an assumption ignores the dynamic nature of the modernization process, which requires different kinds of adaptive strategies at different stages, so that what was once functionally adaptive for Japan's modernization in its early stages may no longer be functional, but instead may even be detrimental. At the same time, some traditional institutions which were beneficial for early modernization may transform themselves in adaptation to the changing situation and continue to play an important role. Let us take a few examples to illustrate these processes.

We have said that the concept of personal loyalty, diffuse and particularistic human relations, and the blurred distinction between kin and non-kin —which were all part of the traditional, pre-modern Japan—played crucial roles in facilitating Japan's early modernization. In the early days of modernization, when the society was close to the traditional past, when most economic enterprises were carried out in small "cottage industries," when there was only a limited degree of mobility, when bureaucracy had its beginnings, but only on a small scale so that the need for impersonal rule was not great, a compromise accommodation between early modern insitutions and traditional values and institutions worked out well. But a hundred years later, modernization has reached another stage. Industries and government agencies employ thousands of workers and universities have tens of thousands of students. There is now a greater and greater need for impersonal but efficient bureaucratic organization. The application of universalistic criteria for hiring and firing and for raises and promotion is highly desirable, and is, in fact, desired by many Japanese. But traditional institutions which were so successful in transforming Japan into a modern nation, partly because of their very success have become deeply entrenched in Japanese society. They have become "ossified" in the contemporary society to such a degree that even though the transformation of these institutions and values is critically needed in modern industrial society, they do not readily transform. They are thus no longer facilitators of modernization, but to a considerable extent are instead its deterrents.

The same argument may be made regarding Japan's long accustomed pattern of cultural borrowing. As we have noted, the Japanese are not slavish imitators. Certainly they have shown an ability to synthesize and make improvements upon what they borrow. But still the improvements and modifications are minor compared with the basic innovations they borrow. Basic inventions and discoveries are still by and large made outside Japan and are imported. In the early stages of modernization, this was a highly useful and adaptive process, since resisting borrowing and trying to invent is a highly wasteful method of achieving modernization. Japanese were quite ready to take over the latest technological developments, and thus reached in a few decades a high technological stage which Western nations had taken centuries to achieve. But after achieving a level comparable to the West, instead of changing her role from borrower to innovator, Japan has remained, by and large, a borrowing nation. This is clearly evident in the large number of technological innovations with patents and copyrights held in Western nations (especially United States and Germany) which are used in Japan and for which Japanese business firms pay royalties. Japanese business firms have found it less expensive to borrow ideas and pay for them than to carry out basic research which may or may not yield profitable innovations. At present, research institutions in Japan—at universities, in private businesses, and government agencies—are extremely inadequate in most fields. The gap with Western nations in the scale of basic research is now so great that it would require a major shift in national orientation to close the gap, which is not likely to be forthcoming. This gap might not have resulted had Japan made a major effort from the beginning of the modern period to foster basic research and minimize the extent of borrowing from abroad. But the centuries-old pattern of successful borrowing has prevented Japan from developing patterns of basic research and original innovation.

A somewhat different example is Japan's paternalism and its relationship to modernization. Using the traditional kinship structure as the base, various institutional and ideological "extensions" took place in the early modern period. Through continual modification, this extension, which we have called "paternalism," had adapted itself to small family industries, large business firms, small units within large bureaucratic institutions, and many other types of groups and organizations as Japan grew out of the traditional past and began modernizing. Kinship adapted itself to modern conditions by giving rise to paternalism, and paternalism adapted itself to the modernizing environment by diversifying into many different forms, each adapted to its own niche, so to speak (Ishino, 1966).

Thus paternalism, unlike the pattern of cultural borrowing, has gone through numerous modifications and transformations in the past one hundred years in keeping with changing circumstances. An important question for Japan's future is whether paternalism is still capable of modifying itself as industrial technology develops and the society changes, and whether paternalism, no matter how modified, will continue to be adaptive and beneficial for Japan's modernization. We have noted that in contemporary Japan, managerial paternalism only vaguely remains and that its ideological component, in particular, is only weakly present at best. We have also noted the tendency, where paternalism does remain, of those in superordinate positions to exploit their subordinates. In addition, as the government takes on more and more responsibility for social welfare—in health insurance, old age pensions, etc., and in providing adequate living conditions for most citizens—there will be less and less need for private, paternalistic institutions. Thus it is expected that paternalism will continue to weaken and become a less and less prevalent and crucial institution for the society as a whole, although at the same time no one can be so rash as to say that paternalism has completely disappeared in modern Japan.

At any rate, it is clear that paternalism as it operated a generation or two ago is no longer functional in the present-day context of Japan, although western social scientists who have analyzed the institution have tended to see only its beneficial, functional aspects, while ignoring its detrimental and disfunctional features. The majority of Japanese do not accept any more the paternalistic ideology in its pristine form, including complete submission to the authority figure and the idea of repayment of *on*. Any attempt to institute it would be strongly resisted. The important question is whether a new institution will emerge which will substitute for the ever-weakening paternalism with the effectiveness with which paternalism once helped modernize Japan.

Let us take another example where change is needed; namely, the practices of lifetime employment and graduated wage scales in business firms, two features which are closely related. As noted earlier, permanent workers in Japanese companies are generally not subject to firing. At the same time there is a strong expectation that once a man is hired, he should stay with the firm for an indefinite period of time, ideally until retirement. Both management and workers often speak of this expectation of lifetime commitment in the idiom of feudal loyalty to one's lord, albeit jokingly. Many overt as well as subtle institutional arrangements support this expectation. For example, companies, especially large ones, expend a considerable amount of effort indoctrinating workers in their loyalty to the company and a sense of pride in belonging to it. Not to be forgotten in this context is the need for emotional interdependence, which can be fulfilled only through long years of association with fellow workers and which in turn tends to discourage workers from shifting employment. At the same time, changing economic conditions—industrial growth and attendant labor scarcity at all levels—have created a situation in which openings cannot be adequately filled through the conventional channels of employing young men out of school. The acute labor shortage favors freer labor market conditions than what prevails now, and there are individual workers who wish to change employment if the change can be executed without loss. However, because of the norm of lifetime commitment which the majority of workers still adhere to, anyone changing his job is suspect simply because he is changing jobs, the assumption being that no normal person would or should have to change his job and that if one changes jobs it is because there is something wrong with his character, not with his job.

In addition, the graduated wage scale, in which one's basic wage is a function of the length of service, amount of education at the time of entrance to the company, and age, prevents workers from changing jobs even if they wish to do so. Since the length of service is such a major factor, anyone changing jobs after several years of service in a company is bound to take a drastic cut in salary. And the rigidity of the wage-scale system prevents any older person coming into the company from receiving a wage comparable to his age mates in the company with the same amount of education. In short, the wage system has no way of giving extra reward to a person of exceptional talent.

These features of lifetime commitment and graduated wage scale, which are closely tied historically with the managerial paternalism we discussed earlier, successfully adapted themselves to early Japanese industrialism, so successfully, in fact, that they are now deeply entrenched components of the Japanese employment structure. It is this past success in adaptation which has caused them to "ossify" into relatively unchangeable practices even in the face of a need for change. To be sure, to a small extent changes are taking place. The Laobr Ministry's 1967 employment survey shows that job changing is a growing trend. Yet, compared with the United States the proportion of male workers changing jobs in one year in Japan is about one-half to one-third for any age-specific group (Japan Report, August 31, 1969). Whether phenomena such as this are signs of a more drastic and fundamental change in the future and whether changes will come fast enough in Japan no one can say yet. The demands of the economic world seem to be pushing toward the direction of change; but whether the psychological dispostion of Japanese and the Japanese social structure will manage to meet these demands is another question.

Herein lies the dilemma of Japan's future. Whether Japan can rid itself of what are now no longer useful institutions, no matter how adaptive they may have been in earlier periods of modernization, and substitute for them new ones which are adapted to the advanced stage of modernization that Japan is now entering is one of the most crucial areas of investigation for the understanding of modern Japan and for predicting Japan's future.

SUGGESTED READINGS

Bellah, Robert N.
1957   *Tokugawa Religion: The Values of Pre-industrial Japan.* Glencoe: The Free Press.

Burke, William
1962   "Creative response and adaptive response in Japanese society." *American Journal of Economics and Sociology* 21: 103–112.

DeVos, George
1965   "Achievement orientations, social self-identity, and Japanese economic growth." *Asian Survey* 5: 575–589.

Dore, Ronald P.

1965 "The legacy of Tokugawa education," in Marius B. Jansen, ed., *Changing Japanese Attitudes Toward Modernization.* Princeton: Princeton University Press, pp. 99–131.

Horie, Yasuzo

1965 "Modern entrepreneurship in Meiji Japan," in W. M. Lockwood, ed., *The State and Economic Enterprise in Japan.* Princeton: Princeton University Press, pp. 183–208.

Levy, Marion J., Jr.

1966 *Modernization and the Structure of Societies: A Setting for International Affairs.* Princeton: Princeton University Press.

Lockwood, William W.

1956 "Japan's response to the West, the contrast with China." *World Politics* 9: 37–54.

Odaka, Kunio

1964 "Traditionalism and democracy in Japanese industry," in *Transactions of the Fifth World Congress of Sociology,* vol. III. Louvain: International Sociological Association, pp. 39–49.

Index of Japanese Terms

(THE MOST EXPLANATORY REFERENCES
ARE IN (BOLDFACE)

References Cited in the Text

Abegglen, James C.
1958 *Japanese Factory: Aspects of its Social Organization.* Glencoe: The Free Press.

Adachi, Masao
1959 *Kinsei shōnin no bekke seido* [Branching system among merchants of the Tokugawa period]. n.p.: Yūkonsha.

Anonymous
1968 "A report on induced abortion." *East,* vol. 4, no. 6, pp. 5–10.

Ariga, Kizaemon
1939 "Nambu Ninoe-gun Ishigami-mura ni okeru daikazoku seido to nago seido [Large family system and *nago* system in Ishigami village, Ninoe County, Nambu Province]." Tokyo: *Attic Museum Report,* no. 43.
1943 *Nihon kazoku seido to kosaku seido* [Japanese family system and tenant system]. Tokyo: Kawade Shobō.
1947 "Dōzoku to shinzoku [*Dōzoku* and kinship]," in *Nihon minzokugaku no tame ni,* ed. Shinobu Origuchi. vol. 2, pp. 1–70. Tokyo:Minkan Denshō no Kai.
1959 "Nihon ni okeru senzo no kannen—ie no keifu to ie no hommatsu no keifu to [The idea of the ancestor in Japan—relation to the genealogy and the main-branch relationship of the *ie*]," in *Ie: Sono kōzō bunseki,* eds. Seiichi Kitano and Yuzuru Okada, pp. 1–23. Tokyo: Sōbunsha

Asahi Shimbunsha
1967 *Asahi nenkan* [Asahi yearbook]. Tokyo; Osaka; Kita-Kyūshū, and Nagoya.

Befu, Harumi
1962 "Corporate emphasis and patterns of descent in the Japanese family," in *Japanese Culture: Its Development and Characteristics,* eds. Robert J. Smith and Richard K. Beardsley, pp. 34–41. Chicago: Aldine Publishing Company.
1963 "Patrilineal descent and personal kindred in Japan." *American Anthropologist* 65: 1328–41.
1964 "Ritual kinship in Japan, its variability and resiliency." *Sociologus* 14: 150–69.

1965 "Village autonomy and articulation with the state: The case of Tokugawa Japan." *Journal of Asian Studies* 25: 19–32.

1967 "The political relation of the village to the state." *World Politics* 19: 610–20.

1968 "Ecology, residence, and authority: The corporate household in central Japan." *Ethnology* 7: 25–42.

Benedict, Burton
1968 "Family firms and economic development." *Southwestern Journal of Anthropology* 24: 1–19.

Benedict, Ruth
1946 *The Chrysanthemum and the Sword.* Boston: Houghton Mifflin.

Bennett, John W. and Iwano Ishino
1963 *Paternalism in the Japanese Economy: Anthropological Studies of Oyabun-kobun Patterns.* Minneapolis: University of Minnesota Press.

Blood, Robert O.
1967 *Love Match and Arranged Marriage: A Tokyo-Detroit Comparison.* New York: The Free Press.

Blyth, R. H.
1952 *Haiku.* Vol. 3. Tokyo, Hokuseidō.

Brown, Keith
1966 "*Dōzoku* and the ideology of descent in rural Japan." *American Anthropologist* 68: 1129–51.

1968 "The content of *dōzoku* relationships in Japan." *Ethnology* 7: 113–38.

Caudill, William
1961 "Around the clock patient care in Japanese psychiatric hospitals: The role of the tsukisoi." *American Sociological Review* 26: 204–14.

1962 "Patterns of emotion in modern Japan," in *Japanese Culture, Its Development and Characteristics,* eds. Robert J. Smith and Richard K. Beardsley, pp. 115–31. Chicago: Aldine Publishing Company.

1964 "Sibling rank and style of life among Japanese psychiatric patients." *Folia Psychiatria et Neurologia Japonica,* supplement no. 7, pp. 35–40.

Caudill, William and David W. Plath
1966 "Who sleeps by whom? Parent-child involvement in urban Japanese families." *Psychiatry* 29: 344–66.

Caudill, William and Harry A. Scarr
1962 "Japanese value orientations and culture change." *Ethnology* 1: 53–91.

Caudill, William and Helen Weinstein
1969 "Maternal care and infant behavior in Japan and America." *Psychiatry* 32: 12–43.

Chard, Chester S.
1971 "Prehistoric Japan: A survey of cultural development down to the late Jōmon stage (approximately 2000 B.C.)," in *Early Chinese Art and its Possible Influence in the Pacific Basin.* New York: Intercultural Arts Press.

Crump, James I., Jr.
1952   " 'Borrowed' T'ang titles and offices in the Yōrō code." *University of Michigan Center for Japanese Studies Occasional Papers* 2, pp. 35–58.

Davis, Kingsley
1963   "The theory of change in response to modern demographic history." *Population Index* 29: 345–66.

DeVos, George
1960   "The relation of guilt toward parents to achievement and arranged marriage among the Japanese." *Psychiatry* 23: 287–301.

DeVos, George and Hiroshi Wagatsuma, eds.
1966   *Japan's Invisible Race: Caste in Culture and Personality* Berkeley and Los Angeles: University of California Press.

Doi, L. Takeo
1962   " 'Amae': A key concept for understanding Japanese personality structure," in *Japanese Culture, It's Development and Characteristics,* eds. Robert J. Smith and Richard K. Beardsley, pp. 132–39. Chicago: Aldine Publishing Company.

Dore, Ronald P.
1958   *City Life in Japan.* Berkeley and Los Angeles: University of California Press.
1965   "The legacy of Tokugawa education," in *Changing Japanese Attitudes Toward Modernization,* ed. Marius B. Jansen. Princeton: Princeton University Press.

Egami, Namio
1962   "Light on Japanese cultural origins from historical archaeology and legend," in *Japanese Culture: Its Development and Characteristics,* eds. Robert J. Smith and Richard K. Beardsley, pp. 11–16. Chicago: Aldine Publishing Company.
1968   *Kiba minzoku kokka* [Nation of an equestrian tribe]. Tokyo: Chūō Kōronsha.

Embree, John F.
1939   *Suye mura: A Japanese Village.* Chicago: University of Chicago Press.
1941   "Some social functions of religion in rural Japan." *American Journal of Sociology* 47: 184–89.

Erasmus, Charles
1966   "Monument building: Some field experiments." *Southwestern Journal of Anthropology* 21: 277–301.

Esaka, Teruya
1967   *Nihon bunka no kigen*—Jōmon jidai ni nōkō wa hassei shita [Origins of Japanese culture—horticulture began in the Jōmon period]. Tokyo: Kōdansha.

Foster, George M.
1960   *Culture and Conquest: America's Spanish Heritage. Viking Fund Publications in Anthropology,* no. 27. New York: Wenner–Gren Foundation for Anthropological Research.

Fried, Morton H.
1967   *The Evolution of Political Society: An Essay in Political Anthropology.* New York: Random House, Inc.

Fujishima, Taisuke
1965   *Nihon no jōryū shakai* [Japan's upper-crust society]. Tokyo: Kōbunsha.

Fukutake, Tadashi
1967   *Japanese Rural Society.* Tokyo: Oxford University Press.

Fuse, Akiko
1967   "Toshi kazoku no naibu kōzō no hen'yō ni kansuru ichi kōsatsu [An analysis of the change of the internal structure of urban family]." *Shakaigaku Hyōron* 17, 4: 45–71.

Gamō, Masao
1962   "Shinzoku [Kinship]," in *Nihon minzokugaku taikei* 3:233–58. Tokyo: Heibonsha.
1967   "Nihon no kon'in girei [Marriage rituals in Japan]." *Meiji Daigaku Shakai Kagaku Kenkyusho Kiyo* 5, pp. 23–40.

Gōda, Hirofumi
1958   "Kagoshima-ken Madomari buraku no tsumakata ottokata kyojū hōshiki —duopatrilocal residence [Field report on duopatrilocal residence in a fishing village: Madomari *buraku* of Kagoshima Prefecture in the southern part of Kyūshū]." *Shakai Jinruigaku* no 4, pp. 55–63.

Hall, John W.
1965   "Education and modern national development," in *Twelve Doors to Japan,* eds. John W. Hall and Richard K. Beardsley. New York: McGraw-Hill, Inc.

Hasebe, Kotondo
1956   "Nihonjin no sosen [Ancestors of Japanese]," in *Zusetsu Nihon bunkashi taikei,* vol. 1: Jōmon, Yayoi, Kofun jidai, pp. 94–105. Tokyo: Shōgakkan.

Hattori, Shirō
1955   "Gengo nendaigaku' sunawachi 'goi tōkeigaku' no hōhō ni tsuite—Nihon sogo no nendai [On the method of glottochronology]," *Minzokugaku Kenkyū,* vol. 19, no 1, pp. 100–01.
1956   "Nihongo no keitō [Derivation of Japanese]," in *Zusetsu Nihon bunkashi taikei,* vol. 1: Jōmon, Yayoi, kofun jidai, pp. 117–30. Tokyo: Shōgakkan.

Hattori, Shirō, and Mashiho Chiri
1960   "Ainu-go shohōgen no kiso goi tōkeigaku-teki kenkyū [A lexico-statistical study of the Ainu dialects]," *Minzokugaku Kenkyū* 24: 307–42. (English summary on p. 307.)

Hayashi, Chikio
1954   "Tōkeiteki tachiba kara mita kokuminsei no kenkyū [A statistical study of (Japanese) national character]," *Kyōiku Tōkei* no. 30, pp. 16–53.

Hayashi, Chikio, Shigeru Suri, and Tatsuzō Suzuki
1964   *Nihon no howaito karā* [Japan's whitecollar class]. Tokyo: Daiyamondosha.

Hazama, Hiroshi
1963   *Nihonteki keiei no fukei* [Development of Japanese-style management].
Tokyo: Nihon Nōritsu Kyōkai.

Hori, Ichirō
1962   "Shokugyō no kami [Occupational gods]," in *Nihon minzokugaku taikei*
8: 91–135. Tokyo: Heibonsha.

Howells, William
1959   *Mankind in the Making.* Garden City, New York: Doubleday & Company, Inc.
1966   "Jomon population of Japan: A study by discriminant analysis of Japanese
and Ainu crania." *Papers of the Peabody Museum of Archaeology and Ethnology,
Harvard University,* vol. 57, no. 1, pp. 1–43.

Inkeles, Alex and Peter H. Rossi
1956   "National comparisons of occupational prestige." *American Journal of
Sociology* 61: 329–39.

Ishida, Eiichiro and Seiichi Izumi, eds.
1968   *Shimpojium Nihon nōkō bunka no kigen* [Symposium on the origins of
agriculture in Japan]. Tokyo: Kadokawa Shobō.

Ishino, Iwao
1966   "Paternalism in Japanese industry'" (Paper presented at the annual meeting of the American Anthropological Association, Pittsburgh, Pa.).

Isomura, Eiichi
1956   "Boshi kazoku [The fatherless family]," in *Gendai kazoku kōza,* eds.
Eiichi Isomura, Takenori Kawashima, and Takashi Koyama, vol. 6: Kazoku no
fuyō, pp. 141–76. Tokyo: Kawade Shobō.

Kamaki, Yoshiaki
1965   "Jinki bunka [Blade culture]," in *Nihon no Kōkogaku,* vol. 1: Sendoki
jidai, ed. Sōsuke Sugihara, pp. 131–37. Tokyo: Kawade Shobō Shinsha.

Kanaseki, Takeo
1966   "Yayoi jidaijin [People of the Yayoi period]," in *Nihon no kōkogaku,*
vol. 3: Yayoi jidai, ed., Seiichi Wajima, pp. 460–71. Tokyo: Kawade Shobō Shinsha.

Kaplan, David
1963   "Men, monuments, and political systems." *Southwestern Journal of Anthropology* 19: 397–410.

Kawashima, Takeyoshi and Kurt Steiner
1960   "Modernization and divorce rate trends in Japan," in *City and Village in
Japan,* ed. Thomas C. Smith, pp. 213–39. (Published in *Economic Development and
Cultural Change,* vol. 9, no. 1, part 2.)

Kimura, Seiji
1963   *Genshi no nōkō bunka* [Primitive agriculture]. Tokyo: Nihon Nōgyō
Shimbun.

Kitano, Seiichi

1951   "Dōzoku soshiki to hōken isei [*Dōzoku* organization and feudalistic vestiges]," in *Hōken isei,* ed. Nihon Jimbun Kagakkai, pp. 175–95. Tokyo: Yūhikaku.

Kluckhohn, Florence R. and Fred L. Strodtbeck

1961   *Variations in Value Orientation.* Evanston, Illinois and Elmsford, New York: Ron Peterson.

Kobayashi, Kazumasa

1964   "Jōmon jidaijin chikotsu no keitai to shibō nenrei no suitei [Estimation of age at death from pubic symphysis for the prehistoric human skeletons in Japan]." *Zinruigaku Zasshi* 72, no. 2, pp. 43–55 (English summary on p. 54).

Kobayashi, Yukio

1959   *Kofun no hanashi* [The story of tumuli]. Tokyo: Iwanami Shoten.

Kokubu, Naoichi

1966   "Shina-kai sho chiiki to senshi Nihon bunka [The China Seas areas and prehistoric Japan]." *Minzokugaku Kenkyū* 30: 277–300.

Koyama, Takashi

1959   "Kazoku keitai no shūki-teki henka [Cyclical changes in the family form]," in *Ie—sono kōzō bunseki,* ed. Seiichi Kitano and Yuzuru Okada, pp. 67–83. Tokyo: Sōbunsha.

1962   "Changing family structure in Japan," in *Japanese Culture: Its Development and Characteristics,* ed. Robert J. Smith and Richard K. Beardsley, pp. 47–54. Chicago: Aldine Publishing Company.

Koyama, Takashi, ed.

1960   *Gendai kazoku no kenkyū* [An investigation of the contemporary family]. Tokyo: Kōbundō.

Koyama, Takashi, et al.

1965   "The family in postwar Japan." *Journal of Social and Political Ideas in Japan* 3, no. 3, pp. 11–16.

Kroeber, Alfred L.

1948   *Anthropology: Race, Language, Culture, Psychology, Prehistory.* New York: Harcourt, Brace, Inc.

1952   *The Nature of Culture.* Chicago: University of Chicago Press.

Lanham, Betty B.

1965   "Aspects of child care in Japan: Preliminary report," in *Personal Character and Cultural Milieu,* ed. Douglas G. Haring, pp. 565–83. Syracuse: Syracuse University Press.

Lewis, Oscar

1966   "Culture of Poverty." *Scientific American* 205, no. 4, pp. 19–25.

Lifton, Robert

1967   *Death in Life: Survivors of Hiroshima.* New York: Random House, Inc.

Maringer, J.

1957a   "A stone industry of Patjitanian tradition from central Japan." *Artibus Asiae* 19, no. 2, pp. 111–26.

1957b   "Some stone tools of early Hoabinhian type from central Japan." *Man* 57, article 1.

Masuda, Yoshirō
1967   *Junsui bunka no jōken: Nihon bunka was shōgeki no dō taetaka* [Conditions of a pure culture: the history of Japan's acculturation]. Tokyo: Kōdansha.

Matsuda, Michio
1964   *Nihonshiki ikujihō* [Child-rearing, Japanese style]. Tokyo: Kōdansha.

Matsushima, Shizou and Takashi Nakano
1962   *Nihon shakai yōron* [Introduction to Japanese society] Tokyo: Tokyo University Press.

Meggers, Betty J., Clifford Evans, and Emilio Estrada
1965   "Early formative period of coastal Ecuador: The Valdivia and Machalilla phases." *Smithsonian Contributions to Anthropology,* vol. 1.

Minami, Hiroshi
1953   *Nihonjin no shinri* [Psychology of the Japanese] Tokyo: Iwanami Shoten.

Mitsukawa, Harunori
1966   "Kesson kazoku [Defective family]," in *Kazoku shakaigaku,* ed. Kaoru Ōhashi and Kōkichi Masuda. Tokyo: Kawashima Shoten.

Montagu, M. F. Ashley
1960   *An Introduction to Physical Anthropology.* Springfield, Illinois: Charles C. Thomas, Publisher.

Mori, Teijirō
1966   "Kyūshū [Kyūshū Island]," in *Nihon no Kōkogaku,* vol 3: Yayoi jidai, ed. Seiichi Wajima. pp. 32–80. Tokyo: Kawade Shobō Shinsha.

Morioka, Kiyomi
1962   "Buddhist orders and the Japanese family system." *Orient/West* 7, pp. 55–59.
1967   "The social network around old people in a suburb of Tokyo," *International Christian University: The Final Report of the Ford Research Project,* pp. 237–52.

Morlan, Richard E.
1967   "ChronometricdatinginJapan."*ArcticAnthropology*4,no.2,pp.180–211.

Murayama, Schichirō
1962   "Nihongo no Tsungūsugo-teki kōsei yōso [Tungusic elements in the Japanese language]," *Minzokugaku Kenkyū* 26, no. 3, pp. 157–69.

Nagashima, Fukutarō
1959   Shoki chōnin to dōzoku soshiki [Early merchants and the dōzoku organization]," in *Ie: sono kōzō bunseki,* ed. Seiichi Kitano and Yuzuru Okada, pp. 237–57. Tokyo: Sōbunsha.

Nakane, Chie
1965   "Toward a theory of Japanese social structure: An unilateral society." *Economic Weekly* (Bombay), vol. 17, pp. 197–201, 203–7, 209–11, 213, 215–16.
1967   *Kinship and Economic Organization in Rural Japan.* London: Athlone.

Nakano, Takashi

1957 "Kazoku to shinzoku [Family and kinship]," in *Kōza shakaigaku,* ed. Tadashi Fukutake, vol. 4, pp. 44–70. Tokyo: Tokyo University Press.

1964 *Shōka dōzokudan no kenkyū: noren o meguru ie no kenkyū* [A study of merchant dōzoku groups], Tokyo: Miraisha.

Nihon Shakai Gakkai Chōsa Iinkai

1958 *Nihon shakai no kaisōteki kōzō* [Class structure of Japanese society]. Tokyo: Yūhikaku.

Nishihira, Shigeki

1964 "Shokugyō no shakaiteki hyōka [Social evaluation of occupations]." Tōtei Sūri Kenkyūsho Sūken Kenkyū Report 12, pp. 21–40.

1968 "Le prestige social des différentes professions." *Revue francais de Sociologie* 9, pp. 548–57.

Nishiyama, Matsunosuke

1959 *Iemoto no kenkyū* [Studies in schools of arts]. Tokyo: Kōsō Shobō.

Norbeck, Edward

1953 "Age-grading in Japan." *American Anthropologist* 55, pp. 373–84.

1962 "Common-interest associations in rural Japan," in *Japanese Culture: Its Development and Characteristics,* ed. Robert J. Smith and Richard K. Beardsley, pp. 73–85. Chicago: Aldine Publishing Company.

1966 "Little known minority groups of Japan," in *Japan's Invisible Race: Caste in Culture and Personality,* ed. George DeVose and Hiroshi Wagatsuma, pp. 184–99. Berkeley and Los Angeles: University of California Press.

1967 "Associations and democracy in Japan," in *Aspects of Social Change in Modern Japan,* ed. Ronald P. Dore, pp. 185–200. Princeton: Princeton University Press.

Norbeck, Edward and Harumi Befu

1958 "Informal fictive kinship in Japan." *American Anthropologist* 60: 102–17.

Norbeck, Edward and Margaret Norbeck

1956 "Child training in a Japanese fishing community," in *Personal Character and Cultural Milieu,* ed. Douglas G. Haring, pp. 651–73. Syracuse: Syracuse University Press.

Odaka, Kunio

1964–65 "The middle classes in Japan." *Contemporary Japan* 28, no. 1–2, pp. 1–52.

Oikawa, Hiroshi

1939 "Dōzoku soshiki to kon'in oyobi sōsō no girei [Dōzoku organization and its relation to wedding and funeral ceremonies]." *Minzokugaku Nempō* 2, pp. 1–40.

Oka, Masao

1965 "Nihon minzoku bunka no keisei [Formation of Japanese culture]," in *Zusetsu Nihon bunkashi taikei,* vol. 1: Jōmon, Yayoi, Kofun jidai, pp. 110–120. Tokyo: Shōgakkan.

Ōmachi, Tokuzō
1963 "Ashiire-kon, putting-one's-feet-in marriage," in *Studies in Japanese Folklore*, ed. Richard M. Dorson, pp. 251–266. Bloomington, Indiana: Indiana University Press.

Ōnishi, Yoshinori
1939 *Yūgen to aware* [Yūgen and Aware]. Tokyo: Iwanami Shoten.

Ōno, Susumu
1957 *Nihongo no kigen* [The origin of the Japanese language]. Tokyo: Iwanami Shoten.
1962 "The Japanese language: Its origins and its sources," in *Japanese Culture: Its Development and Characteristics*, ed. Robert J. Smith and Richard K. Beardsley, pp. 17–21. Chicago: Aldine Publishing Company.

Otomasu, Shigetaka
1965 "Kyūshū seihoku [Northwestern Kyūshū]," in *Nihon no kōkogaku*, vol. 2: Jōmon jidai, ed. Shigeaki Kamaki, pp. 250–67. Tokyo: Kawade Shobō Shinsha.

Ōyama, Hikoichi
1960 *Nansei Shotō no kazoku seido no kenkyū: Maki hara no chōsa* [A study of the family system of the Nansei Islands: An investigation into *maki* and *hara*]. Tokyo: Seki Shoin.

Pelzel, John and Florence Kluckhohn
1957 "A theory of variation in values applied to aspects of Japanese social structure." *Bulletin of the Research Institute of Comparative Education and Culture*, Kyūshū University (English Edition), no. 1, pp. 62–76.

Plath, David W.
1964a *The After Hours: Modern Japan and the Search for Enjoyment*. Berkeley and Los Angeles: University of California Press.
1964b "Where the family of God is the family." *American Anthropologist* 66: 300–17.
1966 "Japan and the ethics of fatalism." *Anthropological Quarterly* 39: 161–70.

Seikatsu Kagaku Chōsakai
1963 *Danchi no subete* [All about the *danchi*]. Tokyo: Ishiyaku Shuppan.

Seki, Teigo
1954 "Tatari [Retribution]," in *Nihon shakai minzoku jiten*, vol. 2, p. 885. Tokyo: Seibundō Shinkōsha.

Seki, Kiyohide
1966 *Toshi no kazoku* [The urban family]. Tokyo: Seishin Shobō.

Serizawa, Chōsuke
1965 Ōita-ken Sōzudai ni okeru zenki kyūsekki no kenkyū [A lower paleolithic industry from the Sōzudai site, Ōita prefecture, Japan]." *Nihon Bunka Kenkyūjo Kenkyū Hōkoku*, Tōhoku University, no. 1, pp. 1–119.
1967 "Nihon ni okeru kyūsekki no sōi-teki shutsudorei to C 14 nendai [The chronology of Paleolithic industries and the carbon 14 dates in Japan]." *Nihon Bunka Kenkyūjo Kenkyū Hōkoku*, Tōhoku University, no. 3, pp. 59–110.

Service, Elmer R.

1962   *Primitive Social Organization: An Evolutionary Perspective.* New York: Random House, Inc.

Shikata, Hisao

_ 1966   "Rikon iede [Divorce and desertion]," in *Kazoku shakaigaku,* ed. Kaoru Ōhashi and Kōkichi Masuda, pp. 256–79. Tokyo: Kawashima Shoten.

Smith, Robert J.

1960   "Pre-industrial urbanism in Japan: A consideration of multiple traditions in feudal society," in *City and Village in Japan,* ed. Thomas C. Smith, pp. 241–257. (Published in *Economic Development and Cultural Change,* vol. 9, no. 1, part 2.)

1961   "The Japanese rural community: Norms, sanctions, and ostracism." *American Anthropologist* 63, pp. 522–33.

Smith, Thomas C.

1959   *The Agrarian Origins of Modern Japan.* Stanford: Stanford University Press.

Suzuki, Hisashi

1956   Jōmon jidai jinkotsu [Human skeletons of the Jōmon period]," in *Nihon kōkogaku kōza,* ed. Sōsuke Sugihara, vol. 3: jōmon bunka, pp. 353–75. Tokyo: Kawade Shobō.

1965   "Nihon kōseki-sō no jinrui [Man in Pleistocene Japan]," in *Nihon no kōkogaku,* vol. 1: Sendoki jidai, ed. Sōsuke Sugihara, pp. 102–16. Tokyo: Kawade Shobo Shinsha.

1966   "Hamakita jinkotsu no keishitsu [Skeletal remains of the Hamakita man]." *Zinruigaku Zasshi,* vol. 74, pp. 119–36 and 172–74 (English summary).

Suzuki, Tatsuzo

1970   "A study of the Japanese national character—part IV." *Annals of the Institute of Statistical Mathematics, Supplement* 6

Taira, Koji

1968   "Ragpickers and community development: 'ant's villa' in Tokyo." *Industrial and Labor Relations Review* 22: 3–19.

Tōkei Sūri Kenkyūjo [Institute of Statistical Mathematics]

1966   "Kokuminsei no kenyū [A study in (Japanese) national character]," *Sū-ken kenkyū ripōto,* no. 14.

Tōkei Sūri Kenkyūjo: Kokuminsei Chōsa Iinkai. [Institute of Statistical Mathematics: Research Committee on Japanese National Character]

1961   *Nihonjin no kokuminsei* [National character of Japanese]. Tokyo: Shiseidō

Ueno, Kazuo

1967   "San riku kaison no shinzoku soshiki [Kinship organization of Shimo-Hoei, Iwate Prefecture]." *Minzokugaku Kenkyū* 32: 155–65.

United States Bureau of the Census

1940   Marriage and Divorce Statistics: United States 1887–1937. *Special Reports,* vol. 9, no. 60.

1968   *Statistical Abstract of the United States: 1968.* (89th edition.) Washington, D. C.

United States Department of Health, Education and Welfare, Public Health Service, National Center for Health Statistics

1967   *Vital Statistics of the United States,* 1963, Marriage and Divorce, Vol. 3.

Vogel, Ezra

1962   "Entrance examinations and emotional disturbances in Japan's 'new middle class'," in *Japanese Culture: Its Development and Characteristics,* ed. Robert J. Smith and Richard K. Beardsley, pp. 140–152. Chicago: Aldine Publishing Company.

1963   *Japan's New Middle Class.* Berkeley and Los Angeles: University of California Press.

Watanabe, Hitoshi

1966   "Jōmon jidaijin no seikatsu: Jūkyo no anteisei to sono seibutsugaku-teki minzokushi-teki igi [Ecology of the Jōmon people: Stability of habitation and its biological and ethnohistorical implications]." *Zinruigaku Zasshi* 74: 73–84 (English summary, pp. 83–84).

Watsuji, Tetsurō

1961   *A Climate: A Philosophical Study.* Tokyo: Japanese Government Printing Bureau.

Whitehill, Arthur M., Jr. and Shin'ichi Takezawa

1961   "Cultural values in management-worker relations Japan: Gimu in transition." *University of North Carolina School of Business Administration,* Research Paper no. 5.

Yanagita, Kunio

1937   "Oyakata kokata [*Oyakata* and *kokata*]," in *Kazoku seidoshi zenshū*, part 1: Shiron-hen, vol. 3: Oyako, pp. 89–124. Tokyo: Kawade Shobō

Yonemura, Shōji

1966   "Ichi sanson ni okeru dōzoku to shinzoku [*Dōzoku* and kindred in a mountain village]." *Okayama Daigaku. Kyōikugaku-bu. Kenkyū shūroku,* no. 22, pp. 57–119.

Yoshida, Teigo

1967   "Mystical retribution, spirit possession, and social structure in a Japanese village." *Ethnology* 6: 237–62.

General Index